12 Sermons
of Comfort & Cheer

Charles H. Spurgeon

Baker Books

A Division of Baker Book House Co.
Grand Rapids, Michigan 49516

First reprinted 1976 by Baker Books
a division of Baker Book House Company
P.O. Box 6287, Grand Rapids, MI 49516-6287

Formerly published under the title
12 Sermons for the New Year

ISBN: 0-8010-8082-7

Sixth printing, June 1994

Printed in the United States of America

CONTENTS

Healing by the Stripes of Jesus

"With his stripes we are healed."—Isaiah liii. 5.

BEING one evening in Exeter Hall, I heard our late beloved brother, Mr. Mackay, of Hull, make a speech, in which he told us of a person who was under very deep concern of soul, and felt that he could never rest till he found salvation. So, taking the Bible into his hand, he said to himself, "Eternal life is to be found somewhere in this Word of God; and if it be here, I will find it, for I will read the Book right through, praying to God over every page of it, if perchance it may contain some saving message for me." He told us that the earnest seeker read on through Genesis, Exodus, Leviticus, and so on; and though Christ is there very evidently, he could not find him in the types and symbols. Neither did the holy histories yield him comfort, nor the book of Job. He passed through the Psalms, but did not find his Saviour there; and the same was the case with the other books till he reached Isaiah. In this prophet he read on till near the end, and then in the fifty-third chapter, these words arrested his delighted attention, "*With his stripes we are healed.*" "Now I have found it," says he. "Here is the healing that I need for my sin-sick soul, and I see how it comes to me through the sufferings of the Lord Jesus Christ. Blessed be his name, I am healed!" It was well that the seeker was wise enough to search the sacred volume; it was better still that in that volume there should be such a life-giving word, and that the Holy Spirit should reveal it to the seeker's heart. I said to myself, "That text will suit me well, and peradventure a voice from God may speak through it yet again to some other awakened sinner." May he, who by these words spoke to the chamberlain of the Ethiopian queen, who also was impressed with them while in the act of searching the Scripture, speak also to many who shall hear or read this sermon! Let us pray that it may be so. God is very gracious, and he will hear our prayers.

The object of my discourse is very simple: I would come *to* the text, and I would come *at* you. May the Holy Spirit give me power to do both to the glory of God!

I. In endeavouring to come to the full meaning of the text, I would remark, first, that God, IN INFINITE MERCY, HERE TREATS SIN AS A DISEASE. "With his stripes"—that is, the stripes of the Lord Jesus—" we are healed." Through the sufferings of our Lord, sin is pardoned, and we are delivered from the power of evil: this is regarded as the healing of a deadly malady. The Lord in this present life treats sin as a disease. If he were to treat it at once as sin, and summon us to his bar to answer for it, we should at once sink beyond the reach of hope, for we could not answer his accusations, nor defend ourselves from his justice. In great mercy he looks upon us with pity, and for the while treats our ill manners as if they were diseases to be cured rather than rebellions to be punished. It is most gracious on his part to do so; for while sin is a disease, it is a great deal more. If our iniquities were the result of an unavoidable sickness, we might claim pity rather than censure; but we sin wilfully, we choose evil, we transgress in heart, and therefore we bear a moral responsibility which makes sin an infinite evil. Our sin is our crime rather than our calamity: however, God looks at it in another way for a season. That he may be able to deal with us on hopeful grounds, he looks at the sickness of sin, and not as yet at the wickedness of sin. Nor is this without reason, for men who indulge in gross vices are often charitably judged by their fellows to be not only wholly wicked, but partly mad. Propensities to evil are usually associated with a greater or less degree of mental disease; perhaps, also, of physical disease. At any rate, sin is a spiritual malady of the worst kind.

Sin is a disease, for *it is not essential to manhood*, nor an integral part of human nature as God created it. Man was never more fully and truly man than he was before he fell; and he who is specially called "the Son of man" knew no sin, neither was guile found in his mouth; yet was he perfectly man. Sin is abnormal; a sort of cancerous growth, which ought not to be within the soul. Sin is disturbing to manhood: sin unmans a man. Sin is sadly destructive to man; it takes the crown from his head, the light from his mind, and the joy from his heart. We may name many grievous diseases which are the destroyers of our race, but the greatest of these is sin: sin, indeed, is the fatal egg from which all other sicknesses have been hatched. It is the fountain and source of all mortal maladies.

It is a disease, because *it puts the whole system of the man out of order*. It places the lower faculties in the higher place, for it makes the body master over the soul. The man should ride the horse; but in the sinner the horse rides the man. The mind should keep the animal instincts and propensities in check; but in many men the animal crushes the mental and the spiritual. For instance, how many live as if eating and drinking were the chief objects of existence: they live to eat, instead of eating to live! The faculties are thrown out of gear by sin, so that they act fitfully and irregularly; you cannot depend upon any one of them keeping its place. The equilibrium of the life-forces is grievously disturbed. Even as a sickness of body is called a disorder, so is sin the disorder of the soul. Human nature is out of joint, and out of health, and man is no longer man: he is dead through sin, even as he was warned of old, " in the day that thou eatest thereof thou shalt surely die." Man is marred, bruised, sick, paralyzed, polluted, rotten with disease, just in proportion as sin has shown its true character.

Sin, like disease, operates to weaken man. The moral energy is broken down so as scarcely to exist in some men. The conscience labours under a fatal consumption, and is gradually ruined by a decline; the understanding has been lamed by evil, and the will is rendered feeble for good, though forcible for evil. The principle of integrity, the resolve of virtue, in which a man's true strength really lies, is sapped and undermined by wrong-doing. Sin is like a secret flow of blood, which robs the vital parts of their essential nourishment. How near to death in some men is even the power to discern between good and evil! The apostle tells us that, when we were yet without strength, in due time Christ died for the ungodly; and this being without strength is the direct result of the sickness of sin, which has weakened our whole manhood.

Sin is a disease which in some cases causes extreme pain and anguish, but in other instances deadens sensibility. It frequently happens that, the more sinful a man is, the less he is conscious of it. It was remarked of a certain notorious criminal that many thought him innocent because, when he was charged with murder, he did not betray the least emotion. In that wretched self-possession there was to my mind presumptive proof of his great familiarity with crime : if an innocent person is charged with a great offence, the mere charge horrifies him. It is only by weighing all the circumstances, and distinguishing between sin and shame, that he recovers himself. He who can do the deed of shame does not blush when he is charged with it. The deeper a man goes in sin, the less does he allow that it is sin. Like a man who takes opium, he acquires the power to take larger and larger doses, till that which would kill a hundred other men has but slight effect upon him. A man who readily lies is scarcely conscious of the moral degradation involved in being a liar, though he may think it shameful to be called so. It is one of the worst points of this disease of sin that it stupefies the understanding, and causes a paralysis of the conscience.

By-and-by sin is sure to cause pain, like other diseases which flesh is heir to; and when its awakening comes, what a start it gives! Conscience one day will awake, and fill the guilty soul with alarm and distress, if not in this world, yet certainly in the next. Then will it be seen what an awful thing it is to offend against the law of the Lord.

Sin is a disease which pollutes a man. Certain diseases render a man horribly impure. God is the best judge of purity, for he is thrice-holy, and he cannot endure sin. The Lord puts sin from him with abhorrence, and prepares a place where the finally-unclean shall be shut up by themselves. He will not dwell with them here, neither can they dwell with him in heaven. As men *must* put lepers apart by themselves, so justice must put out of the heavenly world everything which defileth. O my hearer, shall the Lord be compelled to put you out of his presence because you persist in wickedness?

And this disease, which is so polluting, is, at the same time, *most injurious* to us, from the fact that it prevents the higher enjoyment and employment of life. Men exist in sin, but they do not truly live :

as the Scripture saith, such an one is dead while he liveth. While we continue in sin, we cannot serve God on earth, nor hope to enjoy him for ever above. We are incapable of communion with perfect spirits, and with God himself; and the loss of this communion is the greatest of all evils. Sin deprives us of spiritual sight, hearing, feeling, and taste, and thus deprives us of those joys which turn existence into life. It brings upon us true death, so that we exist in ruins, deprived of all which can be called life.

This disease is fatal. Is it not written, "The soul that sinneth, it shall die"? "Sin, when it is finished, bringeth forth death." There is no hope of eternal life for any man unless sin be put away. This disease never exhausts itself so as to be its own destroyer. Evil men wax worse and worse. In another world, as well as in this present state, character will, no doubt, go on to develop and ripen, and so the sinner will become more and more corrupt as the result of his spiritual death. O my friends, if you refuse Christ, sin will be the death of your peace, your joy, your prospects, your hopes, and thus the death of all that is worth having! In the case of other diseases nature may conquer the malady, and you may be restored; but in this case, apart from divine interposition, nothing lies before you but eternal death.

God, therefore, treats sin as a disease, because it is a disease; and I want you to feel that it is so, for then you will thank the Lord for thus dealing with you. Many of us have felt that sin is a disease, and we have been healed of it. Oh, that others could see what an exceedingly evil thing it is to sin against the Lord! It is a contagious, defiling, incurable, mortal sickness.

Perhaps somebody says, "Why do you raise these points? They fill us with unpleasant thoughts." I do it for the reason given by the engineer who built the great Menai Tubular Bridge. When it was being erected, some brother engineers said to him, "You raise all manner of difficulties." "Yes," he said, "I raise them that I may solve them." So do we at this time dilate upon the sad state of man by nature, that we may the better set forth the glorious remedy of which our text so sweetly speaks.

II. God treats sin as a disease, and HE HERE DECLARES THE REMEDY WHICH HE HAS PROVIDED: "With his stripes we are healed."

I ask you very solemnly to accompany me in your meditations, for a few minutes, while I bring before you the stripes of the Lord Jesus. The Lord resolved to restore us, and therefore he sent his Only-begotten Son, "Very God of very God," that he might descend into this world to take upon himself our nature, in order to our redemption. He lived as a man among men; and, in due time, after thirty years or more of service, the time came when he should do us the greatest service of all, namely, stand in our stead, and bear the chastisement of our peace. He went to Gethsemane, and there, at the first taste of our bitter cup, he sweat great drops of blood. He went to Pilate's hall, and Herod's judgment-seat, and there drank draughts of pain and scorn in our room and place. Last of all, they took him to the cross, and nailed him there to die—to die in our stead, "the Just for the unjust, to bring us to God." The word "stripes" is used to set forth his sufferings, both of body and of soul. The whole of Christ was made a sacrifice for us:

his whole manhood suffered. As to his body, it shared with his mind in a grief that never can be described. In the beginning of his passion, when he emphatically suffered instead of us, he was in an agony, and from his bodily frame a bloody sweat distilled so copiously as to fall to the ground. It is very rarely that a man sweats blood. There have been one or two instances of it, and they have been followed by almost immediate death; but our Saviour lived—lived after an agony which, to any one else, would have proved fatal. Ere he could cleanse his face from this dreadful crimson, they hurried him to the high-priest's hall. In the dead of night they bound him and led him away. Anon they took him to Pilate and to Herod. These scourged him, and their soldiers spat in his face, and buffeted him, and put on his head a crown of thorns. Scourging is one of the most awful tortures that can be inflicted by malice. It is to the eternal disgrace of Englishmen that they should have permitted the "cat" to be used upon the soldier; but to the Roman cruelty was so natural that he made his common punishments worse than brutal. The Roman scourge is said to have been made of the sinews of oxen, twisted into knots, and into these knots were inserted slivers of bone, and huckle-bones of sheep; so that every time the scourge fell upon the bare back, "the plowers made deep furrows." Our Saviour was called upon to endure the fierce pain of the Roman scourge, and this not as the *finis* of his punishment, but as a preliminary to crucifixion. To this they added buffeting, and plucking of the hair: they spared him no form of pain. In all his faintness, through bleeding and fasting, they made him carry his cross until another was forced, by the forethought of their cruelty, to bear it, lest their victim should die on the road. They stripped him, and threw him down, and nailed him to the wood. They pierced his hands and his feet. They lifted up the tree, with him upon it, and then dashed it down into its place in the ground, so that all his limbs were dislocated, according to the lament of the twenty-second psalm, "I am poured out like water, and all my bones are out of joint." He hung in the burning sun till the fever dissolved his strength, and he said, "My heart is like wax; it is melted in the midst of my bowels. My strength is dried up like a potsherd; and my tongue cleaveth to my jaws; and thou hast brought me into the dust of death." There he hung, a spectacle to God and men. The weight of his body was first sustained by his feet, till the nails tore through the tender nerves: and then the painful load began to drag upon his hands, and rend those sensitive parts of his frame. How small a wound in the hand has brought on lockjaw! How awful must have been the torment caused by that dragging iron tearing through the delicate parts of the hands and feet! Now were all manner of bodily pains centred in his tortured frame. All the while his enemies stood around, pointing at him in scorn, thrusting out their tongues in mockery, jesting at his prayers, and gloating over his sufferings. He cried, "I thirst," and then they gave him vinegar mingled with gall. After a while he said, "It is finished." He had endured the utmost of appointed grief, and had made full vindication to divine justice: then, and not till then, he gave up the ghost. Holy men of old have enlarged most lovingly upon the bodily sufferings of our Lord, and I have no hesitation in doing the same, trusting that trembling sinners may see salvation in these painful "stripes" of the Redeemer.

To describe the outward sufferings of our Lord is not easy: I acknowledge that I have failed. But his soul-sufferings, which were the soul of his sufferings, who can even conceive, much less express, what they were? At the very first I told you that he sweat great drops of blood. That was his heart driving out its life-floods to the surface through the terrible depression of spirit which was upon him. He said, "My soul is exceeding sorrowful, even unto death." The betrayal by Judas, and the desertion of the twelve, grieved our Lord; but the weight of our sin was the real pressure on his heart. Our guilt was the olive-press which forced from him the moisture of his life. No language can ever tell his agony in prospect of his passion; how little then can we conceive the passion itself? When nailed to the cross he endured what no martyr ever suffered; for martyrs, when they have died, have been so sustained of God that they have rejoiced amid their pain; but our Redeemer was forsaken of his Father, until he cried, "My God, my God, why hast thou forsaken me?" That was the bitterest cry of all, the utmost depth of his unfathomable grief. Yet was it needful that he should be deserted, because God must turn his back on sin, and consequently upon him who was made sin for us. The soul of the great Substitute suffered a horror of misery, instead of that horror of hell into which sinners would have been plunged had he not taken their sin upon himself, and been made a curse for them. It is written, "Cursed is every one that hangeth on a tree"; but who knows what that curse means?

The remedy for your sins and mine is found in the substitutionary sufferings of the Lord Jesus, and in these only. These "stripes" of the Lord Jesus Christ were on our behalf. Do you enquire, "Is there anything for us to do, to remove the guilt of sin?" I answer: There is nothing whatever for you to do. By the stripes of Jesus we are healed. All those stripes he has endured, and left not one of them for us to bear.

"But must we not believe on him?" Ay, certainly. If I say of a certain ointment that it heals, I do not deny that you need a bandage with which to apply it to the wound. Faith is the linen which binds the plaster of Christ's reconciliation to the sore of our sin. The linen does not heal; that is the work of the ointment. So faith does not heal; that is the work of the atonement of Christ.

Does an enquirer reply, "But surely I must do something, or suffer something"? I answer: You must put nothing with Jesus Christ, or you greatly dishonour him. In order to your salvation, you must rely upon the wounds of Jesus Christ, and nothing else; for the text does not say, "His stripes help to heal us," but, "With his stripes we are healed."

"But we must repent," cries another. Assuredly we must, and shall, for repentance is the first sign of healing; but the stripes of Jesus heal us, and not our repentance. These stripes, when applied to the heart, work repentance in us: we hate sin because it made Jesus suffer.

When you intelligently trust in Jesus as having suffered for you, then you discover the fact that God will never punish you for the same offence for which Jesus died. His justice will not permit him to see the debt paid, first, by the Surety, and then again by the debtor. Justice cannot twice demand a recompense : if my bleeding Surety has borne my guilt, then I cannot bear it. Accepting Christ Jesus as suffering for me, I have accepted a complete discharge from judicial liability. I have been condemned in Christ, and there is, therefore, now no condemnation to me any more. This is the groundwork of the security of the sinner who believes in Jesus : he lives because Jesus died in his room, and place, and stead; and he is acceptable before God because Jesus is accepted. The person for whom Jesus is an accepted Substitute must go free ; none can touch him ; he is clear. O my hearer, wilt thou have Jesus Christ to be thy Substitute ? If so, thou art free. "He that believeth on him is not condemned." Thus "with his stripes we are healed."

III. I have tried to put before you the disease and the remedy; I now desire to notice the fact that THIS REMEDY IS IMMEDIATELY EFFECTIVE WHEREVER IT IS APPLIED. The stripes of Jesus do heal men : they have healed many of us. It does not look as if it could effect so great a cure, but the fact is undeniable. I often hear people say, "If you preach up this faith in Jesus Christ as saving men, they will be careless about holy living." I am as good a witness on that point as anybody, for I live every day in the midst of men who are trusting to the stripes of Jesus for their salvation, and I have seen no ill effect following from such a trust; but I have seen the very reverse. I bear testimony that I have seen the very worst of men become the very best of men by believing in the Lord Jesus Christ. These stripes heal in a surprising manner the moral diseases of those who seemed past remedy.

The character is healed. I have seen the drunkard become sober, the harlot become chaste, the passionate man become gentle, the covetous man become liberal, and the liar become truthful, simply by trusting in the sufferings of Jesus. If it did not make good men of them, it would not really do anything for them, for you must judge men by their fruits after all ; and if the fruits are not changed the tree is not changed. Character is everything : if the character be not set right, the man is not saved. But we say it without fear of contradiction, that the atoning sacrifice, applied to the heart, heals the disease of sin. If you doubt it, try it. He that believes in Jesus is sanctified as well as justified ; by faith he becomes henceforth an altogether changed man.

The conscience is healed of its smart. Sin crushed the man's soul ; he was spiritless and joyless, but the moment he believed in Jesus he leaped into light. Often you can see a change in the very look of the man's face ; the cloud flies from the countenance when guilt goes from the conscience. Scores of times, when I have been talking with those bowed down with sin's burden, they have looked as though they were qualifying for an asylum through inward grief ; but they have caught the thought, "Christ stood for me ; and if I trust in him, I have the sign that he did so, and I am clear," and their faces have been lit up as with a glimpse of heaven.

Gratitude for such great mercy causes a change of thought towards God, and so *it heals the judgment*, and by this means the affections are turned in the right way, and *the heart is healed*. Sin is no longer loved, but God is loved, and holiness is desired. *The whole man is healed*, and the whole life changed. Many of you know how light of heart faith in Jesus makes you, how the troubles of life lose their weight, and the fear of death ceases to cause bondage. You rejoice in the Lord, for the blessed remedy of the stripes of Jesus is applied to your soul by faith in him.

The fact that "with his stripes we are healed" is a matter in evidence. I shall take liberty to bear my own witness. If it were necessary, I could call thousands of persons, my daily acquaintances, who can say that with the stripes of Christ they are healed; but I must not therefore withhold my personal testimony. If I had suffered from a dreadful disease, and a physician had given me a remedy which had healed me, I should not be ashamed to tell you all about it; but I would quote my own case as an argument with you to try my physician. Years ago, when I was a youth, the burden of my sin was exceedingly heavy upon me. I had fallen into no gross vices, and should not have been regarded by any one as being specially a transgressor; but I regarded myself as such, and I had good reason for so doing. My conscience was sensitive because it was enlightened; and I judged that, having had a godly father, and a praying mother, and having been trained in the ways of piety, I had sinned against much light, and consequently there was a greater degree of guilt in my sin than in that of others who were my youthful associates, but had not enjoyed my advantages. I could not enjoy the sports of youth because I felt that I had done violence to my conscience. I would seek my chamber, and there sit alone, read my Bible, and pray for forgiveness; but peace did not come to me. Books such as Baxter's "Call to the Unconverted," and Doddridge's "Rise and Progress," I read over and over again. Early in the morning I would awake, and read the most earnest religious books I could find, desiring to be eased of my burden of sin. I was not always thus dull, but at times my misery of soul was very great. The words of the weeping prophet and of Job were such as suited my mournful case. I would have chosen death rather than life. I tried to do as well as I could, and to behave myself aright; but in my own judgment I grew worse and worse. I felt more and more despondent. I attended every place of worship within my reach, but I heard nothing which gave me lasting comfort till one day I heard a simple preacher of the gospel speak from the text, "Look unto me, and be ye saved, all the ends of the earth." When he told me that all I had to do was to "look" to Jesus—to Jesus the crucified One, I could scarcely believe it. He went on, and said, "Look, look, look!" He added, "There is a young man, under the left-hand gallery there, who is very miserable: he will have no peace until he looks to Jesus"; and then he cried, "Look! Look! Young man, look!" I did look; and in that moment relief came to me, and I felt such overflowing joy that I could have stood up, and cried, "Hallelujah! Glory be to God, I am delivered from the burden of my sin!" Many days have passed since then; but my faith has held me up, and compelled me to tell out the story of free grace and dying love. I can truly say—

> " E'er since by faith I saw the stream
> Thy flowing wounds supply,
> Redeeming love has been my theme,
> And shall be till I die."

I hope to sit up in my bed in my last hours, and tell of the stripes that healed me. I hope some young men, yea, and old men before me, will at once try this remedy; it is good for all characters, and all ages. "With his stripes we are healed." Thousands upon thousands of us have tried and proved this remedy. We speak what we do know, and testify what we have seen. God grant that men may receive our witness through the power of the Holy Spirit !

I want a few minutes' talk with those who have not tried this marvellous heal-all. Let us come to close quarters. Friend, you are by nature in need of soul-healing as much as any of us, and one reason why you do not care about the remedy is, because you do not believe that you are sick. I saw a pedlar one day, as I was walking out : he was selling walking-sticks. He followed me, and offered me one of the sticks. I showed him mine—a far better one than any he had to sell—and he withdrew at once. He could see that I was not likely to be a purchaser. I have often thought of that when I have been preaching : I show men the righteousness of the Lord Jesus, but they show me their own, and all hope of dealing with them is gone. Unless I can prove that their righteousness is worthless, they will not seek the righteousness which is of God by faith. Oh, that the Lord would show you your disease, and then you would desire the remedy !

It may be that you do not care to hear of the Lord Jesus Christ. Ah, my dear friends ! you will have to hear of him one of these days, either for your salvation or your condemnation. The Lord has the key of your heart, and I trust he will give you a better mind; and whenever this shall happen, your memory will recall my simple discourse, and you will say, "I do remember. Yes, I heard the preacher declare that there is healing in the wounds of Christ."

I pray you do not put off seeking the Lord; that would be great presumption on your part, and a sad provocation to him. But, should you have put it off, I pray you do not let the devil tell you it is too late. It is never too late while life lasts. I have read in books that very few people are converted after they are forty years of age. My solemn conviction is that there is but little truth in such a statement. I have seen as many people converted at one age as at another in proportion to the number of people who are living at that age. Any first Sunday in the month you may see the right-hand of fellowship given to from thirty to eighty people who have been brought in during the month; and if you take stock of them, there will be found to be a selection representing every age, from childhood up to old age. The precious blood of Jesus has power to heal long-rooted sin. It makes old hearts new. If you were a thousand years old, I would exhort you to believe in Jesus, and I should be sure that his stripes would heal you. Your hair is nearly gone, old friend, and furrows appear on your brow; but come along! You are rotting away with sin, but this medicine meets desperate cases! Poor, old, tottering pensioner, put your trust in Jesus, for with his stripes the old and the dying are healed!

Now, my dear hearers, you are at this moment either healed or not. You are either healed by grace, or you are still in your natural sickness. Will you be so kind to yourselves as to enquire which it is? Many say, "We know what we are"; but certain more thoughtful ones reply, "We don't quite know." Friend, you ought to know, and you should know. Suppose I asked a man, "Are you a bankrupt or not?" and he said, "I really have no time to look at my books, and therefore I am not sure." I should suspect that he could not pay twenty shillings in the pound: should not you? Whenever a man is afraid to look at his books, I suspect that he has something to be afraid of. So, whenever a person says, "I don't know my condition, and I don't care to think much about it," you may pretty safely conclude that things are wrong with him. *You ought to know whether you are saved or not.*

"I hope I am saved," says one, "but I do not know the date of my conversion." That does not matter at all. It is a pleasant thing for a person to know his birthday; but when persons are not sure of the exact date of their birth, they do not, therefore, infer that they are not alive. If a person does not know *when* he was converted, that is no proof that he is not converted. The point is, do you trust Jesus Christ? Has that trust made a new man of you? Has your confidence in Christ made you feel that you have been forgiven? Has that made you love God for having forgiven you, and has that love become the mainspring of your being, so that out of love to God you delight to obey him? Then you are a healed man. If you do not believe in Jesus, be sure that you are still unhealed, and I pray you look at my text until you are led by grace to say, "I am healed, for I have trusted in the stripes of Jesus."

Suppose, for a moment, you are not healed, let me ask the question, "*Why are you not?*" You know the gospel: why are you not healed by Christ? "I don't know," says one. But, my dear friend, I beseech you do not rest until you do know.

"I can't get at it," says somebody. The other day a young girl was putting a button on her father's coat. She was sitting with her back to the window, and she said, "Father, I can't see; I am in my own light." He said, "Ah, my daughter, that is where you have been all your life!" This is the position of some of you spiritually. You are in your own light: you think too much of yourselves. There is plenty of light in the Sun of Righteousness, but you get in the dark by putting self in the way of that Sun. Oh, that your self might be put away! I read a touching story the other day as to how one found peace. A young man had been for some time under a sense of sin, longing to find mercy; but he could not reach it. He was a telegraph clerk, and being in the office one morning he had to receive and transmit a telegram. To his great surprise, he spelt out these words —"Behold the Lamb of God, which taketh away the sin of the world." A gentleman out for a holiday was telegraphing a message in answer to a letter from a friend who was in trouble of soul.

It was meant for another, but he that transmitted it received eternal life, as the words came flashing into his soul.

O dear friends, get out of your own light, and at once, "Behold the Lamb of God, which taketh away the sin of the world"! I cannot telegraph the words to you, but I would put them before you so plainly and distinctly that every one in trouble of soul may know that they are meant for him. There lies your hope—not in yourself, but in the Lamb of God. Behold him; and as you behold him your sin shall be put away, and by his stripes you shall be healed.

If, dear friend, you are healed, this is my last word to you; then *get out of diseased company*. Come away from the companions that have infected you with sin. Come ye out from among them, be ye separate, and touch not the unclean thing. If you are healed, praise the Healer, and acknowledge what he has done for you. There were ten lepers healed, but only one returned to praise the healing hand. Do not be among the ungrateful nine. If you have found Christ, confess his name. Confess it in his own appointed way. "He that believeth and is baptized shall be saved." When you have thus confessed him, speak out for him. Tell what Jesus has done for your soul, and dedicate yourself to the holy purpose of spreading abroad the message by which you have been healed.

I met this week with something that pleased me—how one man, being healed, may be the means of blessing to another. Many years ago I preached a sermon in Exeter Hall, which was printed, and entitled, "Salvation to the uttermost." A friend, who lives not very far from this place, was in the city of Para, in Brazil. Here he heard of an Englishman in prison, who had in a state of drunkenness committed a murder, for which he was confined for life. Our friend went to see him, and found him deeply penitent, but quietly restful, and happy in the Lord. He had felt the terrible wound of blood-guiltiness in his soul, but it had been healed, and he felt the bliss of pardon. Here is the story of the poor man's conversion as I have it:—"A young man, who had just completed his contract with the gas-works, was returning to England, but before doing so he called to see me, and brought with him a parcel of books. When I opened it, I found that they were novels; but, being able to read, I was thankful for anything. After I had read several of the books, I found a sermon (No. 84), preached by C. H. Spurgeon, in Exeter Hall, on June 8th, 1856, from the words, 'Wherefore he is able also to save them to the uttermost,' &c. (Hebrews vii. 25.) In his discourse, Mr. Spurgeon referred to Palmer, who was then lying under sentence of death in Stafford Gaol, and in order to bring home this text to his hearers, he said that if Palmer had committed many other murders, if he repents and seeks God's pardoning love in Christ, even he will be forgiven! I then felt that if Palmer could be forgiven, so might I. I sought, and blessed be God, I found. I am pardoned, I am free; I am a sinner saved by grace. Though a murderer, I have not yet sinned 'beyond the uttermost,' blessed be his holy name!" It made me very happy to think that a poor condemned murderer could thus be converted. Surely there is hope for every hearer and reader of this sermon, however guilty he may be!

If you know Christ, tell others about him. You do not know what good there is in making Jesus known, even though all you can do is to give a tract, or repeat a verse. Dr. Valpy, the author of a great many class-books, wrote the following simple lines as his confession of faith :—

> "In peace let me resign my breath,
> And thy salvation see;
> My sins deserve eternal death,
> But Jesus died for me."

Valpy is dead and gone; but he gave those lines to dear old Dr. Marsh, the Rector of Beckenham, who put them over his study mantel-shelf. The Earl of Roden came in, and read them. "Will you give me a copy of those lines?" said the good earl. "I shall be glad," said Dr. Marsh, and he copied them. Lord Roden took them home, and put them over *his* mantel-shelf. General Taylor, a Waterloo hero, came into the room, and noticed them. He read them over and over again, while staying with Earl Roden, till his Lordship remarked, "I say, friend Taylor, I should think you know those lines by heart." He answered, "I do know them by heart; indeed, my very heart has grasped their meaning." He was brought to Christ by that humble rhyme. General Taylor handed those lines to an officer in the army, who was going out to the Crimean war. He came home to die; and when Dr. Marsh went to see him, the poor soul in his weakness said, "Good sir, do you know this verse which General Taylor gave to me? It brought me to my Saviour, and I die in peace." To Dr. Marsh's surprise, he repeated the lines :—

> "In peace let me resign my breath,
> And thy salvation see;
> My sins deserve eternal death,
> But Jesus died for me."

Only think of the good which four simple lines may do. Be encouraged all of you who know the healing power of the wounds of Jesus. Spread this truth by all means. Never mind how simple the language. Tell it out: tell it out everywhere, and in every way, even if you cannot do it in any other way than by copying a verse out of a hymn-book. Tell it out that by the stripes of Jesus we are healed. May God bless you, dear friends! Pray for me that this sermon of mine, which is numbered TWO-THOUSAND, may be a very fruitful one.

A Psalm for the New Year

"But grow in grace and in the knowledge of our Lord and Saviour Jesus Christ. To him be glory both now and for ever. Amen."—2 Peter iii. 18.

BEHOLD, beloved, our perpetual dangers. Whither can we go to escape from peril? Where shall we fly to avoid temptation? If we venture into business, worldliness is there. If we retire to our homes, trials are there. One would have imagined that in the green pastures of the Word of God there would have been perfect security for God's sheep. Surely no lion shall be there, and no ravenous beast shall go up thereon! Alas! it is not so. For even while we are reading the Bible we are still exposed to peril. Not that the truth is dangerous, but that our corrupt hearts can find poison in the very flowers of Paradise. Mark what our apostle saith of the writings of St. Paul, "Wherein are some things which are hard to be understood." And mark the danger to which we are exposed, lest we, being unlearned and unstable, should wrest even the Word of God itself to our own destruction. With the Bible before our eyes, we may still commit sin; and pondering over the hallowed words of inspiration, we may receive a deadly wound from "the error of the wicked." Even at the horns of the altar we need that God should still cover us with the shadow of his wings. It is a very pleasing reflection that our gracious Father has provided a shield by which we may be sheltered from every ill, and in our text the evil of heterodoxy finds a suitable preventative. We are in danger, lest misinterpreting Scripture we should make God to say what he does not; and lest by departing from the teaching of the Holy Spirit, we should wrest the letter of the Word and lose its spirit, and from the letter draw a meaning which may be for our soul's ruin. How shall we escape this? Peter, speaking by the Holy Ghost, has in the words before us, pointed out our safeguard. While ye search the Scriptures and grow in acquaintance with them, see to it that ye grow in grace; and while ye desire to know the doctrine, long above all to grow in the knowledge of our Lord and Saviour Jesus Christ; and let your study of Scripture, and your growth in grace and in the knowledge of Christ, still be subservient to that higher object, that you may live to bring glory both now and for ever to Him who hath loved you and bought you with his blood. Let your hearts say evermore, "Amen" to the doxology of praise, so shall ye be kept from all pestilent errors, and ye shall not "fall from your own stedfastness." It appears, then, that our text is adapted to be a heavenly remedy for certain diseases to which even students of Scripture are exposed; and I am persuaded it may serve also as a most blessed directory to us through the whole of the coming year.

I might divide my text, this morning, as good old Adams does. He says there are here two trumpets. One is blown from heaven to earth— "Grow in grace and in the knowledge of our Lord and Saviour Jesus Christ;" the other sounds from earth to heaven—"To him be glory both now and for ever." Or I might quote him again. He says, here is first a point of *theology*, "Grow in grace;" secondly, a point of *doxology*, "To him be glory both now and for ever." We will take the text in the same natural divisions with other headings, and just notice, first, that we have here *a divine injunction, with a special direction:* and secondly, *a grateful doxology, with a suggestive conclusion.*

I. To begin, then, at the beginning, we have here first of all, A DIVINE INJUNCTION WITH A SPECIAL DIRECTION: "Grow in grace, and in the knowledge of our Lord and Saviour Jesus Christ."

"*Grow in grace.*" *What* is this? It must be in the outset implied that we have been quickened by grace, otherwise this text cannot apply to us at all. Dead things cannot grow. Only those who are alive unto God by the resurrection of Jesus Christ from the dead, have in them any power or capability of growth. The great Quickener must first implant the seeds of life, then afterwards those seeds can germinate and grow. To you, therefore, who are dead in trespasses and sins, this text has no application. You cannot grow in grace, because as yet you are under the curse of the law, and the wrath of God abideth on you. Tremble, repent, believe, and may God have mercy on you. But being alive from the dead, and quickened by the Spirit of God which is in you, beloved brethren, *you* who are born again are bidden to grow, for growth shall prove your life. A post planted in the earth grows not; but a tree rooted there, increases from a sapling to a forest king. Drop a pebble into the richest soil, and it will be a pebble still of the same size; put in there the grain or the pulse, and it will spring up and produce its stalk and its flower. Ye who are alive unto God, see to it that ye grow in all the graces. Grow in that root-grace, *faith*. Seek to believe the promises better than ye have done. Go from that trembling faith which says, "Lord, I believe : help thou my unbelief," upward to that which staggers not at the promise, but which, like Abraham, believes that he who has promised is able also to perform. Let your faith increase in extent, believing more truth; let it increase in firmness, getting a tighter grip of every truth; let it increase in constancy, not being feeble or wavering, nor always tossed about with every wind; let your faith daily increase in simplicity, resting more fully, and more entirely, and more completely upon the finished work of your Lord Jesus Christ. See to it that your *love* also grows. If ye have loved with a spark, pray that the spark may

16

become an all-consuming flame. If ye have brought to Christ some little, pray that ye may bring your all; and may offer that all in such a fashion, that like Mary's broken alabaster box, the king himself may be satisfied with the perfume. Ask that your love may become more extended—that ye may have love unto all the saints; more practical, that it may move your every thought, your every word and deed; more intense, that ye may become as burning and shining lights whose flame is love to God and man. Pray that ye may grow in *hope*, that "the eyes of your understanding being enlightened, ye may know what is the hope of his calling, and what the riches of the glory of his inheritance in the saints: that ye may be looking for that blessed hope, the glorious appearing of our Lord and Saviour Jesus Christ; that the hope not seen as yet may enable you with patience to wait for it; that ye may by hope enter into the joys of heaven while ye are on earth; that hope may give you immortality while you are yet mortal—may give you resurrection before you die—may give you to see God, while as yet the glass darkly parts you from him. Ask that you may grow in *humility*, till you can say, "I am less than the least of all the saints;" that ye may grow in *consecration* till ye can cry, "For me to live is Christ: to die is gain;" that ye may grow in *contentment* till ye can feel, "In whatsoever state I am, I have learned therewith to be content." Advance in likeness to the Lord Jesus, that your very enemies may take knowledge of you that ye have been with Jesus, and have learned of him. In fine, if there be any virtue, if there be any praise, if there be anything that is lovely and of good repute, if there be anything that can increase your usefulness, that can add to your happiness, that can make you more serviceable to man and more glorious towards God, grow in it, for ye have not yet attained, neither are ye yet already perfect.

Following up an illustration furnished by the holy Scriptures, let me remind you all, ye faithful believers in Christ, that ye are compared to *trees*—trees of the Lord's right hand planting. Seek to grow as the tree grows. Pray that this year ye may grow *downward;* that ye may know more of your own vileness, more of your own nothingness ; and so be rooted in humility. Pray that your roots may penetrate below the mere topsoil of truth, into the great rocks which underlie the uppermost stratum; that ye may get a good hold of the doctrines of eternal love, of immutable faithfulness, of complete satisfaction, of union to Christ, of the eternal purpose of God, which he purposed in Christ Jesus before the world was. These deep things of God will yield a rich and abundant sap, and your roots shall drink from the hidden fountains of "the depth which lieth under." This will be a growth which will not add to your fame, which will not minister to your vanity: but it will be invaluable in the hour of storm, a growth the value of which no heart can conceive when the hurricane is tearing up the hypocrite, and hurling into the sea of destruction the "trees whose fruit withereth, without fruit, twice dead, plucked up by the roots." As ye root downward, seek to grow *upward*. Send out the topshoot of your love towards heaven. As the trees send out their spring shoot and their midsummer shoot; and as you see upon the top of the fir that new green child of spring, the fresh shoot which lifts its hand towards the sun, so pant to have more love and greater desires after God, a nearer approach towards him in prayer, a sweeter spirit of adoption, a more intense and intimate fellowship with the Father and with his son Jesus Christ. This mounting upwards will add to your beauty and to your delight. Then pray to grow *on either side*. Stretch out your branches; let the shadow of your holy influence extend as far as God has given you opportunities. But see to it also that ye grow in *fruitfulness*, for to increase the bough without adding to the fruit is to diminish the beauty of the tree. Labour this year by God's grace to bring forth more fruit unto him than ye have ever done. Lord, give to this congregation more of the fruits of penitence for sin, of faith in the great sacrifice, of love to Jesus, of zeal for the conversion of souls. We would not be as the gleanings of the vintage when there is only here and there a cluster upon the uppermost bough, we would be as the valley of Eshcol, whose presses burst with new wine. This is to grow in grace: to root downward, to shoot upward, to extend your influences like far-reaching branches, and to bring forth fruit unto the Lord's glory.

But we will borrow another figure from Scripture. Brethren in Jesus Christ, we are not only compared to trees, but to *children*. Let us grow as babes do, nourished by unadulterated milk. Steadily, slowly, but surely and certainly. Little each day, but much in years. Oh that we may grow as a child does in strength, till the little tottering limbs of our faith shall be firm muscular legs with which the young man may run without weariness, and feet upon which the strong man may walk without fainting. As yet our wings are callow, and we can hardly leave the nest. Lord, bid our growth proceed till we can mount as with the wings of eagles towards thyself, surmounting clouds and storms, and dwelling in the serene presence of the Most High. Let us grow in the development of all our powers. Let us ask that we may be no more little infants of a span long, but that many cubits may be added to our stature till we ripen to perfect men in Christ Jesus. And let us specially pray that we may grow as healthy children, uniformly. Brethren, it is an ill sign if a child's head enlarges, but not the rest of his body, or if its arm or foot should be swollen to an ill proportion. Beauty consists in the proportion of every part. A vigorous judgment should not be yoked with a cold heart, nor a clear eye with a withered hand. A giant's head rides ill on a dwarf's shoulders. A virtue nourished at the expense of others is a fattened cannibal fed upon the flesh and blood of its murdered kinsmen; and it ill becomes a Christian to harbour such a monster. Let us pray that faith and love and every grace may be developed; that not one power of the man may be left unnurtured or ungrown, for only thus we can truly grow in grace and in the knowledge of our Lord and Saviour Jesus Christ.

But do ye inquire *why* and wherefore we should thus grow in grace? Let us say, brethren, that if we do not advance in grace it is a sorrowful sign. It is a mark of *unhealthiness*. It is an unhealthy child that grows not, a cankered tree that sends forth no fresh shoots. More ; it may be not only a sign of unhealthiness but of *deformity*. If a man's shoulders have come to a certain breadth, and his lower limbs refuse to lift him aloft, we call him a dwarf, and we look upon him with some degree of pity. He is ill-formed. O Lord, let us grow, for we would not be abortions, we would not be deformities. We would be children like unto God our Father : we would be comely ones, every one of us like the sons of a king. Not to grow may be, moreover, the sign of *death.* It may say to us, Inasmuch as thou growest not, thou livest not ; inasmuch as thou dost not increase in faith, and love, and grace ; and inasmuch as thou dost not ripen towards the harvest, fear and tremble lest thou shouldst only have a name to live and be destitute of life, lest thou shouldst be the painted counterfeit ; a lovely flower-picture drawn by the painter's skilful hand, but without reality, because without the life-power which should make it bud and germinate, and blossom and bring forth fruit. Advance in grace, because not to progress augurs many evils things, and may teach that worst of all things, the want of spiritual life. Grow in grace, because, beloved, to increase in grace is the only pathway to enduring nobility. Oh! wc.uld ye not wish to stand with that noble host who have served their Master well, and have entered into their eternal rest. Who among ye does not wish to have his name written w'th the missionaries of modern times—with Judson and with Carey, with Williams and with Moffat ? Who amongst us is there who has no ambition to find his name written among those servants of God—Whitfield, Grimshaw, Newton, Romaine, Toplady and others who preached the Word with power ? Are there any of us who wish to go back to the vile dust from whence we sprung, " unwept, unhonoured, and unsung ?" Then let us be as we are ; let us cease our march. Meanness lies at your door, be stunted and be ignoble. But if we would be princes in God's Israel, if we would be mighty warriors for the cross of Christ, let us pray this prayer, " Lord, bid us grow in grace, that we may be faithful servants, and receive thy commendation at the last." But to grow is not only to be noble, it is to be happy. That man who stays growing, refuses to be blessed. With most men in business, if they do not win, they lose. With the warrior, if he gains not in the battle, his enemy is getting an advantage. That wise man who gets no wiser, grows more foolish. That Christian who does not know more of his Lord, and become more like him, knows less of his Lord and becomes less like him. Our armour if unused will tarnish, and our arms if not strengthened by effort will be weakened by indolence. Our *happiness* declines as our spirituality fades. To be happy, I say, we must go forward. Forward is the sunlight ! forward is victory ! forward is heaven ! forward is Christ ! But here, to stand still is danger ; nay, it is death. O Lord, for our happiness' sake bid thou us advance, and for our usefulness' sake let us ascend. Oh! if we as a congregation and as a Church grew in grace more; if we were stronger in faith, mightier in prayer, more fervent in heart, more holy in life, who can tell how much we might effect for our age. Men who walk but lightly, leave but faint steps ; but men who tread with the tramp of Roman soldiers stamp their foot-prints on the sands of time, never to be erased. So let us live, that in our day and in after days the world may be the better, and Christ's Church the more prosperous for our having lived. For this reason, if for no other, let us grow in grace.

Oh, could I fire you with some hallowed ambition to-day I were but too happy! Could I snatch from some ancient altar a live coal such as that which fell upon the lip of Esaias, I would say unto you, Lo, this has touched your lip—go forth in the spirit and power of God, even the Most High; and live as they lived who counted not their lives dear unto them that they might serve their Master and be found in him. I point you to the spirits who have entered within the veil and who rest upon the couches of eternal glory, and I say, they won the victory by grace, and growth in grace was the means of their triumph. Emulate them; press forward as they did, and through grace you shall inherit their rest and their triumph, and sit down with them for ever.

But do ye inquire *how* ye shall grow in grace? The answer is simple. He who gave you grace must give you more of it. Where ye first received your grace there ye must receive the increase of that grace. He who made the cattle and who created man, was the same who afterwards said "Be fruitful and multiply and replenish the earth." So he that has given you grace must speak with the fiat of his omnipotence in your heart and say to that grace, "Be fruitful and multiply and replenish the soul till its native emptiness shall be filled, and the natural wilderness shall rejoice and blossom like a rose." But at the same time we would have you use the means; and those means are much prayer, a more diligent search of the sacred Scriptures, a more constant fellowship with the Lord Jesus Christ, greater activity in his cause, an earnest attendance upon the means of grace, a devout reception of all revealed truth, and so forth. If ye do these things ye shall never be stunted or dwarfed, for he that has given you life will thus enable you to fulfil the word which he spake to you by his apostle, "Grow in grace and in the knowledge of our Lord and Saviour Jesus Christ."

I have thus explained the divine exhortation; but you perceive it contains a *special injunction*, upon which we must pause a moment. "And in the knowledge of our Lord and Saviour Jesus Christ."

My beloved brethren in the Lord Jesus, we must see to it that we ripen in the knowledge of *Him*. Oh that this year we may know more of him in his divine nature, and in his human relationship to us ; in his finished work, in his death, in his resurrection, in his present glorious intercession, and in his future royal advent. To know more of Christ in his work is, I think, a blessed means of enabling us to work more for Christ.

We must study to know more of Christ also in his character—in that divine compound of every perfection, faith, zeal, deference to his Father's will, courage, meekness and love. He was the lion of the tribe of Judah, and yet the man upon whom the dove descended in the waters of baptism. Let us thirst to know him of whom even his enemies said, "Never man spake like this man," and his unrighteous judge said, "I find no fault in him."

Above all, let us long to know Christ in his person. This year endeavour to make a better acquaintance with the crucified one. Study his hands and his feet; abide ye hard by the cross, and let the sponge, the vinegar and the nails, be subjects of your devout attention. This year seek to penetrate into his very heart, and to search those deep far-reaching caverns of his unknown love, that love which can never find a rival, and can never know a parallel. If ye can add to this a knowledge of his sufferings, ye will do well. Oh! if ye can grow in the knowledge of fellowship if ye shall this year drink of his cup, and be baptized with his baptism—if ye shall this year abide in him and he in you—blessed shall ye be. This is the only growth in grace which is true growth; and all other growth which leads us not to increase in the knowledge of Christ is but the puffing up of the flesh and not the building up of the Spirit.

Grow in the knowledge of Christ, then. And do ye ask me *why?* Oh! if ye have ever known Him you will not ask that question. He that longs not to know more of Christ, knows nothing of him yet. He that ever sipped this wine will thirst for more, for although Christ doth satisfy, yet it is such a satisfaction, that we want to taste more, and more, and more, and more. Oh! if ye know the love of Jesus, I am sure as the hart panteth for the water-brooks, so will you pant after him. If ye say ye do not desire to know him better, then I tell you ye love him not, for love always cries, "Nearer, nearer, nearer." Absence from Christ is hell; but presence with Christ is heaven; and, as we get nearer to him, our heaven becomes more heavenly, and we enjoy it more, and feel more that it is of God. Oh! may you this year come to the very well of Bethlehem, and not merely receive a vessel from it, as David did, at the risk of the lives of three mighty men; but may you come to the well and drink—drink from the well itself, from that bottomless well-spring of eternal love. Oh, this year may the secret of the Lord be with you, and may you be in the secret place of the Most High! My Master, shouldest thou permit me to ask thee one thing as a special favour, it should be this, that I may "know him and the power of his resurrection, being made conformable to his death!" Nearer to thee, blessed Lord, nearer to thee: this all our cry shall be. The Lord grant that our cry may be heard, that we may grow in the knowledge of Christ!

We wish to know Christ this year as our *Lord*—Lord of every thought and every desire, of every word and every act. And as our *Saviour* too, our Saviour from every indwelling sin, our Saviour from every evil past, from every trial to come. All hail, Jesu! we salute thee as Lord. Teach us to feel thy Kingship over us, and to feel it every hour. All hail, thou crucified One! We acknowledge thee as Saviour; help us to rejoice in thy salvation, and to feel the plenitude of that salvation in all and every part of spirit, soul, and body, being wholly saved by thee.

I have thus, men and brethren, sought to expound the point of theology; I lift up my heart in prayer for you all that you may grow in grace, and in the knowledge of our Lord and Saviour Jesus Christ.

II. In the second place, we have A GRATEFUL THANKSGIVING, WITH A MOST SUGGESTIVE TERMINATION : "To him be glory both now and for ever. Amen."

The apostles, we must remark, very frequently suspended their writing in order to lift up their hearts in praise. Praise is never out of season, and it is no interruption to interrupt any engagement in order to laud and magnify our God. "To him be glory." Brethren, do not let me preach now, but let me interpret your emotions. Let it be not so much my utterance, as your utterance by my lips. Let every heart joyously feel this doxology, To him, the God that made the heavens and the earth, without whom was not anything made; to him who in his infinite compassion became the surety of the covenant—to him who became a babe of a span long—to him who was despised and rejected of men, a man of sorrows and acquainted with grief—to him who on the bloody tree poured out his heart's life that he might redeem his people—to *him* who said "I thirst," and "It is finished!"—to *him* whose lifeless body slumbered in the grave—to him be glory. To him that burst the bonds of death—to him who ascended on high and led captivity captive—to him who sitteth at the right hand of the Father and who shall soon come to be our Judge—"to him be glory." Yes, to him, ye atheists, who deny him—to him, ye Socinians, who doubt his Deity—to him, ye kings, who vaunt your splendour, and will not have this man to reign over you—to him, ye people, who against him stand up, and ye rulers who against him take counsel—to him, the King whom God hath set upon his holy hill of Zion—to him be glory. To him be glory as the Lord: King of kings and Lords; "Wonderful, Counsellor, the mighty God, the everlasting Father, the Prince of Peace." And yet again Hosannah in the highest—Hallelujah! King of kings and Lord of lords. To him be glory as *Lord.* To him be glory as *Saviour.* He alone hath redeemed us unto God by his blood; he alone hath "trodden the wine-press," and "cometh from Edom, with dyed garments from Bozrah, glorious in his apparel, travelling in the greatness of his strength." "To him be glory." Hear it ye angels : "To him be glory." Clap your wings. Cry "Hallelujah! to him be glory." Hear it ye spirits of the just made perfect; sweep the strings of your celestial harps, and say, "Hallelujah, glory to him who hath redeemed us unto God by his own blood." "*To him be glory.*" Church of God respond! Let every pious heart say " *To him be glory.*" Yes, unto him be glory, ye fiends of hell, as ye tremble at his presence, and see the key of your prison-house swinging at his girdle. Let heaven, and earth, and hell—let things that are, and were, and shall be, cry, "To him be glory."

But the apostle adds, "*now*"—"to him be glory, *now.*" O brethren, postpone not the day of his triumph; put not off the hour of his coronation. *Now*, NOW.

> "Bring forth the royal diadem,
> And crown him Lord of all."

Now, now; for now, to-day, he hath raised us up together, and made us sit in heavenly places with Christ Jesus. "Beloved, now are we the sons of God;" now are our sins forgiven; now are we robed in his righteousness; now are our feet upon a rock, and our goings are established. Who is there among you that would defer the time of your hosannahs? "To him be glory *now*." O cherubim above, "To him be glory now!" for ye "continually do cry, Holy, holy, holy, Lord God of hosts." Adore him yet again, for, "To him be glory now."

"*And for ever*." Never shall we cease our praise. Time! thou shalt grow old and die. Eternity! thine unnumbered years shall speed their everlasting course; but for ever, for ever, for ever, "to him be glory." Is he not a "Priest for ever, after the order of Melchisedek?" "To him be glory." Is he not king for ever?—King of kings and Lord of lords, the everlasting Father? "To him be glory *for ever*." Never shall his praises cease. That which was bought with blood deserves to last while immortality endures. The glory of the cross must never be eclipsed; the lustre of the grave and of the resurrection must never be dimmed. Oh, my beloved brethren, my spirit begins to feel the ardour of the immortals. I would anticipate the songs of heaven. My tongue, had it but celestial liberty, would begin e'en now, to join those thrice-melodious sonnets sung by flaming tongues above. O Jesus! thou shalt be praised for ever. Long as immortal spirits live—long as the Father's throne endures—for ever, for ever, for ever, unto thee shall be glory.

But now, there is a conclusion to this of the most suggestive kind, "*Amen*." Brethren, I want to work this amen out—not as a matter of doctrine, but as a matter of blessed transport. Come, give me your hearts again. "To him be glory both now and for ever, *Amen*." What means this Amen? Amen has four meanings in Scripture. By the way, the Puritan's remark—it is a very remarkable thing—that under the old law, there was no amen to the blessings; the only amen was to the curses. When they pronounced the curses, "All the people said Amen." Under the law, there never was an amen to the blessing. Now, it is an equally remarkable, and more blessed thing, that under the gospel, there is no amen to the curses, the only amen is to the blessings. "May the grace of our Lord Jesus Christ, and the love of God our Father, and the communion of the Holy Ghost, be with you all, Amen." "If any man love not the Lord Jesus Christ, let him be Anathema Maran-atha." No amen. There is no amen to the curse under the gospel. But "all the promises of God are yea and amen, in Christ Jesus." Now, the ' Amen,"—and here I am greatly indebted to good old Thomas Adams—means four things. First, it is *the desire of the heart*, "Behold, I come quickly; Amen. Even so, come, Lord Jesus." We say amen at the end of the prayer, to signify, "Lord, let it be so,"—it is our heart's desire. Now, brethren, give me your hearts, then—for it is all a heart-matter here. "To him be glory both now and for ever, Amen." Is that your heart's desire? If not, you cannot say amen to it. Does your heart long, pant, thirst, groan, and cry out after Christ, so that you *can* say, every time you bend your knee, "Thy kingdom come, thy will be done on earth as it is in heaven, for thine is the kingdom, the power, and the glory, for ever and ever, Amen." Can you say, "Amen, Lord, let thy kingdom come." Brethren, if you can say it in this sense, if it be your heart's desire that Christ's glory should be extended, and his kingdom should come, say "Amen," aloud this morning. Now join with me, for my heart glows with it. I can say it,—and the Judge of all knows how my heart longs to see Jesus magnified; join with me then, ye who can

23

do it honestly, while I repeat the doxology—" To him be glory both now and for ever. Amen."

[The congregation very heartily, aloud said, " Amen."]

So be it Lord. Thou hearest thy Church as it cries " Amen;" verily, it is our heart's desire.

> " Amen, with joy divine, let earth's
> Unnumber'd myriads cry ;
> Amen, with joy divine, let heaven's
> Unnumber'd choirs reply."

But it signifies more than this ; it means *the affirmation of our faith.* We only say amen to that which we really believe to be true. We add our affidavit as it were to God's promise, that we believe him to be faithful and true. Have you any doubts but that Jesus Christ is glorious now and for ever ? Do you doubt his being glorified of angels, cherubim and seraphim, to-day ? And do you not believe, my brethren, that they that dwell in the wilderness shall bow before him, and that his enemies shall lick the dust ? If you so believe, if you have faith to-day amid the world's obstinacy and the sinner's pride, amid abounding superstition and dominant evil, if you have faith still to believe that Christ shall be glorious for ever and ever, then join with me and again say Amen. " To him be glory both now and for ever, Amen." [The congregation again said " Amen."]

Lord, thou hearest it, though it is a feebler cry than aforetime, for there are more who can desire it than there are who believe it. Nevertheless, thou abidest faithful.

> " This little seed from heaven
> Shall soon become a tree ;
> This ever-blessed leaven
> Diffused abroad must be :
> Till God the Son shall come again,
> It must go on. Amen ! Amen."

But there is yet a third meaning to this amen ; it often expresses *the joy of the heart.* When of old they brought forth a Jewish king, the High Priest took a horn of oil and poured it on his head; then came forward a herald, and the moment he had sounded the trumpet, one with a loud voice said, " God save the king ! God save the king !" and all the people said " Amen," and one shout went up to heaven, while with joy of heart they saluted the king in whom they hoped to see a prosperous ruler through whom God would bless them and make them victorious. Now, what say you ? As you see King Jesus sitting upon Mount Zion with death and hell beneath his feet, as to day you anticipate the glory of his Advent, as to day you are expecting the time when you shall reign with him for ever and ever, does not your heart say " Amen ?" I can remember, in a season of the greatest darkness of mind and weakness of body, there was one text which used to cheer me beyond all measure ; there was nothing in the text about myself; it was no promise to *me*, but it was something about *him*. It was this—" Him hath God highly exalted and given him a name which is above every name, that at the name of Jesus every knee should bow, of things in heaven, and things in earth, and things under the earth." Oh! it seemed so joyous that *he* was exalted. What did it matter what became of me? What did it signify what should become of all of us? King David is worth ten thousand of us. Let our name perish, but let his name last for ever. Brethren, this morning I bring forth the King to you. I bring him before the eyes of your faith to-day; I proclaim him king again, and do you if you desire him to be king, and if you rejoice in his reign, say "Amen." Here, here he stands in vision before your eyes. Crown him! Crown him! Lo, he is to-day crowned afresh. "To him be glory both now and for ever." Joyous hearts lift up your voices, and with one accord say "Amen." [The congregation again said "Amen."] Amen, Lord, be thou King in the midst of us all.

> " Yea, amen, let all adore thee,
> High on thine exalted throne!
> Saviour, take thy power and glory;
> Claim the kingdoms for thine own:
> O come quickly!
> Hallelujah! Come, Lord, come."

But, lastly, and this is a very solemn point. Amen is sometimes used in scripture as an amen of resolution. It means, " I, in the name of God, solemnly pledge myself that in his strength I will seek to make it so; to him be glory both now and for ever." Now I shall not want you to say "Amen" to this *aloud*, but I shall pause to let you say it silently in your own souls by-and-bye. I walked last week through the long galleries which vanity has dedicated to all the glories of France. You pass through room after room where especially you see the triumphs of Napoleon in writhing bodies, and in the blood, and vapour, and smoke. Surely as you walk through the pages of Scripture, you walk through a much more marvellous picture gallery, in which you see the glories of Christ. This book contains the memorials of his honours. In another place in Paris there stands a column made with the cannons taken by the Emperor in battle. A mighty trophy, certainly. O Jesus! thou hast a better than this; a trophy made of souls forgiven; of eyes which wept, but whose tears have been wiped away; of broken hearts that have been healed, and of saved souls that for evermore rejoice. But what trophies Christ has to make him glorious, both now and for ever; trophies of living hearts that love him; trophies of immortal spirits who find their heaven in gazing upon his beauties! What must the glories of Christ be for ever when you and I and all the ten thousand millions he has bought with his blood shall be in heaven. Oh! when we have been there many a thousand years we shall feel as fresh a rapture as when we came there, and if our spirits should be sent on any errand from our Master, and we should have to leave the presence-chamber for a moment, oh! with what wings of a dove we will fly back to behold his face again. When we shall all surround that throne, what songs will I give him, the chief of sinners saved by blood! What hymns will you give him; you who have had your iniquities cleansed and are to day saved? What praise will all those multitudes give him who have all been partakers of his grace? But this has more to do with "for ever." Now, what say you about our glorifying him *now?* Oh, brothers and sisters, do you make it your prayer this morning, "Lord, help me to glorify thee; I am poor, help me to glorify thee by contentment; I am sick, help me to give thee honour by patience; I have talents, help me to extol thee by spending them for thee; I have time, Lord, help me to redeem it, that I may serve thee; I have a heart to feel, Lord, let that heart feel no love but thine, and glow with no flame, but affection for thee; I have a head to think, Lord help me to think *of* thee and *for* thee; thou hast put me in this world for something, Lord, show me what that is, and help me to work out my life-purpose; for I do desire to say amen. I cannot do much; my amen is but a feeble one, but as the widow put in her two mites, which made a farthing, which was all her living, so, Lord, I put my time and eternity too into thy treasury; 'tis all thine; take it, and thus I say, 'Amen' to Peter's apostolical doxology."

And now, throughout this year will you go forth, my brothers and sisters, and say, amen to this? I pray you do so. You who love not Christ, cannot say amen. Remember you are under the law. There is an amen to all the curses to you; there is none to the blessings while you are under the law. O poor sinner, under the law, may this be the day when thy law-slavery shall come to an end! "How can it be?" you say. By faith in Christ, I answer. "He that believeth on him is not condemned." Oh that thou mayest believe on him, and then thy joyful heart will say, amen. Then wilt thou say, "Loudest of all the saints in heaven, I will shout amen, when I see the royal crown brought forth, and Jesus is acknowledged Lord of all." May God grant that this year may be the best year this Church has ever had. This year concludes eight years of my ministry among you, and seven years of Printed Sermons are now before the public. How much of blessedness God has caused to pass through our mind, and how much he has been pleased to own his Word, we cannot fully measure. But we know that he *has* been with us in deed and in truth. Now that we begin this year, may the Lord make it so that all the past shall seem to be as nothing compared with that which is to come. I bless you my brothers and sisters in the name of the Lord, and commencing this year, I beg again for renewed tokens of your affection by a renewal of your prayers; and on my part, I only trust that it may be mine through this year, and long as I live, to be giving my amen to that doxology— "To him be glory both now and for ever. Amen."

A Tempted Saviour—Our Best Succour

"For in that he himself hath suffered being tempted, he is able to succour them that are tempted."—Hebrews ii. 18.

MY text, furnishing the motto for the congregation for the New Year, is, as you know, always supplied to me by a most venerable clergyman of the Church of England, who has ever showed to me the most constant and affectionate regard. I have no doubt that the present text has been suggested to this aged servant of the Lord by his deep experience at once of affliction and deliverance: for thence he has learned his need of solid, substantial food, fat things full of marrow, fit for the veteran warriors of the cross. Having been tempted these many years in the wilderness, my esteemed friend finds that as his natural strength decays, he needs more and more to cast himself upon the tenderness of the Redeemer's love; and he is led more fully to look to Him who is his only help and succour in every day of trouble, finding consolation alone in the person of Christ Jesus the Lord. My text seems to me to be a staff fitted for hoary age to lean upon in the rough places of the way; a sword, with which the strong man may fight in all hours of conflict; a shield, with which youth may cover itself in the time of peril; and a royal chariot in which babes in grace may ride in safety. There is something here for every one of us, as Solomon puts it, a portion for seven and also for eight. If we consider the Great Prophet and High Priest of our profession—Jesus Christ—as being tempted in all points, we shall not grow weary or faint in our minds, but shall gird up our loins for our future journey, and like Elijah go in the strength of this meat for many days to come.

Ye that are tempted—and I suppose the major part of this present congregation are included in the list;—ye that are tempted—and indeed if you know yourselves you are all in your measure thus exercised—ye that are tempted, listen to me this morning whilst I endeavour to speak of your temptations, and in parallel lines of the temptations of Him who, having known your trials is able to succour you at all times.

I. Our first point this morning is this—MANY SOULS ARE TEMPTED —CHRIST WAS TEMPTED. All the heirs of heaven pass under the yoke;

27

all true gold must feel the fire; all wheat must be threshed; all diamonds must be cut; all saints must endure temptation.

1. They are tempted *from all quarters.* It is as Christ's parable puts it concerning the house whose foundation was on the rock: " The rain descended, the floods came, and the winds blew and beat upon that house but it fell not, for it was founded upon a rock." The descending rain may represent temptations from above; the floods pouring their devastating torrents upon the land may well denote the trials which spring from the world; while the howling winds may typify those mysterious influences of evil which issue from the Prince of the power of the air. Now whether we shudder at the descending rain, or fear before the uprising flood, or are amazed at the mysterious energy of the winds, it is well to recollect our blessed Lord was tempted in all points like as we are. This is to be our consolation, that nothing strange to the Head has happened to the members.

Beloved friends, it is possible that we may be tempted *by God.* I know it is written that " God is not tempted, neither tempteth he any man;" yet I read in Scripture "It came to pass that God did tempt Abraham," and I know it is a part of the prayer which we are taught to offer before God—" Lead us not into temptation," by which it is clearly implied that God does lead into temptation, or why else should we be taught to entreat him not to do so. In one sense of the term " tempt," a pure and holy God can have no share, but in another sense he does tempt his people. The temptation which comes from God is altogether that of trial; trial, not with an ill-design as are the temptations of Satan, but trial meant to prove and strengthen our graces, and so at once to illustrate the power of divine grace, to test the genuineness of our virtues, and to add to their energy. You remember that Abraham was tried and tested of God when he was bidden to go to a mountain that God would show him, there to offer up his son Isaac. You and I may have the like experience. God may call us in the path of obedience to a great and singular sacrifice, the desire of our eyes may be demanded of us in an hour; or he may summon us to a tremendous duty far surpassing all our strength, and we may be tempted by the weight of the responsibility, like Jonah, to flee from the presence of the Lord. We can only know when placed in the position what temptations the Lord's message may involve, but, beloved, whatever these may be, our Great High Priest has felt them all. His Father called him to a work of the most terrific character. He laid upon him the iniquity of us all. He ordained him the second Adam, the bearer of the curse, the destroyer of death, the conqueror of hell, the seed of the woman doomed to be wounded in the heel, and elected to bruise the serpent's head. Our Lord was appointed to toil at the loom, and there, with ever-flying shuttle, to weave a perfect garment of righteousness for all his people. Now, beloved, this was a strong and mighty testing of the character of him who was found in fashion as a man, and it is not possible that we can ever be thrust into such a refiner's fire as that which tried this most pure gold. No other can be in the crucible so long, or subjected to such a tremendous heat as that which was endured by Christ Jesus. If, then, the trial be sent direct from our heavenly Father, we may solace ourselves with this reflection—in that he himself hath suffered, being tried of God, he is able also to succour them that are likewise tried. But, dear friends, our God not only tries us directly but *indirectly*. All is under the Lord's control of Providence; everything that happeneth to us is meted out by the decree and settled by his purpose. We know that nothing can occur to us save as it is written in the secret roll of providential predestination; consequently all the trials resulting from circumstances are traceable at once to the great First Cause. Out of the golden gate of God's ordinance the armies of trial march forth in array. No shower falls unpermitted from the threatening cloud; every drop has its order ere it hastens to the earth. Consider poverty for instance. How many are made to feel its pinching necessities. They shiver in the cold for want of raiment; they are hungry and athirst; they are houseless, friendless, despised. This is a temptation from God, but all this Christ knew—"Foxes have holes, and the birds of the air have nests, but I, the Son of Man, have not where to lay my head." When he had fasted forty days and forty nights he was an hungered, and then it was that he was tempted of the devil. Nor does the scant table and the ragged garment alone invite temptation, for all Providences are doors to trial. Even our mercies, like roses, have their thorns. Men may be drowned in seas of prosperity as well as in rivers of affliction. Our mountains are not too high, and our valleys are not too low for temptation to travel. Whither shall we flee from their presence? What wings of wind can carry us? What beams of light can bear us? Everywhere, above and beneath, we are beset and surrounded with dangers. Now, since all these are under the superintendence and direction of the great Lord of Providence, we may look upon them all as temptations which come from him. But in every one of these Christ had his part. Let us choose the special one of *sickness;* sickness is a strong temptation to impatience, rebellion, and murmuring, but he himself took our infirmities and bare our sicknesses. That visage had not been marred more than that of any man, had not the soul been sore vexed, and the body consequently much tormented. *Bereavement,* too, what a trial is this to the tender heart! Ye arrows of death, ye kill, but ye wound with wounds worse than death. "Jesus wept," because his friend Lazarus slept in the tomb. In that great loss he was schooled to sympathize with the widow in her weeds, with the orphan in his fatherless estate, and with the friend whose acquaintance has been thrust into darkness. Nothing can come from God to the sons of men the like of which did not also happen unto the Lord Jesus Christ. Herein let us wrap ourselves about with the warm mantle of consolation, since Christ was tempted in this point iike as we are.

1. But still more do temptations *arise from men.* God doth try us now and then, but our fellow-men every day. Our foes are found in our own household, among our friends. Out of a mistaken kindness, it often happeneth that they would lead us to prefer our own ease to the service of God. Links of love have made iron chains for saints. It is hard to ride to heaven over our own flesh and blood. Kinsfolk and acquaintance may much hinder young disciples. This, however, is no novelty to our Lord. You know how he had to say to Peter, well-

beloved disciple though he was, "Get thee behind me, Satan; thou savourest not the things that be of God." Poor, ignorant human friendship, would have kept him back from the cross; would have made him miss his great object in being fashioned as a man, and so have despoiled him of all the honour which only shame and death could win him. Not only true, but false friends attempt our ruin. Treason creeps like a snake in the grass, and falsehood, like an adder, biteth the horse's heels. Doth treachery assault us, let us remember how the Son of David was betrayed. "He that eateth bread with me hath lifted up his heel against me." "Yea, mine own familiar friend, in whom I trusted, which did eat of my bread, hath lifted up his heel against me." What shall be done unto thee, thou false tongue? Eternal silence rest on thee! And yet, thou hast spent thy venom on my Lord; why need I marvel if thou try thy worst on me?

As by friends you and I are tempted, so often are we assailed by enemies. Enemies will waylay us with subtle questions, seeking to entrap us in our speech. O cunning devices of a generation of vipers! They did the same with Christ. The Herodian, the Sadducee, the Pharisee, the lawyer, each one has his riddle, and each one is answered—answered gloriously by the Great Teacher, who is not to be entrapped. You and I are sometimes asked queer questions; doctrines are set in controversy with doctrines; texts of Scripture are made to clash with other portions of God's Word, and we hardly know how to reply. Let us retire into the secret chamber of this great fact—that, in this point, also, Christ was tempted. And then, when his foes could not prevail against him thus, they slandered his character. "A drunken man and a winebibber, a friend of publicans and sinners," said they, and he became the song of the drunkard, till their reproach had broken his heart. This may happen to us. We may be subjected to slander just in that very point where we are most clear. Our good may be evil spoken of; our motives misinterpreted; our words misreported; our actions misconstrued; but here, also, we may shelter ourselves beneath the eagle wings of this great truth, that our glorious Head hath suffered, and, being tempted, he can afford us aid. But his foes did even more than this: when they found him in an agony of pain, they taunted him to his face; pointing with the finger, they mocked his nakedness; thrusting out the tongue, they jeered at his claims, and hissed out that more than diabolical temptation, "If thou be the Son of God, come down from the cross, and we will believe in thee." How often do the sons of men, when they have gone to the full length of their tether, charge us in like manner. They have caught us in some unhappy moment—surprised us when our spirits were broken, when our circumstances were unhappy, and then they say, "Now—now where is your God? If you be what you profess to be, now prove it." They ask us to prove our faith by a sinful action, which they know would destroy our characters —some rash deed, which would be contrary to the profession we have espoused. Here, too, we may remember that, having been tempted, our High Priest is able to succour those that are tempted. Moreover, remember that there are temptations which come from persons who are neither friends nor foes, from those with whom we are compelled to mix in ordinary society. Jesus went to the pharisee's table; the example of the pharisee reeked with infectious pride; he sat with the publicans, whose characters were contagious with impurity; but, whether it was in one lazar-house or another, the Great Physician walked through the midst of moral plagues and leprosies unharmed. He associated with sinners, but was not a sinner; he touched disease, but was not diseased himself; he could enter into the chambers of evil, but evil could not find a chamber in him. You and I are thrown by our daily avocations into constant contact with evil. It were impossible, I suppose, to walk among men without being tempted by them. Inadvertently, men who have no studied design to betray us, by the mere force of their ordinary behaviour entice us to evil, and corrupt our good manners. Here, too, if we have to cry, "Woe is me, for I dwell in Meshech, and sojourn in the tents of Kedar," we may remember that our great Leader sojurned here too, and being here he was tempted even as we are.

Dear friends, we shall not complete the list of temptations if we forget that a vast host, and those of a most violent character, can only be ascribed to *Satanic influence.* These are usually threefold; for Christ's temptation in the wilderness, if I read it aright, was a true picture of all the temptations which Satan uses against God's people. The first grand temptation of Satan is usually made against our faith. Being an hungered, Satan came to our Lord and said, "If thou be the Son of God, command that these stones be made bread." Here it was that devilish "if," that cunning suggestion of a doubt concerning his Sonship, coupled with the enticement to commit a selfish act, to prove whether he were the Son or no. Ah! how often doth Satan tempt us to unbelief. "God hath forsaken thee," saith he; "God hath no love to thee; thine experience has been a delusion; thy profession is a falsehood; all thy hopes will fail thee; thou art but a poor miserable dupe; there is no truth in religion; if there be, how is it that you are in this trouble? Why not do as you like, live as you list, and enjoy yourself?" Ah! foul fiend, how craftily dost thou spread thy net; but it is all in vain, for Jesus has passed through and broken the snare. My hearers, beware of intermeddling with divine providence; Satan tempts many believers to run before the cloud, to carve their own fortunes, build their own house, to steer their own vessels; mischief will surely befall all who yield to this temptation. Beware of becoming the keepers of your own souls, for evil will soon o'ertake you. Ah! when you are thus tempted by Satan, and your adoption seems in jeopardy, and your experience appears to melt, fly at once to the good shepherd, remembering this, "In that he himself hath suffered being tempted, he is able to succour them that are tempted." The next foul temptation of Satan with Christ, was not to unbelief, but to the very reverse—presumption. "Cast thyself down," said he, as he poised the Saviour on the pinnacle of the temple. Even so he whispers to some of us, "You are a child of God; you know that, and therefore you are safe; live as you like; cast thyself down, for it is written, 'He shall give his angels charge over thee to keep the.'" Oh! that foul temptation. Many an Antinomian is led by the nose by this, driven like a fatted bullock to the slaughter, and like a fool to the correction of the stocks: for many an Antinomian will say, "I am safe, therefore I may indulge my lusts with impunity." But you who know better, when you are thus molested, when the devil brings the doctrine of election, or the great truth of the final perseverance of the saints, and seeks to soil your purity, and stain your innocency by temptations drawn from the mercy and love of God, then console yourselves by this fact, that Christ was tempted in this point too, and is able to succour you even here. The last temptation of Christ in the wilderness was to idolatry; ambition was the temptation, but idolatry was the end at which the tempter aimed. "All these things will I give thee if thou wilt fall down and worship me." The old serpent will suggest, "I will make you rich if you will only venture upon that one swindling transaction; you shall be famous, only palm off that one falsehood; you shall be perfectly at ease, only wink at one small evil; all these things will I give thee if thou wilt make me Lord of thy heart." Ah! then it will be a noble thing if you can look up to Him who endured this temptation aforetime, and bid the fiend depart with "It is written, thou shalt worship the Lord with all thy heart, and him only shalt thou serve." Thus shall Satan leave thee, and angels minister unto thee as they did to the tempted one of old.

Still further, to enlarge on this point, let me observe that we are tempted not only from all quarters, but *in all positions*. No man too lowly for the shafts of hell: no person too elevated for the arrows of evil. Poverty has its dangers—"Lest I be poor and steal"—Christ knew these. Contempt has its aggravated temptations—to be despised often makes men bitter of spirit, exasperates them into savage selfishness, and wolfish cruelty of revenge. Our great Prophet knew experimentally the temptations of contempt. It is no small trial to be filled with pain; when all the strings of our manhood are strained and twisted, it is little wonder if they make a discord. Christ endured the greatest amount of physical pain, especially upon the cross. And on the cross, where all the rivers of human agony met in one deep lake within his heart, he bore all that it was possible for the human frame to bear; here, then, without limit he learned the ills of pain. Turn the picture— Christ knew the temptations of riches. You will say, "How?" He had the opportunities to be rich. Mary, and Martha, and Lazarus, would have been too glad to give him their substance; the honourable women who ministered to him, would have grudged him nothing. There were many opportunities when he might have made himself a king; he might have become famous and great like other teachers, and so have earned emolument; but as he knew, so also he overcame the temptations of wealth. The temptations of ease—and these are not small—Christ readily escaped. There would always have been a comfortable home for him at Bethany; there were many disciples who would have thought themselves but too honoured to have found for him the softest couch on which head ever rested; but he who came not to enjoy but to endure, spurned all, but not without knowing the temptation. He learned, too, the trials of honour, of popularity, and of applause. "Hosanna, hosanna, hosanna," said the multitudes in the streets of Jerusalem, when palm-branches were strewed in the way, and he rode in triumph over the garments of his disciples ; but, knowing all this, he was still meek and lowly, and in him was no sin. We cannot either be cast down or lifted up, we cannot be put into the most strange and singular positions, without still being able to remember that Christ has made a pilgrimage over the least trodden of our paths, and is therefore able to succour them that are tempted.

3. Further, let me remark *that every age has its temptations.* The young while yet children, if believers, will discover that there are peculiar snares for the little ones. Christ knew these. It was no small temptation to a youth, a lad of some twelve years of age, to be found sitting in the midst of the doctors, hearing them and answering their questions; it would have turned the heads of most boys, and yet Jesus went down to Nazareth and was subject unto his parents. It is small peril to grow in knowledge and in favour with God and man, if it were not for the word "God" put in it; to grow in favour constantly with men would be too much of a temptation for most youths. It is good for a man that he bear the yoke in his youth, for youth, when honoured and esteemed, is too apt to lift its head and grow self-conceited, vain, and froward. When a young man knows that by-and-bye he shall become something great, it is not easy to keep him balanced. Suppose that he is born to an estate, and knows that when he comes of full age he will be lord and master, and will be courted by everybody, why he is apt to be very wayward and self-willed. Now there were prophecies that went before concerning Mary's son—which marked him out as King of the Jews and a Mighty One in Israel, and yet I find not that the holy child Jesus was ever decoyed by his coming greatness into any actions inconsistent with the duty of a child. So young believers, you who are like Samuels and Timothys, you can look to Christ and know that he can succour you. In his full manhood it is unnecessary for me to repeat the various afflictions which beat upon him. You who to-day bear the burden and heat of the day will find an example here; nor need old age look elsewhere, for we may view our Redeemer with admiration as he goes up to Jerusalem to die. His last moments are manifestly near at hand; he knows the temptations of an expected dissolution; he sees death more clearly than any of you, even though your temples are covered with hoar hairs; and yet, whether in life or in death, on Tabor's summit or on the banks of the river of death, he is still the same; tempted ever, but never sinning; tried always, but never found wanting.

O Lord! thou art able thus to succour them that are tempted; help thou us! I need not say more. If I have not mentioned the particular trial of every one here to-day, yet I think it may be included in some one of the general descriptions, and whatever it may happen to be, it cannot be so out of the catalogue as not to come in somewhere or other in the temptations of our Lord and Saviour Jesus Christ. I, therefore, now turn to the second part of the discourse upon which I shall speak with brevity.

II. Our second point is THAT AS THE TEMPTED OFTEN SUFFERED; CHRIST ALSO SUFFERED.

Notice, the text does not run—"In that he himself also hath been tempted, he is able to succour them that are tempted." It is better than that—"In that he himself *hath suffered,* being tempted, he is able to succour them that are tempted." Temptation, even when overcome, brings with it to the true child of God a great degree of suffering. The suffering consists in two or three things. It lies, mainly, *in the shock which sin gives to the sensitive, regenerate nature.* A man who is clothed in armour may walk in a brake through the midst of tearing thorns and brambles without being hurt, but let the man be stripped of his garments, and then let him attempt the same journey, and how sadly will he be rent and torn. Sin, to the man who is used to it, is no suffering; if he be tempted it is no pain to him; in fact, frequently temptation yields pleasure to the sinner. To look at the bait is sweet to the fish which means to swallow it by-and-bye. But to the child of God, who is new-made and quickened, the very thought of sin makes him shudder; he cannot look at it without abhorrence and detestation, and without being alarmed to think that he is likely ever to fall into so abominable a crime. Now, dear friends, in this case, Christ indeed has fellowship, and far outruns us. His detestation of sin must have been much more deep than ours. A word of blasphemy, a thought of sin, must have cut him to the very quick. We cannot get a complete idea of the degree of wretchedness which Jesus must have endured in merely being upon earth among the ungodly. For infinite purity to dwell among sinners must be something as if you could suppose the best educated, the most pure, the most amiable person, condemned to live in a den of burglars, blasphemers, and filthy wretches: such a man's life must be a misery; no whip, no chain would be needed ; merely associating with such people would be pain and torment enough. So, the Lord Jesus, in merely bearing the neighbourhood of sin, without any other troubles, would have had to suffer a vast, incalculable amount of woe. Suffering, too, arises to the people of God *from a dread of the temptation when its shadow falls upon us ere it comes.* At times there is more dread in the prospect of a trial than there is in the trial itself. We feel a thousand temptations in fearing one. Christ knew this. What an awful dread was that which came over him in the black night of Gethsemane! 'Twas not the cup, 'twas the fear of drinking it. "Let this cup pass from me," just seemed to indicate what the sorrow was. He knew how black, how foul, how fiery were its deeps, and it was the dread of drinking of it that bowed him to the ground till he sweat as it were great drops of blood falling to the ground. When you have the like overwhelming pressure upon your spirit in the prospect of a trial yet to come, fly you to the loving heart of your sympathising Lord, for he has suffered all this, having been himself tempted.

The suffering of temptation also lies often *in the source of it.* Have you not often felt that you would not mind the temptation if it had not come from where it did? "Oh!" say you, "to think that my own friend, my dearly beloved friend, should try me!" You are a child, and you have said, "I think I could bear anything but my father's frown, or my mother's sneer." You are a husband, and you say, "My thorn in the flesh is too sharp, for it is an ungodly wife;" or you are a wife, and this is more frequently the case, and you think there is no temptation like yours, because it is your husband who assaults your religion, and who speaks evil of your good. It makes all the difference where the temptation comes from. If some scoundrel mocks us we think it honour, but when it is an honoured companion we feel his taunt. A friend can cut under our armour and stab us the more dangerously. Ah! but the Man of Sorrows knew all this, since it was one of the chosen twelve who betrayed him. And besides, "it pleased the Father to bruise him, He hath put him to grief." To find God to be in arms against us is a huge affliction. "Eloi, Eloi, lama Sabacthani! My God, my God, why hast thou forsaken me?" is the very emphasis of woe. Jesus surely has suffered your griefs, come whence they may.

I have no doubt, too, that a portion of the sorrow and suffering of temptation may also lie in the fact *that God's name and honour are often involved in our temptation.* It happens to some of us who are more publicly placed than others to be reviled, and when the reviling is merely against our own personal character, against our modes of speech or habit, we cannot only receive it gratefully but thankfully, blessing God that he has counted us worthy to suffer for his Name's sake. But sometimes the attack is very plainly not against us but against God, and there will be things said of which we should say with the Psalmist David—"Horror hath taken hold upon me, because of the wicked that keep not thy law?" When direct blasphemies are uttered against the person of Christ, or against the doctrine of his holy gospel, we have been "very heavy," because we have thought—"If I have opened this dog's mouth against myself it matters not, but if I have made him roar against God, then how should I answer, and what should I speak." This has often been the bitterness of it—"If I fall, God's cause is stained; if I slip through the vehemence of this assault, then one of the gates of the church will be carried by storm; mischief cometh not to me alone, but to many of the Israel of God." David says, of grieving the saints—"When I thought to know this it was too painful for me." David's Lord had to suffer this, for he says, "The reproaches of them that reproached thee fell on me." He was made the target for those errors which were really shot at God, and so he had to feel first this bitterness of sympathy with his ill-used God.

I cannot, of course, particularize this morning so as to hit upon the precise sorrow which you, beloved brother in Christ, are enduring as the result of temptation, but whatever phase your sorrow may have assumed, this should always be your comfort, that he has suffered in temptation; that he has not merely known the temptation as you sometimes have known it, when it rattled on your harness and fell harmless to the ground, but it has rankled in his flesh. It has not made him sin, but it has made him smart; it has not made him err, but it has caused him to mourn. Oh! child of God, I know not a deeper well of purer consolation than this—"He himself hath suffered being tempted."

III. Now for the third and last point. THEY THAT ARE TEMPTED HAVE GREAT NEED OF SUCCOUR, AND CHRIST IS ABLE, HAVING HIMSELF BEEN TEMPTED, TO SUCCOUR THEM THAT ARE TEMPTED.

Of course this is true of Christ as God. Apart from any temptation he has ever endured, he would be able to succour the tempted, but we are now speaking in our text of Christ as a High Priest, in which we are to regard him in his complex character as God-man, for Christ is not only God but man, and not only man but God. The *Christos*, the anointed one, the High Priest of our profession, is in his complex character able to succour them that are tempted. How? Why, first, *the very fact that he was tempted has some succour in it to us.* If we had to walk through the darkness alone we should know the very extremity of misery, but having a companion we have comfort; having such a companion, we have joy. It is all black about me, and the path is miry, and I sink in it and can find no standing; but I plunge onwards, desperately set on reaching my journey's end. It frets me that I am alone, but I hear a voice; (I can see nothing,) but I hear a voice which says, "Yea, though I pass through the valley of the shadow of death I will fear no evil." I cry out, "Who goes there?" and an answer comes back to me—"I, the faithful and true witness, the Alpha and the Omega, the sufferer who was despised and rejected of men, I lead the way;" and at once I feel that it is light about me, and there is a rock beneath my feet, for if Christ my Lord hath been here, then the way must be safe, and must conduct to the desired end. The very fact that he has suffered, then, consoles his people.

But further, the fact *that he has suffered without being destroyed is inestimably comforting to us.* If you could see a block of ore just ready to be put into the furnace, if that block of ore could look into the flames, and could mark the blast as it blows the coals to a vehement heat, if it could speak it would say, "Ah! woe is me that ever I should be put into such a blazing furnace as that! I shall be burnt up; I shall be melted with the slag; I shall be utterly consumed!" But suppose another lump all bright and glistening could lie by its side, and say, "No, no, you are just like I was, but I went through the fire and I lost nothing thereby; see how bright I am; how I have survived all the flames." Why then that piece of ore would rather anticipate than dread the season when it too should be exposed to the purifying heat, and come out all bright and lustrous like its companion. I see thee, I see thee, thou Son of Mary; bone of our bone, flesh of our flesh; thou hast felt the flames, but thou art not destroyed; not the smell of fire has passed upon thee; thine heel has been bruised, but thou hast broken the serpent's head; there is no scar, nor spot, nor injury in thee; thou hast survived the conflict, and I, bearing thy name, purchased with thy blood, and dear to God as thou art dear to him, I shall survive it too, therefore will I tread the coals with confidence, and bear the heat with patience. Christ's conquest gives me comfort, for I shall conquer too.

And you will please to remember, too, that Christ in going through the suffering of temptation was not simply no loser *but he was a great gainer*, for it is written, it pleased God "to make the captain of their salvation perfect through sufferings." It was through his suffering that he obtained the mediatorial glory which now crowns his head. Had he never carried the cross he had never worn that crown, that transcendently bright and glorious crown which now he wears as King in Zion, and as leader of his people whom he hath redeemed by blood. God **over** all blessed for ever he would have been, but as God-man-mediator he could never have been extolled unless he had been obedient even unto death, so that he was a gainer by his suffering, and glory be to his name, we get comfort from this too, for we also shall be gainers by our temptations. We shall come up out of Egypt enriched; as it is written, "He brought them forth also with silver and gold," so shall we come forth out of trial with better than these treasures. "Blessed is the man that endureth temptation, for when he is tried he shall obtain a crown of life which fadeth not away." The deeper their sorrows the louder their song; the more terrible their toil the sweeter their rest; the more bitter the wormwood the more delightful the wine of consolation. They shall have glory for their share; they shall have honour for their contempt; they shall have songs for their sufferings, and thrones for their tribulations.

But more, in that Christ hath suffered, being tempted, he is able to succour us who are tempted *by sending his grace to help us*. He was always able to send grace, but now as God and man he is able to send just the right grace at the right time, and in the right place. You know a doctor may have all the drugs that can be gathered, but an abundance of medicine does not make him a qualified practitioner; if however he has been himself and seen the case, then he knows just at what crisis of the disease such and such a medicine is wanted. The stores are good, but the wisdom to use the stores —this is even more precious. Now it pleased the Father that in Christ should all fulness dwell, but where should the Son of Man earn his diploma and gain the skill with which to use the fulness aright? Beloved, he won it by experience. He knows what sore temptations mean, for he has felt the same. You know if we had comforting grace given us at one time of our temptation it would tempt us more than before; even as certain medicines given to the patient at one period of the disease would aggravate the malady, though the same medicine would cure him if administered a little later. Now Christ knows how to send his comfort at the very nick of time, to afford his help exactly when it will not be a superfluity; to send his joy when we shall not spend it upon our own lusts; and how knows he this? Why, he recollects his own experience; he has passed through it all. There appeared an angel unto him strengthening him; that angel came just when he was wanted; Jesus knows just when to send his angelic messenger to strengthen you, when to lay on the rod more heavily, and when to stay his hand and say, "I have forgiven thee ; go thou in peace."

Once more, dear friends, lest I keep you too long. Having suffered himself, being tempted, Christ knows how to succour us *by his prayers for us*. There are some people whose prayers are of no use to us because they do not know what to ask for us. Christ is the intercessor for his people; he has prevalence in his intercession, but how shall he learn what to ask for ? How can he know this better than by his own trials? He hath suffered being tempted. You hear some brethren pray with such power, such unction, such fervour. Why ? Part of the reason is that they are experimental prayers; they pray out their own life; they just tell out the great deep waters over which they themselves sail. Now the prayer of our great High Priest in heaven is wonderfully comprehensive; it is drawn from his own life, and it takes in every sorrow and every pang that ever rent a human heart, because he himself hath suffered being tempted. I know you feel safe in trusting your case in the hand of such an intercessor, for he knows which is the precise mercy to ask for, and when he asks for it, he knows how to put the words and frame the petition so that the mercy shall surely come to you at the right time.

Ah, dear friends, it is not in my power to bring out the depth which lieth under my text, but I am certain of this, that when through the deep waters he shall cause you to go, or you are made to pass through furnace after furnace, you cannot want a better rod and staff, nor a better table prepared for you in the wilderness than this my text, " In that he himself hath suffered being tempted, he is able to succour them that are tempted." Hang this text up in your house; read it every day; take it before God in prayer every time you bend the knee, and you shall find it to be like the widow's cruse, which failed not, and like her handful of meal, which wasted not; it shall be unto you till the last of December what now it is when we begin to feed upon it in January.

Will not my text suit the awakened sinner as well as the saint. There are timid souls here. They cannot say they are saved; yet here is a loophole of comfort for you, you poor troubled ones that are not yet able to get a hold of Jesus. "He is able to succour them that are tempted." Go and tell him you are tempted; tempted, perhaps, to despair; tempted to self-destruction ; tempted to go back to your old sins; tempted to think that Christ cannot save you. Go and tell him that he himself has suffered being tempted, and that he is able to succour you. Believe that he will, and he will, for you can never believe anything too much of the love and goodness of my Lord. He will be better than your faith to you. If you can trust him with all your heart to save you, he will do it; if you believe he is able to put away your sin, he will do it; if you can but honour him by giving him a good character for grace, you cannot give him too good a name.

> " Trust him, he will not deceive you,
>   Though you hardly on him lean ;
> He will never, never leave you,
>   Nor will let you quite leave him."

Receive, then, the blessing.

May the grace of our Lord Jesus Christ, and the love of God our Father, and the fellowship of the Holy Ghost, be with you for ever. Amen and Amen.

Suffering and Reigning with Jesus

"If we suffer, we shall also reign with him: if we deny him, he also will deny us."—
2 Timothy ii. 12.

MY venerable friend who has hitherto sent me a text for the new year, still ministers to his parish the Word of life, and has not forgotten to furnish the passage for our meditation to-day. Having preached from one of a very similar character a short time ago, I have felt somewhat embarrassed in preparation; but I will take courage, and say with the apostle, " To write the same things to you, to me indeed is not grievous, but for you it is safe." If I should bring forth old things on this occasion, be ye not unmindful that even the wise householder doth this at times. For oft-recurring sickness the same wine may be prescribed by the most skilful physician without blame; no one scolds the contractor for mending rough roads again and again with stones from the same quarry; the wind which has borne us once into the haven, is not despised for blowing often from the same quarter, for it may do us good service yet again; and therefore, I am assured that you will endure my repetitions of the same truths, since they may assist you to suffer with patience the same trials.

You will observe that our text is a part of one of Paul's *faithful sayings*. If I remember rightly, Paul has four of these. The first occurs in 1 Timothy i. 8, that famous, that chief of all faithful sayings, "This is a faithful saying, and worthy of all acceptation, that Christ Jesus came into the world to save sinners; of whom I am chief." A golden saying, whose value Paul himself had most marvellously proved. What shall I say of this verse, but that like the lamp of a lighthouse, it has darted its ray of comfort through leagues of darkness, and guided millions of tempest-tossed spirits to the port of peace. The next faithful saying is in the same epistle, at the fourth chapter, and the ninth verse, " Godliness is profitable unto all things, having the promise of the life that now is, and of that which is to come. This is a faithful saying, and worthy of all acceptation." This, too, the apostle knew to be true, since he had learned in whatsoever state he was, therewith to be content. Our text is a portion of the third faithful saying; and the last of the four you will find in Titus iii. 8, " This is a faithful saying, and these things I will that thou affirm constantly, that they which have believed in God might be careful to maintain good works. These things are good and profitable unto men." We may trace a connection between these faithful sayings. The first one which speaks of Jesus Christ coming into the world to save sinners, lays the foundation of our eternal salvation in the free grace of God, as shown to us in the mission of the great Redeemer. The next affirms the double blessedness which we obtain through this salvation—the blessings of the upper and nether springs—of time and of eternity. The third faithful saying shows one of the duties to which the chosen people are called; we are ordained to suffer for Christ with the promise that "if we suffer, we shall also reign with him." The last faithful saying sets forth the active form of Christian service, bidding us diligently to maintain good works. Thus you have the root of salvation in free grace; you have, next, the privileges of that salvation in the life which now is, and in that which is to come; and you have also the two great branches of suffering with Christ and service of Christ loaded with the fruits of the Spirit of all grace. Treasure up, dear friends, those faithful sayings, "Lay up these words in your heart; bind them for a sign upon your hand, that they may be as frontlets between your eyes." Let these choice sayings be printed in letters of gold, and set up as tablets upon the door-posts of our house and upon our gates. Let them be the guides of our life, our comfort, and our instruction. The apostle of the Gentiles proved them to be faithful; they are faithful still, not one word shall fall to the ground; they are worthy of all acceptation, let us accept them now, and prove their faithfulness, each man for himself.

This morning's meditation is to be derived from a part of that faithful saying which deals with suffering. We will read the verse preceding our text. "It is a faithful saying: For if we be dead with him, we shall also live with him." All the elect were virtually dead with Christ when he died upon the tree—they were on the cross, crucified with him. In him, as their representative, they rose from the tomb, and live in newness of life: because he lives, they shall live also. In due time the chosen are slain by the Spirit of God, and so made dead with Christ to sin, to self-righteousness, to the world, the flesh, and the powers of darkness; then it is that they live with Jesus, his life becomes their life, and as he was, so are they also in this world. The Spirit of God breathes the quickening grace into those who were once dead in sin, and thus they live in union with Christ Jesus. When believers die, though they may be sawn in sunder, or burnt at the stake, yet, since they sleep in Jesus, they are preserved from the destruction of death by him, and are made partakers of his immortality. May the Lord make us rooted and grounded in the mysterious but most consolatory doctrine of union with Christ Jesus.

We must at once advance to our text—"If we suffer, we shall also reign with him: if we deny him, he also will deny us." The words naturally divide themselves into two parts; *suffering with Jesus, and its reward—denying Jesus, and its penalty.*

I. SUFFERING WITH JESUS, AND ITS REWARD. To suffer, is the common lot of all men. It is not possible for us to escape from it. We come into this world through the gate of suffering, and over death's door hangs the same escutcheon. We must suffer if we live, no matter in what style we spend our existence. The wicked man may cast off all respect for virtue, and riot in excess of vice to the utmost degree, yet, let him not expect to avoid the well-directed shafts of sorrow; nay, rather let him look for a tenfold share of pain of body and remorse of soul. "Many sorrows shall be to the wicked." Even if a man could so completely degrade himself as to lose his intellectual powers, and become a brute, yet even then he could not escape from suffering; for we know that the brute creation is the victim of pain, as much as more lordly man; only, as Dr. Chalmers well remarks, the brutes have the additional misery that they have no mind endowed with reason and cheered by hope to fortify them under their bodily affliction. Seest thou not, O man, that however thou mayst degrade thyself, thou art still under the yoke of suffering: the loftiest bow beneath it, and the meanest cannot avoid it. Every acre of humanity must be furrowed with this plough. There may be a sea without a wave, but never a man without sorrow. He who was God as well as man, had his full measure pressed down and running over; let us be assured that if the sinless one was not spared the rod, the sinful will not go free. "Man that is born of woman is of few days and full of trouble." "Man is born unto trouble as the sparks fly upward."

If, then, a man hath sorrow, it doth not necessarily follow that he shall be rewarded for it, since it is the common lot brought upon all by sin. You may smart under the lashes of sorrow in this life, but this shall not deliver you from the wrath to come. Remember you may live in poverty and drag along a wearisome existence of ill-requited toil; you may be stretched upon a bed of sickness, and be made to experience an agony in every single member of your body; and your mind, too, may be depressed with fears, or plunged in the depths of despair; and yet, by all this you may gain nothing of any value to your immortal spirit; for, "Except a man be born again, he cannot see the kingdom of God;" and no amount of affliction upon earth can alter that unchanging rule, so as to admit an unregenerate man into heaven. To suffer is not peculiar to the Christian, neither doth suffering necessarily bring with it any recompense of reward. The text implies most clearly that we must suffer *with Christ* in order to reign with him. The structure of the preceding verse plainly requires such a reading. The words, "with him," may be as accurately supplied at the close of the one clause as the other. The suffering which brings the reigning with Jesus, must be a suffering with Jesus. There is a very current error among those poor people who are ignorant of true religion, that all poor and afflicted people will be rewarded for it in the next state. I have heard working men refer to the parable of the rich man and Lazarus, with a cruel sort of satisfaction at the pains of Dives, because they have imagined that, in the same manner, all rich people would be cast into the flames of hell without a drop of water to cool their tongue, while all poor persons like Lazarus, would be triumphantly carried into Abraham's bosom. A more fearful mistake could not be made. It was not the suffering of Lazarus which entitled him to a place in Abraham's bosom; he might have been licked by all the dogs on earth and then have been dragged off by the dogs of hell. Many a man goes to hell from a dunghill. A drunkard's hovel is very wretched: is he to be rewarded for bringing himself to rags? Very much of the beggary we see abroad is the result of vice, extravagance, or folly— are these things so meritorious as to be passports to glory? Let no man deceive himself so grossly. On the other hand, the rich man was not cast into hell because he was rich and fared sumptuously; had he been rich in faith, holy in life, and renewed in heart, his purple and fine linen would have done him no hurt. Lazarus was carried above by the angels, because his heart was in heaven; and the rich man lifted up his eyes in hell, because he had never lifted them up towards God and heavenly things. It is a work of grace in the heart and character, which shall decide the future, not poverty or wealth. Let intelligent persons combat this notion whenever they meet with it. Suffering here does not imply happiness hereafter. It is only a certain order of suffering to which a reward is promised, the suffering which comes to us from fellowship with the Lord Jesus, and conformity to his image.

A few words here, by way of aiding you in making the distinction. *We must not imagine that we are suffering for Christ, and with Christ, if we are not in Christ.* If a man be not a branch of the living vine, you may prune and cut until the sap flows, and the branch bleeds, but he will never bring forth heavenly fruit. Prune the bramble as long as ever you like, use the knife until the edge is worn away, the brier will be as sharp and fruitless as ever; you cannot by any process of pruning translate it into one of the vines of Eshcol. If a man remain in a state of nature, he is a member of the earthly Adam, he will not therefore escape suffering, but ensure it; he must not, however, dream that *because* he suffers he is suffering with Christ; he is plagued with the old Adam; he is receiving with all the other heirs of wrath the sure heritage of sin. Let him consider these sufferings of his to be only the first drops of the awful shower which will fall upon him for ever, the first tingling cuts of that terrible whip which will lacerate his soul for ever. If a man be in Christ, he may then claim fellowship with the second Man, who is the Lord from heaven, and he may expect to bear the image of the heavenly in the glory to be revealed. O my hearers, are you in Christ by a living faith? Are you trusting to Jesus only? If not, whatever you may have to mourn over on earth, you have no hope of reigning with Jesus in heaven.

Supposing a man to be in Christ, yet it does not even then follow that all his sufferings are sufferings with Christ, for *it is essential that he be called by God to suffer.* If a good man were, out of mistaken views of mortification and self-denial, to mutilate his body, or to flog his flesh as many a sincere enthusiast has done, I might admire the man's fortitude, but I should not allow for an instant that he was suffering with Christ. Who called men to such austerities? Certainly not the God of love. If, therefore, they torture themselves at the command of their own fancies, fancy must reward them, for God will not. If I am rash and imprudent, and run into positions for which neither providence nor grace has fitted me, I ought to question whether I am not rather sinning than communing with Christ. Peter drew his sword, and cut off the ear of Malchus. If somebody had cut *his* ear off, what would you say? He took the sword, and he feels the sword. He was never commanded to cut off the ear of Malchus, and it was his Master's gentleness which saved him from the soldiers' rage. If we let passion take the place of judgment, and self-will reign instead of Scriptural authority, we shall fight the Lord's battles with the devil's weapons, and if we cut our own fingers we must not be surprised. On several occasions, excited Protestants have rushed into Romish cathedrals, have knocked down the priest, and dashed the wafer upon the ground, trod upon it, and in other ways exhibited their hatred of idolatry; now when the law has interposed to punish such outrages, the offenders are hardly to be considered as suffering with Christ. This I give as one instance of a class of actions to which overheated brains sometimes lead men, under the supposition that they will join the noble army of martyrs. The martyrs were all chosen to their honourable estate; and I may say of martyrdom as of priesthood, " No man taketh that honour upon himself but he that is called thereunto as was Aaron." Let us mind we all make a distinction between things which differ, and do not pull a house down on our heads, and then pray the Lord to console us under the trying providence.

Again, *in troubles which come upon us as the result of sin, we must not think we are suffering with Christ*. When Miriam spoke evil of Moses, and the leprosy polluted her, she was not suffering for God. When Uzziah thrust himself into the temple, and became a leper all his days, he could not say that he was afflicted for righteousness' sake. If you speculate and lose your property, do not say that you are losing all for Christ's sake; when you unite with bubble companies and are duped, do not whine about suffering for Christ—call it the fruit of your own folly. If you will put your hand into the fire and it gets burned, why it is the nature of fire to burn you or anybody else; but be not so silly as to boast as though you were a martyr. If you do wrong and suffer for it, what thanks have ye? Go behind the door and weep for your sin, but come not forth in public to claim a reward. Many a hypocrite, when he has had his deserts, and has been called by his proper name, has cried out, " Ah! I am persecuted." It is not an infallible sign of excellence to be in bad repute among men. Who feels any esteem for a cold-blooded murderer? Does not every man reprobate the offender? Is he, therefore, a Christian because he is spoken against, and his name cast out as evil? Assuredly not: he is a heartless villain and nothing more. Brethren, truthfulness and honesty should stop us from using expressions which involve a false claim; we must not talk as if we suffered nobly for Jesus when we are only troubled as the result of sin. O, to be kept from transgression! then it mattereth not how rough the road of obedience may be, our journey shall be pleasant because Jesus walks with us.

Be it observed, moreover, that suffering such as God accepts and rewards for Christ's sake, *must have God's glory as its end*. If I suffer that, I may earn a name, or win applause among men; if I venture into trial merely that I may be respected for it, I shall get my reward; but it will be the reward of the Pharisee, and not the crown of the sincere servant of the Lord Jesus.

I must mind, too, that love to Christ, and love to his elect, is ever the main-spring of all my patience; remembering the apostle's words,

"Though I give my body to be burned, and have not charity, it profiteth me nothing." If I suffer in bravado, filled with proud defiance of my fellow-men; if I love the dignity of singularity, and out of dogged obstinacy hold to an opinion, not because it is right—and I love God too well to deny his truth—but because I choose to think as I like, then I suffer not with Jesus. If there be no love to God in my soul; if I do not endure all things for the elect's sake, I may bear many a cuff and buffetting, but I miss the fellowship of the Spirit, and have no recompense.

I must not forget also that *I must manifest the Spirit of Christ, or else I do not suffer with him.* I have heard of a certain minister, who, having had a great disagreement with many members in his Church, preached from this text, "And Aaron held his peace." The sermon was intended to pourtray himself as an astonishing instance of meekness; but as his previous words and actions had been quite sufficiently violent, a witty hearer observed, that the only likeness he could see between Aaron and the preacher, was this, " Aaron held his peace, and the preacher did not." It is easy enough to discover some parallel between our cases and those of departed saints, but not so easy to establish the parallel by holy patience and Christlike forgiveness. If I have, in the way of virtue, brought down upon myself shame and rebuke; if I am hot to defend myself and punish the slanderer; if I am irritated, unforgiving, and proud, I have lost a noble opportunity of fellowship with Jesus. I must have Christ's spirit in me, or I do not suffer acceptably. If like a sheep before her shearers, I can be dumb; if I can bear insult, and love the man who inflicts it; if I can pray with Christ, "Father, forgive them, for they know not what they do;" if I submit all my case to him who judgeth righteously, and count it even my joy to suffer reproach for the cause of Christ, then, and only then, have I truly suffered with Christ.

These remarks may seem very cutting, and may take away much false but highly-prized comfort from some of you. It is not my intention to take away any true comfort from the humblest believer who really suffers with my Lord; but God grant we may have honesty enough not to pluck flowers out of other men's gardens, or wear other men's honours. Truth only will be desired by true men.

I shall now very briefly show what are the forms of real suffering for Jesus in these days. We have not now to rot in prisons, to wander about in sheep-skins and goat-skins, to be stoned, or to be sawn in sunder, though we ought to be ready to bear all this, if God wills it. The days of Nebuchadnezzar's furnace are past, but the fire is still upon earth. *Some suffer in their estates.* I believe that to many Christians it is rather a gain than a loss, so far as pecuniary matters go, to be believers in Christ; but I meet with many cases—cases which I know to be genuine, where persons have had to suffer severely for conscience sake. There are those present who were once in very comfortable circumstances, but they lived in a neighbourhood where the chief of the business was done on a Sunday; when grace shut up their shop, trade left them; and I know some of them are working very hard for their bread, though once they earned abundance without any great toil; they do it cheerfully for Christ's sake, but the struggle is a hard one. I know other persons who were employed as servants in lucrative positions involving sin, but upon their becoming Christians, they were obliged to resign their former post, and are not at the present moment in anything like such apparent prosperity as they were. I could point to several cases of persons who have really suffered to a very high degree in pecuniary matters for the cross of Christ. Brethren, ye may possess your souls in patience, and expect as a reward of grace that you shall reign with Jesus your beloved. Those feather-bed soldiers who are broken-hearted if fools laugh at them, should blush when they think of those who endure real hardness as good soldiers of Jesus Christ. Who can waste his pity over the small griefs of faint hearts, when cold, and hunger, and poverty are cheerfully endured by the true and brave. Cases of persecution are by no means rare. In many a country village squires and priests rule with a high hand, and smite the godly villagers with a rod of iron. " No blankets, no coals, no alms-house for you, if you venture into the meeting-house. You cannot live in my cottage if you have a prayer-meeting in it. I will have no religious people on my farm." We who live in more enlightened society, little know the terrorism exercised in some of the rural districts over poor men and women who endeavour conscientiously to carry out their convictions and walk with Christ. True Christians of all denominations love each other and hate persecution, but nominal Christians and ungodly men would make our land as hot as in the days of Mary, if they dared. To all saints who are oppressed, this sweet sentence is directed—" If we suffer, we shall also reign with him."

More usually, however, the suffering takes the form of *personal contempt.* It is not pleasant to be pointed at in the streets, and have opprobrious names shouted after you by vulgar tongues; nor is it a small trial to be saluted in the workshop by opprobrious epithets, or to be looked upon as an idiot or a madman; and yet this is the lot of many of the people of God every day of the week. Many of those who are of the humbler classes have to endure constant and open reproach, and those who are richer have to put up with the cold shoulder, and neglect, and sneers, as soon as they become true disciples of Jesus Christ. There is more sting in this than some dream; and we have known strong men who could have borne the lash, brought down by jeers and sarcasms, even just as the wasp may more thoroughly irritate and vex the lion than if the noblest beast of prey should attack him. *Believers have also to suffer slander and falsehood.* It is not expedient for me, doubtless, to glory, but I know a man who scarcely ever speaks a word which is not misrepresented, and hardly performs an action which is not misconstrued. The press at certain seasons, like a pack of hounds, will get upon his track, and worry him with the basest and most undeserved abuse. Publicly and privately he is accustomed to be sneered at. The world whispers, "Ah! he pretends to be zealous for God, but he makes a fine thing of it!" Mark you, when the world shall learn what he does make of it, maybe it will have to eat its words. But I forbear; such is the portion of every servant of God who has to bear public testimony for the truth. Every motive but the right one will be imputed to him; his good will be evil spoken of; his zeal will be called imprudence—his courage, impertinence—his modesty, cowardice—his earnestness, rashness. It is impossible for the true believer in Christ, who is called to any eminent service, to do anything right. He had better at once learn to say with Luther, "The world hates me, and there is no love lost between us, for as much as it hates me, so heartily do I hate it." He meant not the men in the world, for never was there a more loving heart than Luther's; but he meant the fame, the opinion, the honour of the world he trod beneath his feet. If in your measure, you bear undeserved rebuke for Christ's sake, comfort yourselves with these words, "If we suffer, we shall also reign with him: if we deny him, he also will deny us."

Then again, if in your service for Christ, you are enabled so to sacrifice yourself, that you bring upon yourself *inconvenience and pain, labour and loss*, then I think you are suffering with Christ. The missionary who tempts the stormy deep—the herald of the cross who penetrates into unknown regions among savage men—the colporteur toiling up the mountain-side—the teacher going wearily to the class—the village preacher walking many toilsome miles—the minister starving on a miserable pittance—the evangelist content to break down in health—all these and their like, suffer with Christ. We are all too much occupied with taking care of ourselves; we shun the difficulties of excessive labour. And frequently behind the entrenchments of *taking care of our constitution*, we do not half as much as we ought. A minister of God is bound to spurn the suggestions of ignoble ease, it is his calling to labour; and if he destroys his constitution, I for one, only thank God that he permits us the high privilege of so making ourselves living sacrifices. If earnest ministers should bring themselves to the grave, not by imprudence, for that we would not advocate, but by honest labour, such as their ministry and their consciences require of them, they will be better *in* their graves than *out of* their graves, if they come there for the cause of Christ. What, are we never to suffer? Are we to be carpet-knights? Are God's people to be put away in wadding, perfumed with lavender, and boxed up in quiet softnesses? Nay, verily, unless they would lose the reward of true saints!

Let us not forget that *contention with inbred lusts*, denials of proud self, resistance of sin, and agony against Satan, are all forms of suffering with Christ. We may, in the holy war within us, earn as bright a crown as in the wider battle-field beyond us. O for grace to be ever dressed in full armour, fighting with principalities and powers, and spiritual wickedness of every sort.

There is one more class of suffering which I shall mention, and that is, *when friends forsake, or become foes*. Father and mother forsake sometimes. The husband persecutes the wife. We have known even the children turn against the parents. "A man's foes are they of his own household." This is one of the devil's best instruments for making believers suffer; and those who have to drain this cup for the Lord's sake, shall reign with him.

Brethren, if you are thus called to suffer for Christ, will you quarrel with me if I say, in adding all up, what a very little it is compared with reigning with Jesus! "For our light affliction, which is but for a moment, worketh for us a far more exceeding and eternal weight of glory." When I contrast our sufferings of to-day with those of the reign of Mary, or the persecutions of the Albigenses on the mountains, or the sufferings of Christians in Pagan Rome, why ours are scarcely a pin's prick: and yet what is the reward? We shall reign with Christ. There is no comparison between the service and the reward. Therefore it is all of grace. We do but little, and suffer but little—and even that little grace gives us—and yet the Lord grants us "A far more exceeding and eternal weight of glory." We are not merely to sit with Christ, but we are *to reign* with Christ. All that the pomp imperial of his kingship means; all that the treasure of his wide dominions can yield; all that the majesty of his everlasting power can bestow—all this is to belong to you, given to you of his rich, free grace, as the sweet reward of having suffered for a little time with him. Who would draw back then? Who among you will flinch? Young man, have you thought of flying from the cross? Young woman, has Satan whispered to you to shun the thorny pathway? Will you give up the crown? Will you miss the throne? O beloved, it is so blessed to be in the furnace with Christ, and such an honour to stand in the pillory with him, that if there were no reward, we might count ourselves happy; but when the reward is so rich, so super-abundant, so eternal, so infinitely more than we had any right to expect, will we not take up the cross with songs, and go on our way rejoicing in the Lord our God?

II. DENYING CHRIST, AND ITS PENALTY. "If we deny him, he also will deny us." Dreadful "if," and yet an "if" which is applicable to every one of us. If the apostles, when they sat at the Lord's Supper, said, "Lord, is it I?" surely we may say as we sit here, "Lord, shall I ever deny thee?" You who say most loudly, "Though all men shall deny thee, yet will not I"—you are the most likely to do it. In what way can we deny Christ? Some deny him openly as scoffers do, whose tongue walketh through the earth, and defieth heaven. Others do this wilfully and wickedly in a doctrinal way, as the Arians and Socinians do, who deny his deity: those who deny his atonement, who rail against the inspiration of his Word, these come under the condemnation of those who deny Christ. There is a way of denying Christ, without even speaking a word, and this is the more common. In the day of blasphemy and rebuke, many hide their heads. They are in company where they ought to speak up for Christ, but they put their hands upon their mouths; they come not forward to profess their faith in Jesus; they have a sort of faith, but it is one which yields no obedience. Jesus bids each believer to be baptized. They neglect his ordinance. Neglecting that, they also despise the weightier matters of the law. They will go up to the house of God because it is fashionable to go there; but if it were a matter of persecution, they would forsake the assembling of themselves together. In the day of battle, they are never on the Lord's side. If there be a parade, and the banners are flying, and the trumpets are sounding, if there are decorations and medals to be given away, here they are; but if the shots are flying, if trenches have to be carried, and forts to be stormed, where are they? They have gone back to their dens, and there will they hide themselves till fair weather shall return. Mind, mind, mind, for I am giving a description, I am afraid, of some here; mind, I say, ye silent ones, lest ye stand speechless at the bar of judgment. Some, after having been long silent, and so practically denying Christ, go farther, and apostatize altogether from tu. faith they once had. No man who hath a genuine faith in Christ will lose it, for the faith which God gives will live for ever. Hypocrites and formalists have a name to live while yet they are dead, and after a while they return like the dog to its vomit, and the sow which was washed to her wallowing in the mire. Certain professors who do not run this length, yet practically deny Christ by their lives, though they make a profession of faith in him. Are there not here some who have been baptized, and who come to the Lord's table, but what is their character? Follow them home. I would to God they never had made a profession, because in their own houses they deny what in the house of God they have avowed. If I see a man drunk; if I know that a professor indulges in lasciviousness; if I know a man to be harsh, and overbearing, and tyrannical to his servants; if I know another who cheat in his traffic, and another who adulterates his goods, and if I know that such men profess allegiance to Jesus, which am I to believe, their words or their deeds? I will believe that which speaks loudest; and as actions always speak louder than words, I will believe their actions —I believe that they are deceivers whom Jesus will deny at the last. Should we not find many present this morning, belonging to one or other of these grades? Does not this description suit at least some of you? If it should do so, do not be angry with me, but stand still and hear the Word of the Lord. Know, O man, that you will not perish even if you have denied Christ, if now you fly to him for refuge. Peter denied, but yet Peter is in heaven. A transient forsaking of Jesus under temptation will not bring on everlasting ruin, if faith shall step in, and the grace of God shall intervene; but persevere in it, continue still in a denial of the Saviour, and my terrible text will come upon you, "He also will deny you."

In musing over the very dreadful sentence which closes my text, "He also will deny us," I was led to think of various ways in which Jesus will deny us. He does this sometimes on earth. You have read, I suppose, the death of Francis Spira. If you have ever read it, you never can forget it to your dying day. Francis Spira knew the truth; he was a reformer of no mean standing; but when brought to death, out of fear, he recanted. In a short time he fell into despair, and suffered hell upon earth. His shrieks and exclamations were so horrible, that their record is almost too terrible for print. His doom was a warning to the age in which he lived. Another instance is narrated by my predecessor, Benjamin Keach, of one who, during Puritanic times, was very earnest for Puritanism; but afterwards, when times of persecution arose, forsook his profession. The scenes at his death-bed were thrilling and terrible. He declared that though he sought God, heaven was shut against him; gates of brass seemed to be in his way, he was given up to overwhelming despair. At intervals he cursed, at other intervals he prayed, and so perished without hope. If we deny Christ, we may be delivered to such a fate. If we have stood highest and foremost in God's Church, and yet have not been brought to Christ, if we should become apostates, a high soar will bring a deep fall. High pretensions bring down sure destruction when they come to nought. Even upon earth Christ will deny such. There are remarkable instances of persons who sought to save their lives and lost them. One Richard Denton, who had been a very zealous Lollard, and was the means of the conversion of an eminent saint, when he came to the stake, was so afraid of the fire that he renounced everything he held, and went into the Church of Rome. A short time after his own house took fire, and going into it to save some of his money, he perished miserably, being utterly consumed by that fire which he had denied Christ in order to escape. If I must be lost, let it be anyhow rather than as an apostate. If there be any distinction among the damned, those have it who are wandering stars, trees plucked up by the roots, twice dead, for whom Jude tells us, is " reserved the blackness of darkness for ever." *Reserved!* as if nobody else were qualified to occupy that place but themselves. They are to inhabit the darkest, hottest place, because they forsook the Lord. Let us, my dear friends, then rather lose everything than lose Christ. Let us sooner suffer anything than lose our ease of conscience and our peace of mind. When Marcus Arethusus was commanded by Julian the apostate, to subscribe towards the rebuilding of a heathen temple which his people had pulled down upon their conversion to Christianity, he refused to obey; and though he was an aged man, he was stripped naked, and then pierced all over with lancets and knives. The old man still was firm. If he would give but one halfpenny towards the building of the temple, he could be free —if he would cast in but one grain of incense into the censer devoted to the false gods, he might escape. He would not countenance idolatry in any degree. He was smeared with honey, and while his innumerable wounds were yet bleeding, the bees and wasps came upon him and stung him to death. He could die, but he could not deny his Lord. Arethusus entered into the joy of his Lord, for he nobly suffered with him. In the olden time when the gospel was preached in Persia, one Hamedatha, a courtier of the king, having embraced the faith, was stripped of all his offices, driven from the palace, and compelled to feed camels. This he did with great content. The king passing by one day, saw his former favourite at his ignoble work, cleaning out the camel's stables. Taking pity upon him he took him into his palace, clothed him with sumptuous apparel, restored him to all his former honours, and made him sit at the royal table. In the midst of the dainty feast, he asked Hamedatha to renounce his faith. • The courtier, rising from the table, tore off his garments with haste, left all the dainties behind him, and said, "Didst thou think that for such silly things as these I would deny my Lord and Master?" and away he went to the stable to his ignoble work. How honourable is all this! But how shall I execrate the meanness of the apostate, his detestable cowardice, to forsake the bleeding Saviour of Calvary to return to the beggarly elements of the world which he once despised, and to bow his neck again to the yoke of bondage? Will you do this, O followers of the Crucified? You will not; you cannot; I know you cannot, if the spirit of the martyrs dwells in you, and it must dwell in you if you be the children of God. What must be the doom of those who deny Christ, when they reach *another world?* Mayhap, they will appear with a sort of hope in their minds, and they will come before the judge, with "Lord, Lord, open to us?" "Who are you?" saith he. "Lord, we once took the Lord's Supper—Lord, we were members of the Church, but there came very hard times. My mother bade me give up religion; father was angry; trade went bad; I was so mocked at, I could not stand it. Lord, I fell among evil acquaintances and they tempted me —I could not resist. I was thy servant—I did love thee—I always had love towards thee in my heart, but I could not help it—I denied thee and went to the world again." What will Jesus say? "I know ye not, whence ye are." "But, Lord, I want thee to be my advocate." "I know you not!" "But, Lord, I cannot get into heaven unless thou shouldst open the gate—open it for me." "I do not know you; I do not know you." "But, Lord, my name was in the Church Book." "I know you not—I deny you." "But wilt thou not hear my cries?" "Thou didst not hear mine—thou didst deny me, and I deny thee." "Lord, give me the lowest place in heaven, if I may but enter and escape from wrath to come." "No, thou wouldst not brook the lowest place on earth, and thou shalt not enjoy the lowest place here. Thou hadst thy choice, and thou didst choose evil. Keep to thy choice. Thou wast filthy, be thou filthy still. Thou wast unholy, be thou unholy still." O, sirs, if ye would not see the angry face of Jesus! O, sirs, if ye would not behold the lightning flashing from his eye, and hear the thunder of his mouth in the day when he judges the fearful, and the unbelieving, and the hypocrite; if you would not have your portion in the lake which burneth with fire and brimstone, cry this day mightily unto God, " Lord, hold me fast, keep me, keep me. Help me to suffer with thee, that I may reign with thee; but do not, do not let me deny thee, lest thou also shouldst deny me."

True Unity Promoted

" Endeavouring to keep the unity of the Spirit in the bond of peace."--
Ephesians iv. 3.

YOU will remember that for several years I have received my morning's text for the first Sabbath in the year from an esteemed brother, a clergyman of the Church of England. This year he very kindly sends me this verse, which I hope will be useful to us all, reminding us of our former faults, and of our present duty in the matter of "endeavouring to keep the unity of the Spirit in the bond of peace."

The Pope has lately been most lustily cursing us all. According to his nature, of course, must be his utterances. We could not expect a blessing where no blessing abides; and, if we get a curse, we only receive a polluted stream from a polluted fountain. It is an old saying, that England never prospers so well, as when the Pope curses her. I hope to see a year of great prosperity this year. Let the poor deluded priest curse as long as he will, our God shall turn it into a blessing. In former days, when some of the Churches of Christ began to shake off the yoke of Popedom from their necks, the plea urged against reformation was the necessity of maintaining unity. " Ye must bear with this ceremony and that dogma; no matter how antichristian and unholy, you must bear with it, ' endeavouring to keep the unity of the Spirit in the bond of peace.' " So spake the old serpent in those early days. "The Church is one; woe unto those who shall create schism! It may be true that Mary is set up in the place of Christ, that images are worshipped, cast clouts and rotten rags adored, and pardons bought and sold for crimes of every kind; it may be that the so-called Church has become an abomination and a nuisance upon the face of the earth; but still, 'endeavouring to keep the unity of the Spirit in the bond of peace,' you must lie down, restrain the testimony of the Spirit of God within you, keep his truth under a bushel, and let the lie prevail." This was the grand sophistry of the Church of Rome. When, however, she could not seduce men by talking of love and union, she took upon herself to use her natural tone of voice, and cursed right and left right heartily: and let her curse till she expires! Brethren, there was no force in the argument of the Papist, if

51

you will look at the text for a moment: the text bids us endeavour to keep the unity of the *Spirit*, but it does not tell us to endeavour to maintain the unity of evil, the unity of superstition, or the unity of spiritual tyranny. The unity of error, of false doctrine, of priestcraft, may have in it the spirit of Satan; we do not doubt that; but that it is the unity of the Spirit of God we do utterly deny. The unity of evil we are to break down by every weapon which our hand can grasp: the unity of the Spirit which we are to maintain and foster is quite another thing. Remember that we are forbidden to do evil that good may come. But it is to do evil; to restrain the witness of the Spirit of God within us; to conceal any truth which we have learned by revelation of God; to hold back from testifying for God's truth and Word, against the sin and folly of man's inventions, would be sin of the blackest hue. We dare not commit the sin of quenching the Holy Spirit, even though it were with the view of promoting unity. But the unity of the Spirit never requires any sinful support; that is maintained not by suppressing truth, but by publishing it abroad. The unity of the Spirit has for its pillars, among other things, the witnessing of spiritually enlightened saints to the one faith which God has revealed in his Word. That is quite another unity which would gag our mouths and turn us all into dumb driven cattle, to be fed or slaughtered at the will of priestly masters. Dr. Mc Neil has, very properly, said that a man can scarcely be an earnest Christian in the present day without being a controversialist. We are sent forth to-day as sheep in the midst of wolves: can there be agreement? We are kindled as lamps in the midst of darkness: can there be concord? Hath not Christ himself said, "Think not that I am come to send peace on earth: I came not to send peace, but a sword?" You understand how all this is the truest method of endeavouring to keep the unity of the Spirit; for Christ the man of war, is Jesus the Peacemaker; but in order to the creation of lasting, spiritual peace, the phalanx of evil must be broken, and the unity of darkness dashed to shivers. I pray God evermore to preserve us from a unity in which truth shall be considered valueless, in which principle gives place to policy, in which the noble and masculine virtues which adorn the Christian hero are to be supplemented by an effeminate affectation of charity. May the Lord deliver us from indifference to his word and will; for this creates the cold unity of masses of ice frozen into an iceberg, chilling the air for miles around: the unity of the dead as they sleep in their graves, contending for nothing, because they have neither part nor lot in all that belongs to living men. There is a unity which is seldom broken, the unity of devils, who, under the service of their great liege master, never disagree and quarrel: from this terrible unity keep us, O God of heaven! The unity of locusts who have one common object, the glutting of themselves to the ruin of all around, the unity of the waves of Tophet's fire, sweeping myriads into deeper misery: from this also, O King of heaven, save us evermore! May God perpetually send some prophet who shall cry aloud to the world " Your covenant with death shall be disannulled, and your agreement with hell shall not stand." May there ever be found some men, though they be rough as Amos, or stern as Haggai, who shall denounce again and again all league with error and all compromise with sin, and declare that these are the abhorrence of God. Never dream that holy contention is at all a violation of my text. The destruction of every sort of union which is not based on truth, is a preliminary to the edification of the unity of the Spirit. We must first sweep away these walls of untempered mortar —these tottering fences of man's building—before there can be room to lay the goodly stones of Jerusalem's walls one upon the other for lasting and enduring prosperity. In this spirit have I spoken to clear a way to reach my text.

It is clear from the text, *that there is a unity of the Spirit to be kept;* secondly, that *it needs keeping;* and, thirdly, that *a bond is to be used.* When we have enlarged upon these points, we shall use the text in its practical application, first to Christians in their connexion with other Churches, and then to members of the same Church in their connexion with each other.

I. First, THERE IS A UNITY OF THE SPIRIT OF WHICH THE TEXT SPEAKS, WHICH IS WORTHY TO BE KEPT.

You will observe it is not an *ecclesiastical unity,* it is not endeavouring to keep the unity of the denomination, the community, the diocese, the parish—no, it is "endeavouring to keep the unity of the Spirit." Men speak of the Episcopal Church, the Wesleyan Church, or the Presbyterian Church. Now I hesitate not to say that there is nothing whatever in Scripture at all parallel to such language; for there I read of the seven Churches in Asia, the Church in Corinth, Philippi, Antioch, etc. In England, if I speak according to the Word of God, there are some thousands of Churches holding the episcopal form of government; in Scotland, some thousands of godly Churches ordered according to Presbyterian rule; among the Wesleyans, Churches adhering to the form of government first carried out by Mr. Wesley; but it is not according to the method of Scripture but only according to human invention to speak of a whole cluster of Churches as one Church. Although myself much inclined to a Presbyterian union among our Churches, I cannot but perceive in Holy Scripture that each Church is separate and distinct from every other Church; the whole being connected by those divers bonds and ligaments which keep all the separate members together, but not so connected as to run into one another to lose their separateness and individuality. There is nothing in Scripture which says, "Endeavouring to keep up your ecclesiastical arrangements for centralization;" but the exhortation runs thus: "Endeavouring to keep the unity of the Spirit,"

Again, you will observe it does not say, "Endeavouring to keep the *uniformity* of the Spirit." The Spirit does not recognize *uniformity.* The analogy of his work in natrue is against it. The flowers are not all tinted with the same hue, nor do they exhale the same odours. There is variety everywhere in the work of God. If I glance at providence, I do not perceive that any two events happen after the same form—the page of history is varied. If, therefore, I look into the Church of God, I do not expect to find that all Christians pronounce the same shibboleth, or see with the same eyes. The same, "one Lord one faith, one baptism, one God and Father of all, we rejoice to recognize; but as to uniformity of dress, liturgical verbiage, or form of worship, I find nothing of it in Scripture. Men may pray acceptably standing, sitting, kneeling, or lying with their faces upon the earth; they may meet with Jesus by the river's side, in the temple porch, in a prison, or in a private house; and they may be one in the same Spirit although the one regardeth a day, and the other regardeth it not.

But what is this unity of the Spirit? I trust, dear brethren, that we know it by having it in possession; for it is most certain that we cannot *keep* the unity of the Spirit, if we have it not already. Let us ask ourselves the question, "Have we the unity of the Spirit?" None can have it but those who have the Spirit, and the Spirit dwells only in new-born believing souls. By virtue of his having the Spirit, the believer is in union with every other spiritual man, and this is the unity which he is to endeavour to keep. This unity of the Spirit is manifested in *love*. A husband and wife may be, through providence, cast hundreds of miles from one another, but there is a unity of spirit in them because their hearts are one. We, brethren, are divided many thousands of miles from the saints in Australia, America, and the South Sea, but loving as brethren, we feel the unity of the Spirit. I was never a member of a Church meeting in the backwoods of America; I never worshipped God with the Samoans, or with my brethren in New Zealand; but notwithstanding all this, I feel the unity of the Spirit in my soul with them, and everything which concerns their spiritual welfare is interesting to me.

This unity of the Spirit is caused by a *similarity of nature*. Find a drop of water glittering in the rainbow, leaping in the cataract, rippling in the rivulet, lying silent in the stagnant pool, or dashing in spray against the vessel's side, that water claims kinship with every drop of water the wide world over, because it is the same in its elements; and even so there is a unity of the Spirit which we cannot imitate, which consists in our being "begotten again unto a lively hope by the resurrection of Jesus Christ from the dead," bearing in us the Holy Ghost as our daily quickener, and walking in the path of faith in the living God. Here is the unity of spirit, a unity of life, nature working itself out in love. This is sustained daily by the Spirit of God. He who makes us one, keeps us one. Every member of my body must have a communion with every other member of my body. I say *must*. The question never arises, that I know of, between the members of my body whether they will do so or not. As long as there is life in my frame, every separate portion of my body must have communion with every other portion of it. Here is my finger—I may discolour it with some noxious drug; my head may not approve of the staining of my finger; my head may suggest a thousand ways by which that finger ought to be put through a purgation, and this may be all right and proper; but my head never says, "I will cut off that finger from communion." My tongue speaks loudly against the noxious fluid which has done my finger mischief and has blistered it so as to cause pain to the whole body, yet the head cannot say, "I will have that finger cut off," unless the body is willing to be for ever mutilated and incomplete. Now, it is not possible to mutilate the body of Christ. Christ does not lose his members or cast off parts of his mystical body. And therefore it never ought to enter the head of any Christian man whether or not he shall have communion in spirit with any other Christian, for he cannot do without it: as long as he lives he must have it. This does not check him in boldly denouncing the error into which his brother may have fallen, or in avoiding his intimate acquaintance while he continues to sin; but it does forbid the thought that we can ever really sever any true believer from Christ, or even from us, if we be in Christ Jesus.

The unity of the Spirit is preserved, then, by the Holy Ghost infusing daily life-floods into the one mystical body; and in proportion as the life-floods become more strong, that union becomes more manifest. Let a spirit of prayer be poured out on all our Churches, conventionalities will be dashed down, divisions will be forgotten, and, locked in each others arms, the people of God will show to the world that they are one in Christ Jesus.

There are some points in which this unity of the Spirit is certain to discover itself. In *prayer*, how truly does Montgomery put it:—

> " The saints in prayer appear as one
> In word, and deed, and mind,
> While with the Father and the Son,
> Sweet fellowship they find."

There is a unity of *praise* too. Our hymn books differ after all very little; we still sing the same song, the praise of the same Saviour. This unity will soon discover itself in *co-working:* they have a union in their conflict with the common foe, and in their contention for the common truth. This will lead to communion—I do not mean sitting down to the same table to eat bread and drink wine—that is only the outward union—but I mean that communion which consists in heart beating true to heart, and in the feeling that they are one in Christ Jesus. It was a motto with Bucer, "To love all in whom he could see anything of Christ Jesus." Be this your motto, brother in Christ. Make not your love an excuse for not offering stern rebuke, but rebuke because you love. Some persons think that unless you smooth your tongue and cover your words with sugar, no matter though it may be sugar of lead—unless you cringe, and compliment, and conceal, there is no love in your heart; but I trust it will be our privilege to show in our own persons, some of us, how sternly we can dissent and yet love; how truly be Nonconformists to our brethren's error, and yet in our very nonconformity prove our affection to them, and to our common Master. It is said of some men that they appear to have been born upon the mountains of Bether, for they do nothing but cause division; and baptized in the waters of Meribah, for they delight in causing strife. This is not the case with the genuine Christian; he cares only for the truth, for his Master, for the love of souls; and when these things are not imperilled, his own private likes or dislikes never affect him. He loves as much to see another Church prosper as his own: so long as he can know that Christ is glorified it is a matter of comparative indifference to him by what minister God's arm is made bare, in what place souls are converted, or to what particular form of worship men addict themselves: yet ever does he hold to this, that there is no unity of the Spirit where there is a lie in the case; that where the souls of men are concerned he would be a traitor to God if he did not bear witness against the error which damns, and testify to the truth which saves; and where the crown jewels of his Master's kingdom are concerned he dares not traitorously hold his tongue; but though his fellow-subjects cast his name out as evil, he counts it all joy so long as he is faithful to his Master and discharges his conscience as before the Judge of quick and dead.

II. Secondly, THIS UNITY NEEDS KEEPING.

It is a very difficult thing to maintain, and that for several reasons. Our sins would, very naturally, break it. If we were all angels, we should keep the unity of the Spirit, and not need even the exhortation to do so; but, alas! we are proud, and *pride* is the mother of division. Diotrephes, who loves to have the pre-eminence, is very sure to head a faction. *Envy*, too, how that separated very friends! When I cannot be satisfied with anything which is not hammered on my anvil or run in my mould; when another man's candle grieves me because it gives more light than mine; and when another man troubles me because he has more grace than I have—oh! there is no unity in this case. *Anger*—what a deadly foe is that to unity! when we cannot brook the smallest disrespect; when the slightest thing brings the blood into our face; when we speak unadvisedly with our lips: but surely I need not read the long list of sins which spoil this unity of the Spirit, for they are legion. O, may God cast them out from us, for only so can we keep the unity of the Spirit. But, beloved, our very *virtues* may make it difficult for us to keep this unity. Luther is brave and bold, hot and impetuous; he is just the man to lead the van and clear the way for the Reformation. Calvin is logical, clear, cool, precise; he seldom speaks rashly. It is not in the order of things that Luther and Calvin should always agree. Their very virtues cause them to fall out, and, consequently, Luther, in a bad temper, calls Calvin a pig, and a devil; and, albeit, Calvin once replied, "Luther may call me what he will, but I will always call him a dear servant of Christ," yet John Calvin knew how to pierce Luther under the fifth rib when he was in the humour. In those days the courtesies of Christians to one another were generally of the iron-gauntlet order, rather than the naked hand; for all were so much called to war for the sake of the truth, that even their fellow-soldiers were treated with suspicion; and it may be with us that the very watchfulness of truth, which is so valuable, may make us suspect where there is no need for suspicion, and our courage may take us as sometimes a fiery horse has carried a young warrior beyond where he intended to have ridden, where he may be taken prisoner to his own damage. We must watch, the best of us must watch lest we fight the Lord's battles with Satan's weapons, and so even from love to God and his truth, violate the unity of the Spirit.

The unity of the Spirit ought to be kept, dear friends, because Satan is so busy to mar it. He knows that the greatest glory of Christ will spring from the unity of his Church. "That they all may be one; as thou, Father, art in me, and I in thee, that they also may be one in us: that the world may believe that thou hast sent me." There is no Church happiness where there is not Church unity. Let a Church be disaffected and divided, the schism in the body is death to all hallowed fellowship. We cannot enjoy communion with each other unless our hearts be one. Our work for God, how feebly is it done when we are not agreed! The enemy cannot desire a better ally than *strife* in the midst of our camp. "Can ye not agree," said a warrior of old, "when your enemy is in sight!" Christians, can you not agree to keep the unity of the Spirit when a destroying Satan is ever on the watch seeking to drag immortal souls down to perdition? We must be more diligent in this matter; we must seek to purge out from ourselves everything which would divide, and to have in our hearts every holy thought which would tend to unite us with our brethren. I am not, when I join a Christian Church, to say, "I am quite certain I shall never break its unity." I am to suspect myself of a liability to that evil, and I am to watch with all diligence that I keep the unity of the Spirit.

III. In the third place, in order to the keeping of this, THERE IS A BOND PROVIDED, THE BOND OF PEACE.

Beloved, there should be much peace, perfect peace, unbounded peace between the people of God. We are not aliens; we are "*fellow-citizens* with the saints, and of the household of God." Realize your fellow-citizenship; treat not Christian people as foreigners, and this bond of fellow-citizenship will be one bond of peace. You are not enemies. Men may be fellow-citizens and yet hate one another, but you are *friends*, you are all friends to Christ, and in him you are all friends to one another; let that be another bond. But you go farther; you are not mere friends, you are *brethren*, born of the same parent, filled with the same life; and shall not this be a bond? See that ye fall not out by the way; strive not one with another, for ye are brethren. This is not all; you are nearer than this; you are *members of the same body*. Shall this mysterious union fail to be a bond of peace to you? Wilt thou, being the foot, contend with the eye? or wilt thou, being the eye, contend with the hand, and say, "I have no need of thee"? If it be indeed the truth, and not a fiction, that we are members of his body, of his flesh, and of his bones—since the joints and bones in other men's bodies do not disagree, let it never be said of the mystical body of our blessed Lord, that there was such a monstrous thing in it, that the various parts would not co-work, but fell to battling one with another.

I believe I have brought out the meaning of the text. There is a unity of the Spirit which is worthy to be kept—we ought to keep it—we must try to keep it in the bond of peace.

To come to the practical conclusion of the subject. First, *in the connexion of one Church with another;* and, secondly, *in the connexion of one Church member with another.*

It is not a desirable thing that all Churches should melt into one another and become one; for the complete fusion of all Churches into one ecclesiastical corporation would inevitably produce another form of Popery, since history teaches us that large ecclesiastical bodies grow more or less corrupt as a matter of course. Huge spiritual corporations are, as a whole, the strongholds of tyranny and the refuges of abuse; and it is only a matter of time when they shall break to pieces. Disruption and secession must occur, and will occur, where a unity is attempted which is not meant in God's Word; but it will be a blessed thing when all the Churches walk together in the unity of the Spirit when this Church, although it has been baptized into the Lord Jesus

Christ, and laments the neglect of that ordinance by others, yet feels that the unity of the Spirit is not to be broken, and holds out its right hand to all who love our Lord Jesus Christ in sincerity; when yonder Church, governed by its elders, feels a unity with another Church which is presided over by its bishop; when a certain Church, which holds with mutual edification and no ministry, is yet not quarrelsome towards those who love the ministry of the Word; when, in fact, we have agreed in this one thing, that we will search the Word independently and act out according to our light what we find to be true; but having so done we will keep the unity of Spirit in the bond of peace. I say this is most desirable and this it is that we are to seek after; not the fusion of all into one denomination, but the keeping of each Church in its own distinct independent testimony in love with every other Church that is doing the same.

Now, in order to this, I have a few suggestions to offer. It is quite certain we shall never keep the unity of the Spirit if this Church shall declare that it is superior to every other. If there be a Church which says, "We are *the* Church, and all others are mere sects; we are established, and others are only tolerated;" then it is a troubler in Israel, and must hide its head when the unity of the Spirit is so much as hinted at. Any Church which lifts up its head on high and boasts over other Churches has violated the unity of the Spirit. If other Churches reply, "One is our Master and all we are brethren," they do not violate the unity of the Spirit, for they simply claim their rights and speak the truth. That other Church which forgets its true position as one in the family, and begins to set itself up as mistress, and claim pre-eminence over its fellow-servants, has put it out of its own power to keep the unity of the Spirit, for it has violated it once for all.

A Church that would keep the unity of the Spirit, again, must not consider itself to be so infallible, that not to belong to its membership is sin. What right has any one Church to set itself up as the standard, so that those who join it not are necessarily Dissenters? It is true my Episcopal brother is a Dissenter, he dissents from me; it is true he is a Nonconformist, for he does not conform to me: I would not, however, call him by such names, lest I should arrogate to my own Church to be *the one* Church, and so should break the unity of the Spirit. If I turn to history, I may believe that my Church can claim a long line of ancestors descending from the apostles, without ever running through the Church of Rome, but shall I therefore call a brother who does not quite see this succession, a schismatic, and denominate his assembly a conventicle? If he is a schismatic because he does not come to my place, why am I not a schismatic because I do not go to his? Well, but, he divides the Church! He ought to come and worship with me. Ought I not to go and worship with him? Ah! but we are the larger number! Are divine things to be ruled by the majority? Where would the Church of God be any day if it came to polling? I am afraid the devil would always be at the head of the poll. We wish to keep the unity of the Spirit, and if we have a little sister, we will treat her all the more kindly, owing to the fewness of her members. If I want to "keep the unity of the Spirit in the bond of peace," I must never call in the magistrate to force my brother to pay for washing my surplice, ringing my bell, and winding up my clock. I must not tell my brother that he is bound to pay for the support of my worship. "Oh!" he says, "my dear friend, I pay for the maintenance of the worship which I believe to be correct, and I am quite willing that you should do the same for yours; I would voluntarily assist you if you were poor; but you tell me you will put me in prison if I do not pay, and yet tell me to keep the unity of the Spirit; but, my dear friend, it is not keeping the unity of the Spirit to take away my stool, and my table and my candlestick, and say you will put me in 'limbo,' or hale me before an ecclesiastical court. You send the constable after me; and then if I say a word about it, you say, 'Charity hopeth all things.'" Yes, among the rest, it hopes that you will give up your sin in this matter.

If we should stand possessed of a piece of ground where we bury our dead, and if there should happen to come a member of another Christian Church who would wish to lay his poor dead baby in our ground, there being no other convenient spot anywhere, and he asks the favour, I think we can hardly be thought to keep the unity of the Spirit if we tell him, "No, nothing of the kind; you had your child sprinkled, therefore it cannot be buried with us Christians; we will not have your sprinkled baby lying alongside of our baptized dead." I do not think that is keeping the unity of the Spirit. And I do not think when some Churches have turned from their grave-yard gate the mourners who have brought an unbaptized infant, and when the mourners have gone back weeping to their homes—I do not think such Churches have been endeavouring to keep the unity of the Spirit in the bond of peace. Again, if Churches are to agree one with another, they must not make rules that ministers who are not of their own denomination shall not occupy their pulpits. I should be ashamed of you, if you passed a resolution that no one dissenting from us should stand in my pulpit. But we know a Church which says, "No matter how good a man may be; he may be a man as venerated as John Angell James; or he may have all the excellencies of a William Jay—we would not, perhaps, mind hearing him in a Town Hall, but into the sacredness of our particular rostrum these interlopers must not intrude; for, says this Church, "Ours *are* ministers, yours are only lay-teachers; ours *are* sacraments: the cup of blessing which we bless is the blood of Christ, and the bread which we break is the body of Christ; you have no sacramental efficacy with you; you are not a Church in fact, but only a body of schismatics, meeting together to carry out what you think to be right. We tolerate you; that is all we can do." Where is the unity of the Spirit there? My dear friends, I received this text from one of the most holy men in the Church of England: if I expound it slightly for her benefit, he will, I trust, excuse me, for I do so in all honesty, desiring to aid him and many others in revision and reform. If *this* Church were in the same condition as the Church of England, I would pray to be as plain in my remarks. I say it is an anachronism; it is a thing out of date for the nineteenth century, for any one Church in this land, and that Church the only one which defiles her hand by taking State-pay, to stand up and say, " *We* are the Church; our ministers are *the* ministers; our people are *the* people; and now, dear brethren, shake hands, and endeavour to keep the unity of the Spirit of God." Why, it is preposterous. Let us meet on equal ground; let us lay aside all pretences to superiority; let us really aid and not oppress each other; let us mingle in prayer; let us unite in confession of sin; let us join heartily in reforming our errors, and a true Evangelical Alliance will cover our land. If any Church will take the Bible as its standard, and in the power of the Spirit of God preach the name of Jesus, there are thousands of us who will rejoice to give the right hand of fellowship with a hearty greeting to all such, and we are every day striving to get other Churches and ourselves more and more into that condition in which, while holding our own, we can yet keep the unity of the Spirit in the bond of peace.

Now, a few words to you *in regard to your relationship to one another as members of the same Church*. If we are to endeavour to keep the unity of the Spirit in the bond of peace in the same Church, then we must avoid everything that would mar it. *Gossip*—gossip is a very ready means of separating friends from one another. Let us endeavour to talk of something better than each other's characters. Dionysius went down to the Academy to Plato. Plato asked what he came for. "Why," said Dionysius, "I thought that you, Plato, would be talking against me to your students." Plato made this answer: "Dost thou think, Dionysius, we are so destitute of matter to converse upon that we talk of thee?" Truly we must be very short of subjects when we begin to talk of one another. It is better far that we magnify Christ than detract from the honour of his members. We must lay aside all envy. Multitudes of good people liked the Reformation, but they said they did not like the idea of its being done by a poor miserable monk, like Martin Luther; and so there are many who like to see good things done, and good works carried on, but do not care to see it done by that upstart young brother, or that poor man, or that woman who has no particular rank or state. As a Church let us shake off envyings; let us all rejoice in God's light; and as for pride—if any of you have grown vainglorious of late, shake it off. I hope to exercise a ministry in this place which will drive out those of you who will not acknowledge your brethren when they are poorer or of less education than yourselves.

What if the man does mar the Queen's English when he talks—what does that matter, so long as his heart is right? As long as you can feel he loves the Master, surely you can put up with his faults of language, if he can put up with your faults of action. Then let us cultivate everything that would tend to unity. Are any sick? Let us care for them. Are any suffering? Let us weep with them. Do we know one who has less love than others? then let us have more, so as to make up the deficiency. Do we perceive faults in a brother? let us admonish him in love and affection. I pray you be peacemakers, everyone. Let the Church go on as it has done for the last eleven years, in holy concord and blessed unity. Let us remember that we cannot keep the unity of the Spirit unless we all believe the truth of God. Let us search our Bibles, therefore, and conform our views and sentiments to the teaching of God's Word. I have already told you that unity in error is unity in ruin. We want unity in the truth of God through the Spirit of God. This let us seek after; let us live near to Christ, for this is the best way of promoting unity. Divisions in Churches never begin with those full of love to the Saviour. Cold hearts, unholy lives, inconsistent actions, neglected closets; these are the seeds which sow schisms in the body; but he who lives near to Jesus, wears his likeness and copies his example, will be, wherever he goes, a sacred bond, a holy link to bind the Church more closely than ever together. May God give us this, and henceforth let us endeavour to keep the unity of the Spirit in the bond of peace. I commend the text to all believers, to be practised through the coming year. And to those who are not believers, what can I say but that I trust their unity and their peace may be broken for ever, and that they may be led to Christ Jesus to find peace in his death? May faith be given, and then love and every grace will follow, so that they may be one with us in Christ Jesus our Lord. Amen.

Good Cheer for the New Year

"The eyes of the Lord thy God are always upon it, from the beginning of the year even unto the end of the year."—Deut. xi. 12.

The Israelites had sojourned for a while in Egypt, a land which only produces food for its inhabitants by the laborious process of irrigating its fields. They had mingled with the sons of Ham as they watched with anxious eyes the swelling of the river Nile; and they had shared in the incessant labours by which the waters were preserved in reservoirs, and afterwards eked out by slow degrees to nourish the various crops. Moses tells them in this chapter that the land of Palestine was not at all like Egypt; it was a land which did not so much depend on the labour of the inhabitants as upon the good will of the God of heaven. He calls it a land of hills and valleys, a land of springs and rivers, a land dependent not upon the rivers of earth but upon the rain of heaven, and he styles it in conclusion, "A land which the Lord thy God careth for : the eyes of the Lord thy God are always upon it, from the beginning of the year even unto the end of the year."

Observe here a type of the condition of the natural and the spiritual man. In this world in temporals and in all other respects the merely carnal man has to be his own providence, and to look to himself for all his needs. Hence his cares are always many, and frequently they become so heavy that they drive him to desperation. He lives a life of care, anxiety, sorrow, fretfulness and disappointment; he dwells in Egypt, and he knows that there is no joy, or comfort, or provision if it does not wear out his soul in winning it. But the spiritual man dwells in another country; his faith makes him a citizen of another land. It is true he endures the same toils, and experiences the same afflictions as the ungodly, but they deal with him after another fashion, for they come as a gracious Father's appointments, and they go at the bidding of loving wisdom. By faith the godly man casts his care upon God who careth for him, and he walks without carking care because he knows himself to be the child of Heaven's loving-kindness, for whom all things work together for good. God is his great guardian and friend, and all

62

his concerns are safe in the hands of infinite grace. Even in the year of drought the believer dwells in green pastures, and lies down beside the still waters; but as for the ungodly, he abides in the wilderness and hears the mutterings of that curse, "Cursed is he that trusteth in man, and maketh flesh his arm: he shall be like the heath in the desert; he shall not see when good cometh." Do you question my assertion, that Canaan is a fitting type of the present condition of the Christian? We have frequently insisted upon it that it is a far better type of the militant believer here than of the glorified saint in the New Jerusalem. Canaan is sometimes used by us in our hymns as the picture of heaven, but it is scarcely so; a moment's reflection will show that it is far more distinctly the picture of the present state of every believer. While we are under conviction of sin we are like Israel in the wilderness, we have no rest for the sole of our foot; but when we put our trust in Jesus we do as it were cross the river and leave the wilderness behind: "we that have believed do enter into rest," for "there remaineth a rest for the people of God." Believers have entered into the finished salvation which is provided for us in Christ Jesus. The blessings of our inheritance are in a great measure already in our possession; the state of salvation is no longer a land of promise, but it is a land possessed and enjoyed. We have peace with God; we are even now justified by faith. "Beloved, *now* are we the sons of God." Covenant blessings are at this moment actually ours, just as the portions of the land of Canaan became actually in the possession of the various tribes. It is true there is an enemy in Canaan, an enemy to be driven out—indwelling sin, which is entrenched in our hearts as in walled cities; fleshly lusts, which are like the chariots of iron with which we have to do war—but the land is ours; we have the covenanted heritage at this moment in our possession, and the foes who would rob us of it shall, by the sword of faith, and the weapon of all prayer, be utterly rooted out. The Christian, like Israel in Canaan, is not under the government of Moses now; he has done with Moses once for all. Moses was magnified and made honourable as he climbed to the top of the hill, and with a kiss from God's lips was carried into heaven. Even so the law has been magnified and made honourable in the person of Christ, and has ceased to reign over the believer; and as Joshua was the leader of the Israelites when they came into Canaan, so is Jesus our Leader now. He it is who leads us on from victory to victory, and he will not sheathe his sword till he has taken unto himself, and given unto us his followers, the full possession of all the holiness and happiness which covenant engagements have secured to us. For these and many other reasons it is clear that the children of Israel in Canaan were typically in the same condition as we are now who, having believed in Jesus, have our citizenship in heaven.

Beloved, those of you who are in such a state will relish the text. It is to such persons that the text is addressed. The eyes of the Lord thy God are always upon thee, O believer, from the beginning of the year even to the end of the year. You who trust in Jesus are under the guidance of the great Joshua; you are fighting sin; you have obtained salvation; you have left the wilderness of conviction and fear behind you, come into the Canaan of faith, and now the eyes of God are upon you and upon your state from the opening of the year to its close.

May the Holy Spirit bless us; and we shall, first, *take the text as we find it;* secondly, *we shall turn the text over;* thirdly, *we shall blot the text out;* and then, fourthly, *we shall distil practical lessons from the text.*

I. First, we will consider THE TEXT AS WE FIND IT. The first word that glitters before us like a jewel in a crown, is that word "eyes," "The eyes of the Lord." What is meant here? Surely not mere omniscience. In that sense the eyes of the Lord are in every place beholding the evil and the good. God sees Hagar as well as Sarah, and beholds Judas when he gives the traitorous kiss quite as surely as he beholds the holy woman when she washes the feet of the Saviour with her tears. No, there is love in the text to sweeten observation. "The Lord knoweth the righteous" with a knowledge which is over and above that of omniscience. The eyes of the Lord are upon the righteous, not merely to see them, but to view them with complacency and delight; not barely to observe them, but to observe them with affectionate care and interest. The meaning of the text then is, first, that *God's love is always upon his people.* Oh, Christians, think of this (it is rather to be thought of than to be spoken of), that God loves us! The big heart of Deity is set upon us poor, insignificant, undeserving, worthless beings. God loves us, loves us ever, never thinks of us without loving thoughts, never regards us, nor speaks of us, nor acts towards us, except in love. God is love in a certain sense towards all, for he is full of benevolence to all his creatures; love is indeed his essence; but there is a depth unfathomable when that word is used in reference to his elect ones who are the objects of distinguishing grace, redeemed by blood, enfranchised by power, adopted by condescension, and preserved by faithfulness. Beloved, do not ask me to speak of this love, but implore God the Holy Ghost to speak of it to your inmost souls. The loving eyes of God are always upon you, the poorest and most obscure of his people, from the beginning of the year even to the end of the year.

The expression of the text teaches us that *the Lord takes a personal interest in us.* It is not here said that God loves us, and therefore sends an angel to protect and watch over us; but the Lord does it himself. The eyes that observe us are God's own eyes, the guardian under whose protection we are placed is God himself. Some mothers put out their children to nurse, but God never; all his babes hang upon his own breast, and are carried in his own arms. It is little that we could do if we had to perform everything personally, and therefore the most of things are done by proxy. The captain when the vessel is to be steered across the deep must have his hour of sleep, and then the second in command, or some other, must manage the vessel; but you will observe that in times of emergency, the captain is called up and takes upon himself personal responsibility. See him as he himself anxiously heaves the lead, and stands at the helm or at the look-out, for he can trust no one else in perilous moments. It seems from the text that it is always a time of emergency with God's people, for their great Lord always exercises a personal care over them. He has never said to his angels, "I will dispense with my own watching, and you shall guard my saints;" but while he gives them charge concerning his people, yet he himself is personally their keeper and their shield. "I the Lord do keep it, I will water it every moment; lest any hurt it I will keep it night and day." You have sometimes when you have been very sick sent for a physician, and it may be that he has been engaged somewhere else, but he has an assistant who probably is quite as skilful as himself, yet, as soon as that assistant comes, such has been your confidence in the man himself for whom you have sent that you feel quite disappointed; you wanted to see the man whom you had tried in days gone by. There is no fear of our being put off with any substitute for our God. Oh, beloved, when I think of the text, I feel of the same mind as Moses when God said, "I will send my angel before thee." "No," Moses in effect said, "that will not suffice: if *thy presence* go not with us carry us not up hence." My Lord, I cannot be put off with Gabriel or Michael, I cannot be content with the brightest of the seraphs who stand before thy throne; it is thy presence I want, and blessed be thy name, it is thy presence which the text promises to give. The anxious mother is glad to have a careful nurse upon whom she may rely, but in the crisis of the disease when the little one's life trembles in the balance, she says, "Nurse, I must sit up myself with the child to-night;" and though it is the third, perhaps the fourth night, since the mother has had sleep, yet her eyes will not close so long as the particular point of danger is still in view. See, my brethren, see the loving tenderness of our gracious God. Never, never, never, does he delegate to others, however good or kind, or to any secondary agents, however active or powerful, the care of his people, but his own eyes, without a substitute, must watch over us.

Further, the text reminds us of *the unwearied power of God towards his people.* What, can his eyes be always upon us? This were not possible if he were not God. To be always upon one object, man can scarcely effect that; but where there are ten thousand times ten thousand objects, how can the same eyes always be upon every one among so many! I know what unbelief has said to you. It has whispered, "He bringeth forth the stars, he calleth them all by their names, how then can he notice so mean an insect as you are?" Then we have said, "My way is passed over from God: God has forgotten me; my God has forsaken me." But here comes in the text. Not only has he not forgotten you, but he has never once taken his eyes off you, and though you be one among so many, yet he has observed you as narrowly, as carefully, as tenderly, as if there were not another child in the divine family, nor another one whose prayers were to be heard, or whose cares were to be relieved. What would you think of yourself if you knew that you were the only saved soul in the world, the only elect one of God, the only one purchased on the bloody tree? Why you would feel, "How God must care for me! How he must watch over me! Surely he will never take his eyes off such an especial favourite." But it is the same with you, beloved, though the family is so large, as if you were the only one. The eyes of the Lord never grow weary: he neither slumbers nor sleeps; both by day and night he observes each one of his people.

If you put these things together, intense affection, personal interest, and unwearied power, and then if you remember that all this time God's heart is actuated by unchanging purposes of grace towards you, surely there will be enough to make you lose yourself in wonder, love, and praise. You have sinned in the past of your history, but your sin has never made him love you less, because he never looked upon you as you are personally considered, nakedly, and abstractedly in yourself, but he saw you and loved you in Christ in the eternal purpose even when you were dead in trespasses and sins; he has seen you in Christ ever since, and has never ceased to love you. It is true you have been very faulty (what tears this ought to cost you!) but as he never loved you for your good works, he has never cast you away for your bad works, but he has beheld you as washed in the atoning blood of Jesus till you are whiter than snow, and he has seen you clothed in the perfect righteousness of your Surety, and therefore looked upon you and regarded you as though you were without spot, or wrinkle, or any such thing. Grace has always set you before the Lord's eyes as being in his dear Son all fair and lovely—a pleasing prospect for him to look upon. He has gazed upon you, beloved, but never with anger, looked upon you when your infirmities, nay, your wilful wickednesses had made you hate yourself, and yet, though he has seen you in this doleful state, he had such a regard for your relationship to Christ that you have still been accepted in the Beloved.

I wish it were in the power of mortal speech to convey the full glory of that thought, but it is not. You must eat this morsel alone; you must take it like a wafer made with honey and put it under your tongue, and suck the essential sweetness out of it. The eyes of God, *my* God, are always upon his chosen, as eyes of affection, delight, complacency, unwearied power, immutable wisdom, and unchanging love.

The next word that seems to flash and sparkle in the text is that word "ALWAYS." "The eyes of the Lord are always upon it." And it is added, as if that word were not enough for such dull ears as ours, from the beginning of the year even to the end of the year. This is so plain and pointed that we may not imagine that any one single day or hour of the day or minute of the hour we are removed from the eyes or the heart of God. I tried to discover the other day what time there was in one's life when one could best afford to be without God. Perhaps imagination suggests the time of prosperity, when business prospers, wealth is growing, and the mind is happy. Ah, beloved, to be without our God then, why it would be like the marriage feast without the bridegroom, it would be the day of delight and no delight, a sea and no water in it, day and no light. What! all these mercies and no God! Then there is only so much shell and no kernel, so much shadow and no substance. In the midst of such joys as earth can give in the absence of the Lord the soul can hear Satanic laughter, for Satan laughs at the soul because it has tried to make the world its rest, and is sure to be deceived. Do without God in prosperity, beloved! We cannot, for then we should grow worldly, proud, careless, and deep damnation would be our lot. The Christian in prosperity is like a man standing on a pinnacle, he must then be divinely upheld or his fall will be terrible. If you can do without God at all, it certainly is not when you are standing on the pinnacle. What then? Could we do without him in adversity? Ask the heart that is breaking! Ask the tortured spirit that has been deserted by its friend! Ask the child of poverty who has not where to lay his head! Ask the daughter of sickness, tossing by night and day on that uneasy bed, Couldst thou do without thy God? And the very thought causes wailing and gnashing of teeth. *With* God pain becomes pleasure, and dying beds are elevated into thrones, but *without* God—ah! what could we do? Well then, is there no period? Cannot the young Christian, full of freshness and vigour, elated with the novelty of piety, do without his God? Ah, poor puny thing, how can the lamb do without the shepherd to carry it in his arms? Cannot the man in middle life then, whose virtues have been confirmed, do without his God? He tells you that it is the day of battle with him, and that the darts fly so thick in business now-a-days, that the burdens of life are so heavy in this age that without God a man in middle life is like a naked man in the midst of a thicket of briars and thorns—he cannot hope to make his way. Ask yon grey beard with all the experience of seventy years, whether at least he has not attained to an independence of grace, and he will say to you that as the weakness and infirmity of the body press upon him it is his joy that his inner man is renewed day by day, but take away God, who is the spring of that renewal, and old age would be utter wretchedness. Ah! brethren, there is not a moment in any one day that you or I have ever lived, that we could have afforded to dispense with the help of God, for when we have thought ourselves strong, as, alas ! we have been fools enough to do, in one five minutes we have done that which has cost us rivers of tears to undo; in an unguarded moment we have spoken a word which we could not recall, but which we would have recalled if we should have had to bite our tongues in halves to have had it unsaid. We have thought a thought when God has left us which has gone whizzing through our souls like a hellish thunderbolt making a fiery path along the spirit ; we may well wonder how it is that the evil thought did not become a terrible act as it would have done if God whom we had forgotten had forgotten us. We need to set the Lord always before us. Let us then, when we wake in the morning, take this promise with us and say, Lord, thou hast said thou wilt be always with us ; then leave us not till the dews of evening fall, and we return to our couch; leave us not even when we are there, lest in the night temptation should be whispered in our ears and we should wake to defile our mind with unholiness. Leave us never, O our God, but always be our very present help ! Last year was, perhaps, the most gloomy of our lives. All the newspaper summaries of 1866 are like the prophetic roll which was written within and without with lamentations. The year has gone, and everybody is glad to think that we have entered upon a new one ; yet, who knows but what 1867 may be worse ? Who can tell ? Well, brethren, let it be what God chooses it shall be. Let it be what he appoints; for there is this comfort in the assurance that not a moment from this Sabbath night on to the 31st December, 1867, shall be without the tender care of heaven ; not even for a second will the Lord remove his eyes from any one of his people. Here is good cheer for us ! We will march boldly into this wilderness, for the pillar of fire and cloud will never leave us; the manna will never cease to drop, and the rock that followed us will never cease to flow with living streams. Onward, onward, let us go, joyously confident in our God.

The next word that springs from the text is that great word JEHOVAH.

It is a pity that our translators did not give us the names of God as they found them in the original. The word LORD in capitals is well enough, but that grand and glorious name of "Jehovah" should have been retained. In this case we read, "the eyes of Jehovah are always upon it." He who surveys us with love and care is none other than the one and indivisible God, so that we may conclude if we have his eyes to view us we have his heart to love us, and if we have his heart we have his wings to cover us, we have his hands to bear us up; we have the everlasting arms to be underneath us, we have all the attributes of Deity at our command. Oh, Christian, when God says that he always looks at you, he means this, that he is always yours, there is nothing which is necessary for you which he will refuse to do; there is no wisdom stored up in him which he will not use for you, there is no one attribute of all that great mass of splendour which makes up the Deity which shall be withheld from you in any measure, but all that God is shall be yours. He shall be your God for ever and ever. He will give you grace and glory, and be your guide even unto death.

Perhaps the sweetest word of the text is that next one—the eyes of Jehovah "THY GOD." Ah, there is a blessed secret! Why? Ours in covenant, our God, for he chose us to be *his* portion, and by his grace he has made us choose him to be *our* portion. We are his and he is ours.

> "So I my best Beloved's am,
> So he is mine."

"Thy God." Blessed be the Lord, we have learned to view him not as another man's God but as our God. Christian, can you claim a property in God this day? Has your hand by faith grasped him? Has your heart by love twisted its tendrils round him? Do you feel him to be the greatest possession that you have, that all the creatures are but a dream, an empty show, but that God is your substantial treasure; your all in all. Oh then it is not an absolute God whose eyes are upon you, but God in covenant relationship regards you. "Thy God." What a word is this! He who is watching me is my Shepherd; he who cares for me is my Father; not my God alone by way of power, but my Father by way of relationship; one who though he be so great that the heaven of heavens cannot contain him, yet deigned to visit this poor earth robed in mortal flesh that he might become like unto us, and he is now our God, the God of his people by near and dear relationship. In ties of blood Jesus is with sinners one, our husband, our head, our all in all, and we are his fulness, the fulness of him that filleth all in all. Thus the eyes of God, as the covenant God of Israel are upon his people from the beginning of the year to the end of the year.

I must now leave the text to talk to you alone by itself. Much more may be said, but better unsaid by me, if you let the text say it to you. Talk to the text, I pray you, let it journey with you till you can say of it as the disciples said of Christ, "Did not our hearts burn within us while he talked with us by the way?"

II. We are now to TURN THE TEXT OVER; that is to say, we will misread it, yet read it rightly. Suppose the text were to run thus— "The eyes of the Lord's people are always upon him from the beginning of the year to the end of the year." Dear friends, we like the text as it stands, but I do not believe we shall ever comprehend the fulness of it unless we receive it as I have now altered it, for we only understand God's sight of us when we get a sight of him. God, unknown to us, is our protector, but he is not such a protector that we can comfortably repose upon him. We must discern him by the eyes of faith, or else the mercy, though given by God, is not spiritually enjoyed in our hearts. Beloved, if God looks at us, how much more ought we to look at him! When God sees us what does he see? Nothing—I was going to say— nothing, if he looks at us in ourselves, but that which is unworthy to be looked at. Now, on the contrary, when we look at him what do we see? Oh such a sight, that I wonder not that Moses said, "I beseech thee shew me thy glory." What a vision will it be! Will it not be heaven's own vision to see God? Is not it the peculiar prerogative of the pure in heart that they shall see God? And yet, I cannot make it out, some of us have had the right to see God for years, and we have occasionally seen him face to face, as a man speaketh to his friend; by faith we have seen God, but, beloved, what I cannot make out is that we so little see him. Do you never find yourself living all day without God? Not perhaps absolutely so, for you would not like to go to business without a little prayer in the morning; but do you not sometimes get through that morning's prayer without seeing God at all? I mean, is it not just the form of kneeling down, and saying good words and getting up again? And all through the day have you not lived away from God? This is a queer world to live in, there are not many things to make one happy, and yet somehow we forget the very things that could give us happiness, and keep our eyes upon the frivolous cares and teazing troubles which distract us. So do we even close the night—no taste of his love, no kiss of his lips that is better than wine; and our evening prayer—poor moaning it is, hardly a prayer. I fear it is possible to live not only days but months at this dying rate, and it is horrible living, such horrible living that I would infini ely prefer to be locked up in the mouldiest dungeon in which a man of God ever rotted and have the Lord's presence, than I would care to live in the noblest palace in which sinner ever sported himself without God. After all, that which makes life life is the enjoyment of the presence of God. It is not so with the worldling: he can live without God, like the swine, who, being contented with their husks, lie down and sleep and wake again to feed; but the Christian cannot live on husks, he has a stomach above them, and if he does not get his God he must be miserable. God has ordained it so that a spiritual man is wretched without the love of God in his heart. If you and I want present happiness without God, we had better be sinners outright and live upon this world than try to be happy in religion without communion with Jesus. Present happiness for a genuine Christian in the absence of Christ is an absolute impossibility. We must have God or we are of all men most miserable. Suppose that in this year one thousand eight hundred and sixty-seven we were at any rate filled with the desire to have our eyes always upon God from the beginning of the year to the end of the year, to be always conscious that he is seeing us, to be always sensible of his presence—more than that, to be always longing to be obedient to his commands, always wanting to win souls for his dear Son from the beginning of the year to the end of the year; what a happy thing would this be! If we could abide in a spirit of prayerfulness or thankfulness, devout, consecrated, loving, tender, it would be a high thing to attain unto. Brethren, we believe in a great God who is able to do exceeding abundantly above what we ask or even think, why not expect great things from him? I do think of this blessing, and I dare to ask for it; surely then he is able to give it. Do not let us stand back because of unbelief, let us ask that as God's eyes will be upon us our eyes may be upon him. What a blessed meeting of eyes when the Lord looks us full in the face, and we look at him through the Mediator Christ Jesus, and the Lord declares, "I love thee," and we answer, "We also love thee, O our God!" Oh that we may be in harmony with the Lord our God, and find ourselves drawn upwards and bound to him! May the Lord be the Sun, and we the dewdrops which sparkle in his rays and are exhaled and drawn aloft by the heat of his love! May God look down *from* heaven, and we look up *to* heaven, and both of us be happy in the sight of each other, delighting and rejoicing in mutual affection! This is what communion means. I have taken a long while to bring it to that one word, but that is what it means.

> "Daily communion let me prove
> With thee, blest object of my love."

That was Toplady's desire, but I am afraid if I would express my own experience I must close with the other two lines of the verse where Toplady says—

> "But oh, for this no strength have I,
> My strength is at thy feet to lie."

III. In the third place, we will imagine that we BLOT THE TEXT OUT ALTOGETHER. Not that we can blot it out or would do so if we could, but we are to suppose that it is blotted out, to imagine that you and I have to live all the year without the eyes of God upon us, not finding a moment from the beginning of the year to the end of the year in which we perceive the Lord to be caring for us or to be waiting to be gracious to us. Imagine that there is none to whom we may appeal beyond our own fellow-creatures for help. Oh miserable supposition! We have come to the opening of the year, and we have to get through it somehow, we must stumble through January, go muddling through the winter, groaning through the spring, sweating through the summer, fainting through the autumn, and grovelling on to another Christmas, and no God to help us; no prayer when God is gone, no promise when God is no more. There could be no promise, no spiritual succour, no comfort, no help for us if there were no God. I will suppose this to be the case with any one of us here. But I hear you cry out, "Imagine not such a thing, for I should be like an orphan child without a father, I should be helpless—a tree with no water to its roots." But I will suppose this in the case of you sinners. You know you have been living for twenty, or thirty, or forty years without God, without prayer, without trust, without hope, yet I should not wonder that if I were solemnly to tell you that God would not let you pray during the next year, and would not help you if you did pray, I should not wonder if you were greatly startled at it. Though I believe that the Lord will hear you from the beginning of the year to the end of the year, though I believe that he will watch over you and bless you if you seek him, yet I fear that the most of you are despising his care, living without fellowship with him; and so you are without God, without Christ, without hope, and will be so from the beginning of the year to the end of the year. There is a story told of a most eccentric minister, that walking out one morning he saw a man going to work, and said to him, "What a lovely morning! How grateful we ought to be to God for all his mercies! The man said he did not know much about it. "Why," said the minister, "I suppose you always pray to God for your wife and family—for your children—don't you?" "No," said he, "I do not know that I do." "What," said the minister, "do you never pray?" "No." "Then I will give you half-a-crown, if you will promise me you never will as long as ever you live." "Oh," says he, "I shall be very glad of half-a-crown to get me a drop of beer." He took the half-crown, and promised never to pray as long as he lived. He went to his work, and when he had been digging for a little while, he thought to himself, "That's a queer thing I have done this morning—a very strange thing—I've taken money and promised never to pray as long as I live." He thought it over, and it made him feel wretched. He went home to his wife and told her of it. "Well, John," said she, "you may depend upon it it was the devil, you've sold yourself to the devil for half-a-crown." This so bowed the poor wretch down that he did not know what to do with himself. This was all his thought—that he had sold himself to the devil for money, and would soon be carried off to hell. He commenced attending places of worship, conscious that it was of no use, for he had sold himself to the devil, but he was really ill, bodily ill, through the fear and trembling which had come upon him. One night he recognized in the preacher the very man who had given him the half-crown, and probably the preacher recognized him, for the text was, "What shall it profit a man if he shall gain the whole world and lose his own soul?" The preacher remarked that he knew a man who had sold his soul for half-a-crown. The poor man rushed forward and said, "Take it back! Take it back!" "You said you would never pray," said the minister, "if I gave you half-a-crown; do you want to pray?" "Oh yes, I would give the world to be allowed to pray." That man was a great fool to sell his soul for half-a-crown, but some of you are a great deal bigger fools, for *you never had the half-crown*, and yet you do not pray, and I dare say never will, but will go down to hell never having sought God. Perhaps, if I could negative this text, and say to you, "the eyes of God will not be upon you from the beginning of this year to the end of the year, and God will not hear and bless you," it might alarm and awaken you. But though I suggest the thought, I would rather you would say.

"Oh let not such a curse rest upon me, for I may die this year, and I may die this day. O God, hear me now!" Ah, dear hearer, if such a desire be in your heart the Lord will hear you and bless you with his salvation.

III. Let us close with USING THE TEXT. The way to use it is this. If the eyes of the Lord will be upon us his people, from the beginning of the year to the end of the year, what shall we do? Why, let us be as happy as we can during this year. You have your trials and troubles to come—do not expect that you will be free from them. The devil is not dead, and sparks still fly upward. Herein is your joy, the God and Father of our Lord Jesus Christ will never leave you nor forsake you. Up with your standard now and march on boldly! In the name of the Lord set up your banner, and begin to sing. Away with carking care, God cares for us; the sparrows are fed, and shall not the children be? The lilies bloom, and shall not the saints be clothed? Let us roll all our burdens upon the Burden-bearer. You will have enough to care for if you care for his cause as you should. Do not spoil your power to care for God by caring for yourself. This year let your motto be, "Seek first the kingdom of God and his righteousness, and all these things shall be added to you." By taking thought you cannot add a cubit to your stature, nor turn one hair white or black; take then no anxious thought for the morrow, for the morrow shall take thought for the things of itself. Lean upon your God, and remember his promise, that as your day is so shall your strength be. "I would have you," says the apostle, "I would have you without carefulness." He does not mean, I would have you without economy, without prudence and without discretion, but he means, I would have you without fretfulness, without distrustful care, I would have you be without care for yourself, because the Lord's eyes will be upon you.

Further, dear friends, I would have you use the text by the way of seeking greater blessings and richer mercies than you have ever enjoyed. Blessed be God for his merciful kindness towards this church; his loving-kindnesses have been very many; his favours new every morning and fresh every evening; but we want more. Let us not be content with a February blessing, though that is generally the month in which we have had our refreshings; let us seek to get a blessing to-day. I hope you will get it this afternoon in the Sunday-school you workers there, and I hope you will obtain it in the senior classes from the beginning of the year to the end of the year. Let there be no dulness, lethargy, and lukewarmness in the classes this afternoon. The brother who has to address the school will I hope speak to you with fervour and earnestness: there must be no coldness there. And I hope you who are preaching in the street, if it be possible in such weather, or going from house to house with tracts, or doing anything else, will have a blessing on this first Sunday of the year. But then shall we grow cold next Sunday? Not at all. It is from the beginning of the year to the end of the year. Shall we endeavour to get up a little excitement, and have a revival for five or six weeks? No, blessed be God, we must have it from the beginning of the year to the end of the year. While we have a spring which never grows dry, why should the pitcher ever be empty? Surely gratitude can find us fuel enough in the forests of memory to keep the fire of love always flaming. Why should we be weary when the glorious prize is worthy of our constant exertions, when the great crowd of witnesses hold us in full survey? May our Lord by his Spirit bring you and me to a high pitch of prayerfulness, and then let us continue in prayer from the beginning of the year to the end of the year. May God bring you and me to a high degree of generosity, and then may we be always giving from the beginning of the year to the end of the year every week, from the first to the last, always laying by in store as God has prospered us for his cause. May we be always active, always industrious, always hopeful, always spiritual, always heavenly, and always raised up and made to sit together in heavenly places in Christ Jesus. So may our gracious God deal with us from the beginning of the year to the end of the year through Jesus Christ our Lord. Amen.

Creation's Groans and Saints' Sighs

"We know that the whole creation groaneth and travaileth in pain together until now. And not only they, but ourselves also, which have the first-fruits of the Spirit, even we ourselves groan within ourselves, waiting for the adoption, to wit, the redemption of our body."—Romans viii. 22, 23.

MY venerable friend, who, on the first Sabbath of the year, always sends me a text to preach from, has on this occasion selected one which it is very far from easy to handle. The more I have read it, the more certainly have I come to the conclusion that this is one of the things in Paul's epistles to which Peter referred when he said, "Wherein are some things hard to be understood." However, dear friends, we have often found that the nuts which are hardest to crack have the sweetest kernels, and when the bone seems as if it could never be broken, the richest marrow has been found within. So it may by possibility be this morning; so it will be if the Spirit of God shall be our instructor, and fulfil his gracious promise to "lead us into all truth."

The whole creation is fair and beautiful even in its present condition. I have no sort of sympathy with those who cannot enjoy the beauties of nature. Climbing the lofty Alps, or wandering through the charming valley, skimming the blue sea, or traversing the verdant forest, we have felt that this world, however desecrated by sin, was evidently built to be a temple of God, and the grandeur and the glory of it plainly declare that "the earth is the Lord's and the fulness thereof." Like the marvellous structures of Palmyra of Baalbek, in the far off east, the earth in ruins reveals a magnificence which betokens a royal founder, and an extraordinary purpose. Creation glows with a thousand beauties, even in its present fallen condition; yet clearly enough it is not as when it came from the Maker's hand—the slime of the serpent is on it all—this is not the world which God pronounced to be "very good." We hear of tornadoes, of earthquakes, of tempests, of volcanoes, of avalanches, and of the sea which devoureth its thousands: there is sorrow on the sea, and there is misery on the land; and into the highest palaces as well as the poorest cottages, death, the insatiable, is shooting his arrows, while his quiver is still full to bursting with future woes. It is a sad, sad world. The curse has fallen on it since the fall, and thorns and thistles it bringeth forth, not from its soil alone, but from all that comes of it. Earth wears upon her brow, like Cain of old, the brand of transgression. Sad would it be to our thoughts if it were always to be so. If there were no future to this world as well as to ourselves, we might be glad to escape from it, counting it to be nothing better than a huge penal colony, from which it would be a thousand mercies for both body and soul to be emancipated. At this present time, the groaning and travailing which are general throughout creation, are deeply felt among the sons of men. The dreariest thing you can read is the newspaper. I heard of one who sat up at the end of last year to groan last year out; it was ill done, but in truth it was a year of groaning, and the present one opens amid turbulence and distress. We heard of abundant harvests, but we soon discovered that they were all a dream, and that there would be scant in the worker's cottage. And now, what with strifes between men and masters, which are banishing trade from England, and what with political convulsions, which unhinge everything, the vessel of the state is drifting fast to the shallows. May God in mercy put his hand to the helm of the ship, and steer her safely. There is a general wail among nations and peoples. You can hear it in the streets of the city. The Lord reigneth, or we might lament right bitterly.

The apostle tells us that not only is there a groan from creation, but this is shared in by God's people. We shall notice in our text, first, *whereunto the saints have already attained;* secondly, *wherein we are deficient;* and thirdly, *what is the state of mind of the saints in regard to the whole of the matter.*

I. WHEREUNTO THE SAINTS HAVE ATTAINED.

We were once an undistinguished part of the creation, subject to the same curse as the rest of the world, " heirs of wrath, even as others." But distinguishing grace has made a difference where no difference naturally was; we are now no longer treated as criminals condemned, but as children and heirs of God. We have received a divine life, by which we are made partakers of the divine nature, having " escaped the corruption which is in the world through lust." The Spirit of God has come unto us so that our " bodies are the temples of the Holy Ghost." God dwelleth in us, and we are one with Christ. We have at this present moment in us certain priceless things which distinguish us as believers in Christ from all the rest of God's creatures. " *We have,*" says the text, not " we hope and trust sometimes we have," nor yet " possibly we may have," but " we have, we know we have, we are sure we have." Believing in Jesus, we speak confidently, we have unspeakable blessings given to us by the Father of spirits. Not we *shall have,* but *we have.* True, many things are yet in the future, but even at this present moment, we have obtained an inheritance; we have already in our possession a heritage divine which is the beginning of our eternal portion. This is called " the first-fruits of the Spirit," by which I understand the first works of the Spirit in our souls. Brethren, we have repentance, that gem of the first water. We have faith, that priceless, precious jewel. We have hope, which sparkles, a hope most sure and steadfast. We have love, which sweetens all the rest. We have that work of the Spirit within our souls which always comes before admittance into glory. We are already made " new creatures in Christ Jesus," by the effectual working of the mighty power of God the Holy Ghost. This is called the first-fruit because *it comes first.* As the wave-sheaf was the first of the harvest, so the spiritual life which we have, and all the graces which adorn that life, are the first gifts, the first operations of the Spirit of God in our souls. We *have* this.

It is called " first-fruits," again, because *the first-fruits were always the pledge of the harvest.* As soon as the Israelite had plucked the first handful of ripe ears, they were to him so many proofs that the harvest was already come. He looked forward with glad anticipation to the time when the wain should creak beneath the sheaves, and when the harvest-home should be shouted at the door of the barn. So, brethren, when God gives us " Faith, hope, charity—these three," when he gives us " whatsoever things are pure, lovely, and of good report," as the work of the Holy Spirit, these are to us the prognostics of the coming glory. If you have the Spirit of God in your soul, you may rejoice over it as the pledge and token of the fulness of bliss and perfection " which God hath prepared for them that love him."

It is called " first-fruits," again, because *these were always holy to the Lord.* The first ears of corn were offered to the Most High, and surely our new nature, with all its powers, must be regarded by us as a conse-crated thing. The new life which God has given to us is not ours that we should ascribe its excellence to our own merit: the new nature is Christ's peculiarly; as it is Christ's image and Christ's creation, so it is for Christ's glory alone. That secret we must keep separate from all earthly things; that treasure which he has committed to us we must watch both night and day against those profane intruders who would defile the consecrated ground. We would stand upon our watch-towel and cry aloud to the Strong for strength, that the adversary may be re-pelled, that the sacred castle of our heart may be for the habitation of Jesus, and Jesus alone. We have a sacred secret which belongs to Jesus, as the first-fruits belong to Jehovah.

Brethren, the work of the Spirit is called " first-fruits," because *the first-fruits were not the harvest.* No Jew was ever content with the first-fruits. He was content with them for what they were, but the first-fruits enlarged his desires for the harvest. If he had taken the first-fruits home, and said, " I have all I want," and had rested satisfied month after month, he would have given proof of madness, for the first-fruit does but whet the appetite—does but stir up the desire it never was meant to satisfy. So, when we get the first works of the Spirit of God, we are not to say, " I have attained, I am already perfect, there is nothing further for me to do, or to desire." Nay, my brethren, all that the most advanced of God's people know as yet, should but excite in them an insatiable thirst after more. My brother with great ex-perience, my sister with enlarged acquaintance with Christ, ye have not yet known the harvest, you have only reaped the first handful of corn. Open your mouth wide, and God will fill it! Enlarge thine ex-pectations—seek great things from the God of heaven—and he will give them to thee; but by no means fold thine arms in sloth, and sit down upon the bed of carnal security. Forget the steps thou hast already trodden, and reach forward towards that which is before, looking unto Jesus.

Even this first point of what the saint has attained will help us to understand why it is that he groans. Did I not say that we have not received the whole of our portion, and that what we have received is to the whole no more than one handful of wheat is to the whole harvest, a very gracious pledge, but nothing more? Therefore it is that we groan. Having received something, we desire more. Having reaped handfuls, we long for sheaves. For this very reason, that we are saved, we groan for something beyond. Did you hear that groan just now? It is a traveller lost in the deep snow on the mountain pass. No one has come to rescue him, and indeed he has fallen into a place from which escape is impossible. The snow is numbing his limbs, and his soul is breathed out with many a groan. Keep that groan in your ear, for I I want you to hear another. The traveller has reached the hospice. He has been charitably received, he has been warmed at the fire, he has received abundant provision, he is warmly clothed. There is no fear of tempest, that grand old hospice has outstood many a thundering storm. The man is perfectly safe, and quite content, so far as that goes, and exceedingly grateful to think that he has been rescued; but yet I hear him groan because he has a wife and children down in yonder plain, and the snow is lying too deep for travelling, and the wind is howling, and the blinding snow flakes are falling so thickly that he cannot pursue his journey. Ask him whether he is happy and content. He says, "Yes, I am happy and grateful. I have been saved from the snow. I do not wish for anything more than I have here, I am perfectly satisfied, so far as this goes, but I long to look upon my household, and to be once more in my own sweet home, and until I reach it, I shall not cease to groan." Now, the first groan which you heard was deep and dreadful, as though it were fetched from the abyss of hell; that is the groan of the ungodly man as he perishes, and leaves all his dear delights; but the second groan is so softened and sweetened, that it is rather the note of desire than of distress. Such is the groan of the believer, who, though rescued and brought into the hospice of divine mercy, is longing to see his Father's face without a veil between, and to be united with the happy family on the other side the Jordan, where they rejoice for evermore. When the soldiers of Godfrey of Bouillon came in sight of Jerusalem, it is said they shouted for joy at the sight of the holy city. For that very reason they began to groan. Ask ye why? It was because they longed to enter it. Having once looked upon the city of David, they longed to carry the holy city by storm, to overthrow the crescent, and place the cross in its place. He who has never seen the New Jerusalem, has never clapped his hands with holy ecstasy, he has never sighed with the unutterable longing which is expressed in words like these—

> " O my sweet home, Jerusalem,
> Would God I were in thee!
> Would God my woes were at an end,
> Thy joys that I might see!"

Take another picture to illustrate that the obtaining of something makes us groan after more. An exile, far away from his native country, has been long forgotten, but on a sudden a vessel brings him the pardon of his monarch, and presents from his friends who have called him to remembrance. As he turns over each of these love-tokens, and as he reads the words of his reconciled prince, he asks "When will the vessel sail to take me back to my native shore?" If the vessel tarries, he groans over the delay; and if the voyage be tedious, and adverse winds blow back the barque from the white cliffs of Albion, his thirst for his own sweet land compels him to groan. So it is with your children when they look forward to their holidays; they are not unhappy or dissatisfied with the school, but yet they long to be at home. Do not you recollect how, in your schoolboy days, you used to make a little almanack with a square for every day, and how you always crossed off the day as soon as ever it began, as though you would try and make the distance from your joy as short as possible? You groaned for it, not with the unhappy groan that marks one who is to perish, but with the groan of one who, having tasted of the sweets of home, is not content until again he shall be indulged with the fulness of them. So you see, beloved, that because we have the "first-fruits of the Spirit," for that very reason, if for no other, we cannot help but groan for that blissful period which is called "the adoption, to wit, the redemption of the body."

II. Our second point rises before us—WHEREIN ARE BELIEVERS DEFICIENT? We are deficient in those things for which we groan and wait. And these appear to be four at least.

The first is, that *this body of ours is not delivered.* Brethren, as soon as a man believes in Christ, he is no longer under the curse of the law. As to his spirit, sin hath no more dominion over him, and the law hath no further claims against him. His soul is translated from death unto life, but the body, this poor flesh and blood, doth it not remain as before? Not in one sense, for the members of our body, which were instruments of unrighteousness, become by sanctification, the instruments of righteousness unto the glory of God; and the body which was once a workshop for Satan, becomes a temple for the Holy Ghost, wherein he dwells; but we are all perfectly aware that the grace of God makes no change in the body in other respects. It is just as subject to sickness as before, pain thrills quite as sharply through the heart of the saint as the sinner, and he who lives near to God, is no more likely to enjoy bodily health than he who lives at a distance from him. The greatest piety cannot preserve a man from growing old, and although in grace, he may be "like a young cedar, fresh and green," yet the body will have its grey hairs, and the strong man will be brought to totter on the staff. The body is still subject to the evils which Paul mentions, when he says of it that it is subject to corruption, to dishonour, to weakness, and is still a natural body.

Nor is this little, for the body has a depressing effect upon the sou.. A man may be full of faith and joy spiritually, but I will defy him under some forms of disease to feel as he would. The soul is like an eagle, to which the body acts as a chain, which prevents its mounting. Moreover, the appetites of the body have a natural affinity to that which is sinful. The natural desires of the human frame are not in themselves sinful, but through the degeneracy of our nature, they very readily lead us into sin, and through the corruption which is in us, even the natural desires of the body become a very great source of temptation. The body is redeemed with the precious blood of Christ, it is redeemed by price, but it has not as yet been redeemed by power. It still lingers in the realm of bondage, and is not brought into the glorious liberty of the children of God. Now this is the cause of our groaning and mourning, for the soul is so married to the body that when it is itself delivered from condemnation, it sighs to think that its poor friend, the body, should still be under the yoke. If you were a free man, and had married a wife, a slave, you could not feel perfectly content, but the more you enjoyed the sweets of freedom yourself, the more would you pine that she should still be in slavery. So is it with the Spirit, it is free from corruption and death; but the poor body is still under the bondage of corruption, and therefore the soul groans until the body itself shall be set free. Will it ever be set free? O my beloved, do not ask the question. This is the Christian's brightest hope. Many believers make a mistake when they long to die and long for heaven. Those things may be desirable, but they are not the ultimatum of the saints. The saints in heaven are perfectly free from sin, and, so far as they are capable of it, they are perfectly happy; but a disembodied spirit never can be perfect until it is reunited to its body. God made man not pure spirit, but body and spirit, and the spirit alone will never be content until it sees its corporeal frame raised to its own condition of holiness and glory. Think not that our longings here below are not shared in by the saints in heaven. They do not groan, so far as any pain can be, but they long with greater intensity than you and I long, for the "adoption, to wit, the redemption of the body." People have said there is no faith in heaven, and no hope; they know not what they say—in heaven it is that faith and hope have their fullest swing and their brightest sphere, for glorified saints believe in God's promise, and hope for the resurrection of the body. The apostle tells us that "they without us cannot be made perfect;" that is, until our bodies are raised, theirs cannot be raised, until we get our adoption day, neither can they get theirs. The Spirit saith Come, and the bride saith Come—not the bride on earth only, but the bride in heaven saith the same, bidding the happy day speed on when the trumpet shall sound, and the dead shall be raised incorruptible, and we shall be changed. For it is true, beloved, the bodies that have mouldered into dust will rise again, the fabric which has been destroyed by the worm shall start into a nobler being, and you and I, though the worm devour this body, shall in our flesh behold our God.

> " These eyes shall see him in that day,
>   The God that died for me;
> And all my rising bones shall say,
>   ' Lord, who is like to thee ? ' "

Thus we are sighing that our entire manhood, in its trinity of spirit, soul, and body, may be set free from the last vestige of the fall; we long to put off corruption, weakness, and dishonour, and to wrap ourselves in incorruption, in immortality, in glory, in the spiritual body which the Lord Jesus Christ will bestow upon all his people. You can understand in this sense why it is that we groan, for if this body really is still, though redeemed, a captive, and if it is one day to be completely free, and to rise to amazing glory, well may those who believe in this precious doctrine groan after it as they wait for it.

But, again, there is another point in which the saint is deficient as yet, namely, *in the manifestation of our adoption.* You observe the text speaks of waiting for the adoption; and another text further back, explains what that means, waiting for the manifestation of the children of God. In this world, saints are God's children, but you cannot see that they are so, except by certain moral characteristics. That man is God's child, but though he is a prince of the blood royal, his garments are those of toil, the smock frock or the fustian jacket. Yonder woman is one of the daughters of the King, but see how pale she is, what furrows are upon her brow! Many of the daughters of pleasure are far more fair than she! How is this? The adoption is not manifested yet, the children are not yet openly declared. Among the Romans a man might adopt a child, and that child might be treated as his for a long time; but there was a second adoption in public, when the child was brought before the constituted authorities, and in the presence of spectators its ordinary garments which it had worn before were taken off, and the father who took it to be his child put on garments suitable to the condition of life in which it was to live. " Beloved, now are we the sons of God, and it doth not yet appear what we shall be." We have not yet the royal robes which become the princes of the blood; we are wearing in this flesh and blood just what we wore as the sons of Adam; but we know that when *he* shall appear who is the " first born among many brethren," we shall be like him ; that is, God will dress us all as he dresses his eldest son—" We shall be like him, for we shall see him as he is." Cannot you imagine that a child taken from the lowest ranks of society, who is adopted by a Roman senator, will be saying to himself, " I wish the day were come when I shall be publicly revealed as the child of my new father. Then, I shall leave off these plebeian garments, and be robed as becomes my senatorial rank." Happy in what he has received, for that very reason he groans to get the fulness of what is promised him. So it is with us to-day. We are waiting till we shall put on our proper garments, and shall be manifested as the children of God. Ye are young princes, and ye have not been crowned yet. Ye are young brides, and the marriage day is not come, and by the love your spouse bears you, you are led to long and to sigh for the marriage day. Your very happiness makes you groan; your joy, like a swollen spring, longs to leap up like some Iceland Geyser, climbing to the skies, an it heaves and groans within the bowels of your spirit for want of space and room by which to manifest itself to men.

There is a third thing in which we are deficient, namely, *liberty*, the glorious liberty of the children of God. The whole creation is said to be groaning for its share in that freedom. You and I are also groaning for it. Brethren, we are free ! " If the Son therefore shall make you free, ye shall be free indeed." But our liberty is incomplete. When Napoleon was on the island of St. Helena, he was watched by many guards, but after many complaints, he enjoyed comparative liberty, and walked alone. Yet, what liberty was it ? Liberty to walk round the rock of St. Helena, nothing more. You and I are free, but what is our liberty? As to our spirits, we have liberty to soar into the third heaven, and sit in the heavenly places with Christ Jesus; but as for our bodies, we can only roam about this narrow cell of earth, and feel that it is not the place for us. Napoleon had been used to gilded halls, and all the pomp and glory of imperial state, and it was hard to be reduced to a handful of servants. Just so, we are kings—we are of the blood imperial; but we have not our proper state and becoming dignities—we have not our royalties here. We go to our lowly homes; we meet with our brethren and sisters here in their earth-built temples; and we are content, so far as these things go, still, how can kings be content till they mount their thrones? How can a heavenly one be content till he ascends to the heavenlies? How shall a celestial spirit be satisfied until it sees celestial things? How shall the heir of God be content till he rests on his Father's bosom, and is filled with all the fulness of God?

I wish you now to observe that we are linked with the creation. Adam in this world was in liberty, perfect liberty; nothing confined him; paradise was exactly fitted to be his seat. There were no wild beasts to rend him, no rough winds to cause him injury, no blighting heats to bring him harm; but in this present world everything is contrary to us. Evidently we are exotics here. Ungodly men prosper well enough in this world, they root themselves, and spread themselves like green bay trees: it is their native soil; but the Christian needs the hot-house of grace to keep himself alive at all—and out in the world he is like some strange foreign bird, native of a warm and sultry clime, that being let loose here under our wintry skies is ready to perish. Now, God will one day change our bodies and make them fit for our souls, and then he will change this world itself. I must not speculate, for I know nothing about it; but it is no speculation to say that we look for new heavens and a new earth wherein dwelleth righteousness; and that there will come a time when the lion shall eat straw like an ox, and the leopard shall lie down with the kid. We expect to see this world that is now so full of sin as to be an Aceldama, a field of blood, turned into a paradise, a garden of God. We believe that the taber-nacle of God will be among men, that he will dwell among them, and they shall see his face, and his name shall be in their foreheads. We expect to see the New Jerusalem descend out of heaven from God. In this very place, where sin has triumphed, we expect that grace will much more abound. Perhaps after those great fires of which Peter speaks when he says, "The heavens being on fire shall be dissolved, and the elements shall melt with fervent heat," earth will be renewed in more than pristine loveliness. Perhaps since matter may not be annihilated, and probably cannot be, but will be as immortal as spirit, this very world will become the place of an eternal jubilee, from which perpetual hallelujahs shall go up to the throne of God. If such be the bright hope that cheers us, we may well groan for its realisation, crying out,

> "O long-expected day, begin;
> Dawn on these realms of woe and sin."

I shall not enlarge further, except to say that *our glory* is not yet revealed, and that is another subject of sighing. "The glorious liberty" may be translated, "The liberty of glory." Brethren, we are like warriors fighting for the victory; we share not as yet in the shout of them that triumph. Even up in heaven they have not their full reward. When a Roman general came home from the wars, he entered Rome by stealth, and slept at night, and tarried by day, perhaps for a week or two, among his friends. He went through the streets, and people whispered, "That is the general, the valiant one," but he was not publicly acknowledged. But, on a certain set day, the gates were thrown wide open, and the general, victorious from the wars in Africa or Asia, with his snow-white horses bearing the trophies of his many battles, rode through the streets, which were strewn with roses, while the music sounded, and the multitudes, with glad acclaim, accompanied him to the Capitol. That was his triumphant entry. Those in heaven, have, as it were, stolen there. They are blessed, but they have not had their public entrance. They are waiting till their Lord shall descend from heaven with a shout, with the trump of the archangel, and the voice of God; then shall their bodies rise, then shall the world be judged; then shall the righteous be divided from the wicked; and then, upstreaming in marvellous procession, leading captivity captive for the last time, the Prince at their head, the whole of the blood-washed host, wearing their white robes, and bearing their palms of victory, shall march up to their crowns and to their thrones, to reign for ever and ever! After this consummation the believing heart is panting, groaning, and sighing.

Now, I think I hear somebody say, "you see these godly people who profess to be so happy and so safe, they still groan, and they are obliged to confess it." Yes, that is quite true, and it would be a great mercy for you if you knew how to groan in the same way. If you were half as happy as a groaning saint is, you might be content to groan on for ever. I showed you, just now, the difference between a groan and a groan. I will shew you yet again. Go into yonder house. Listen at that door on the left, there is a deep, hollow, awful groan. Go to the next house, and hear another groan. It seems to be, so far as we can judge, much more painful than the first, and has an anguish in it of the severest sort. How are we to judge between them? We will come again in a few days: as we are entering the first house we see weeping faces and flowing tears, a coffin, and a hearse. Ah, it was the groan of death! We will go into the next. Ah, what is this? Here is a smiling cherub, a father with a gladsome face : if you may venture to look at the mother, see how her face smiles for joy that a man is born into the world to cheer a happy and rejoicing family. There is all the difference between the groan of death and the groan of life. Now, the apostle sets the whole matter before us when he said, " The whole creation groaneth," and you know what comes after that, " travaileth." There is a result to come of it of the best kind. We are panting, longing after something greater, better, nobler, and it is coming. It is not the pain of death we feel, but the pain of life. We are thankful to have such a groaning.

The other night, just before Christmas, two men who were working very late, were groaning in two very different ways, one of them saying, " Ah, there's a poor Christmas day in store for me, my house is full of misery." He had been a drunkard, a spendthrift, and had not a penny to bless himself with, and his house had become a little hell; he was groaning at the thought of going home to such a scene of quarrelling and distress. Now, his fellow workman, who worked beside of him, as it was getting very late, wished himself at home, and therefore groaned. A shopmate asked, " What's the matter?" " Oh, I want to get home to my dear wife and children. I have such a happy house, I do not like to be out of it." The other might have said, "Ah, you pretend to be a happy man, and here you are groaning." "Yes," he could say, "and a blessed thing it would be for you if you had the same thing to groan after that I have." So the Christian has a good Father, a blessed, eternal home, and groans to get to it; but, ah! there is more joy even in the groan of a Christian after heaven, than in all the mirth and merriment, and dancing, and lewdness of the ungodly when their mirth is at its greatest height. We are like the dove that flutters, and is weary, but thank God, we have an ark to go to. We are like Israel in the wilderness, and are footsore, but blessed be God, we are on the way to Canaan. We are like Jacob looking at the wagons, and the more we .ook at the wagons, the more we long to see Joseph's face; but our groaning after Jesus is a blessed groan, for

> " 'Tis heaven on earth, 'tis heaven above,
> To see his face, and taste his love."

III. Now I shall conclude with WHAT OUR STATE OF MIND IS.

A Christian's experience is like a rainbow, made up of drops of the griefs of earth, and beams of the bliss of heaven. It is a chequered scene, a garment of many colours. He is sometimes in the light and sometimes in the dark. The text says, " we groan." I have told you what that groan is, I need not explain it further. But it is added, " We groan *within ourselves.*" It is not the hypocrite's groan, when he goes mourning everywhere, wanting to make people believe that he is a saint because he is wretched. We groan *within ourselves.* Our sighs are sacred things; these griefs and sighs are too hallowed for us to tell abroad in the streets. We keep our longings to our Lord, and to our Lord alone. We groan within ourselves. It appears from the text that this groaning is universal among the saints: there are no exceptions; to a greater or less extent we all feel it. He that is most endowed with worldly goods, and he who has the fewest; he that is blessed in health, and he who is racked with sickness; we all have in our measure an earnest inward groaning towards the redemption of our body.

Then the apostle says we are " waiting," by which I understand that we are not to be petulant, like Jonah or Elijah, when they said, " Let me die," nor are we to sit still and look for the end of the day because we are tired of work; nor are we to become impatient, and wish to escape from our present pains and sufferings till the will of the Lord is done. We are to groan after perfection, but we are to wait patiently for it, knowing that what the Lord appoints is best. Waiting implies being ready. We are to stand at the door expecting the Beloved to open it and take us away to himself.

In the next verse we are described as hoping. We are saved by hope. The believer continues to hope for the time when death and sin shall no more annoy his body; when, as his soul has been purified, so shall his body be, and his prayer shall be heard, that the Lord would sanctify him wholly, body, soul, and spirit.

Now, beloved, the practical use to which I put this, I am afraid somewhat discursive, discouse of this morning is just this. Here is a test for us all. You may judge of a man by what he groans after. Some men groan after wealth, they worship Mammon. Some groan continually under the troubles of life; they are merely impatient— there is no virtue in that. Some men groan because of their great losses or sufferings; well, this may be nothing but a rebellious smarting under the rod, and if so, no blessing will come of it. But the man that yearns after more holiness, the man that sighs after God, the man that groans after perfection, the man that is discontented with his sinful self, the man that feels he cannot be easy till he is made like Christ, that is the man who is blessed indeed. May God help you, and help me, to groan all our days with that kind of groaning. I have said before, there is heaven in it, and though the word sounds like sorrow, there is a depth of joy concealed within.

> " Lord, let me weep for nought but sin,
> And after none but thee;
> And then I would, O that I might,
> A constant weeper be."

I do not know a more beautiful sight to be seen on earth than a man who has served his Lord many years, and who, having grown grey in service, feels that, in the order of nature, he must soon be called home. He is rejoicing in the first-fruits of the Spirit which he has obtained, but he is panting after the full harvest of the Spirit which is guaranteed to him. I think I see him sitting on a jutting crag by the edge of Jordan, listening to the harpers on the other side, and waiting till the pitcher shall be broken at the cistern, and the wheel at the fountain, and the spirit shall depart to God that made it. A wife waiting for her husband's footsteps; a child waiting in the darkness of the night till its mother comes to give it the evening's kiss, are portraits of our waiting. It is a pleasant and precious thing so to wait and so to hope.

I fear that some of you, seeing ye have never come and put your trust in Christ, will have to say, when your time comes to die, what Wolsey is said to have declared, with only one word of alteration:—

> "O Cromwell, Cromwell!
> Had I but served my God with half the zeal
> I served *the world*, he would not, in mine age,
> Have left me naked to mine enemies."

Oh, before those days fully come, quit the service of the master who never can reward you except with death! Cast your arms around the cross of Christ, and give up your heart to God, and then, come what may, I am persuaded that "Neither death, nor life, nor angels, nor principalities, nor powers, nor things present, nor things to come. Nor height, nor depth, nor any other creature, shall be able to separate us from the love of God, which is in Christ Jesus our Lord." While you shall for awhile sigh for more of heaven, you shall soon come to the abodes of blessedness where sighing and sorrow shall flee away.

The Lord bless this assembly, for Christ's sake. AMEN.

Jesus Christ Immutable

"Jesus Christ the same yesterday, and to-day, and for ever."—Hebrews xiii. 8.

FOR a very considerable number of years an esteemed and venerable vicar of a Surrey parish has sent me at the New Year a generous testimony of his love, and an acknowledgment of the pleasure which he derives from the weekly reading of my sermons. Enclosed in the parcel which his kindness awards to me, is a text from which he hopes that I may preach on the first Sabbath morning of the New Year. This year he sends me this golden line, "Jesus Christ the same yester-day, and to-day, and for ever." I have preached from it before—you will find a sermon from this text in print;* but we need not be at all afraid of preaching from the same text twice, the word is inexhaustible, it may be trodden in the winepress many times, and yet run with generous wine. We ought not to hesitate to preach a second time from a passage, any more than anyone going to the village well would be ashamed to put down the same bucket twice, or feel at all aggrieved at sailing twice down the same river; for there is always a freshness about gospel truth, and though the matter may be the same, there are ways of putting it in fresh light, so as to bring new joy to those who meditate upon it.

Moreover, what if we should repeat our teachings concerning Christ? What if we should hear over and over again the same things "touching the King"? We can afford to hear them. Repetitions concerning Jesus are better than varieties upon any other subject. As the French monarch declared that he would sooner hear the repetitions of Bourdaloue than the novelties of another; so we may aver concerning our Lord Jesus, we would sooner hear again and again the precious truths which glorify him, than listen to the most eloquent orations upon any other theme in all the world. There are a few works of art and wonders of creation which you might gaze upon every day in your life, and yet not weary of them. A great architect tells us there are but few build-ings of this kind, but he instances Westminster Abbey as one; and everyone knows who has ever looked upon the sea, or upon the Falls of Niagara, that look as often as you may, though you see precisely the same object, yet there are new tints, new motions of the waves, and new flashings of the light, which forbid the least approach of monotony, and give to the assembling of the waters an ever-enduring charm. Even thus is it with that sea of all delights which is found in the dear Lover of our souls.

Come we, then, to the old subject of this old text, and may the blessed Spirit give us new unction while we meditate upon it. Note we, first, our Lord's personal name, *Jesus Christ.* Notice, secondly, his memorable attribute—" *he is the same yesterday, and to-day, and for ever,*" and then let us have a few words about his evident claims, derived from *the possession of such a character.*

I. First, then, the personal names of our Lord here mentioned— " JESUS CHRIST."

" JESUS " stands first. That is our Lord's Hebrew name, " Jesus," or, " Joshua." The word signifies, a Saviour, " for he shall save his people from their sins." It was given to him *in his cradle.*

> " Cold on his cradle the dewdrops are shining;
> Low lies his head with the beasts of the stall ;
> Angels adore him, in slumber reclining,
> Maker, and Monarch, and Saviour of all."

While he was yet an infant hanging on his mother's breast, he was recognised as Saviour, for the fact of God's becoming incarnate was the sure pledge, guarantee, and commencement of human salvation. At the very thought of his birth the virgin sang, " My spirit hath rejoiced in God my Saviour." There is hope that man shall be lifted up to God, when God condescends to come down to man. Jesus in the manger deserves to be called the Saviour, for when it can be said that " the tabernacle of God is with men, and he doth dwell among them," there is hope that all good things will be given to the fallen race. He was called Jesus, *in his childhood*—" The Holy Child Jesus." It was as Jesus that he went up with his parents to the temple and sat down with the doctors, hearing them and asking them questions. Ay, and Jesus as a Teacher in the very first principles of his doctrine is a Saviour, emancipating the minds of men from superstition, setting them loose from the traditions of the fathers, scattering even with his infant hand the seeds of truth, the elements of a glorious liberty which shall emancipate the human mind from the iron bondage of false philosophy and priestcraft. He was Jesus, too, and is commonly called so both by his foes and by his friends *in his active life.* It is as Jesus the Saviour that he heals the sick, that he raises the dead, that he delivers Peter from sinking, that he rescues from shipwreck the ship tossed upon the Galilean lake. In all the teachings of his middle life, in those laborious three years of diligent service, both in his public ministry and in his private prayer, he is still Jesus the Saviour; for by his active, as well as by his passive obedience, we are saved. All through his earthly sojourn he made it clear that the Son of man had come to seek and to save that which was lost. If his blood redeems us from the guilt of sin, his life shows us how to overcome its power. If by his death upon the tree he crushes Satan for us, by his life of holiness he teaches us how to break the dragon's head within us. He is the Saviour as a babe, the Saviour as a child, the Saviour as the toiling, labouring, tempted man. But he comes out most clearly as Jesus *when dying on the cross;* named so in a writing of which the author said, " What I have written I have written," for over the head of the dying Saviour you read, " Jesus of Nazareth, the King of the Jews." There pre-eminently was he the Saviour, being made a curse for us that we might be made the righteousness of God in him. After beholding the dying agonies of his Master, the beloved apostle said, "We have seen and do testify that the Father sent the Son to be the Saviour of the world." On Calvary was it seen that the Son of Man saved others, though, through blessed incapacity of love, "himself he could not save." When he was made to feel the wrath of God on account of sin, and pangs unknown were suffered by him as our substitute, when he was made to pass through the thick darkness and burning heat of divine wrath, then was he, according to Scripture, "the Saviour of all men, specially of those that believe." Yes, it is on the tree that Christ is peculiarly a Saviour. If he were nothing better than our exemplar, alas for us! We might be grateful for the example if we could imitate it, but without the pardon which spares us, and the grace which gives us power for holiness, the brightest example were a tantalising of our grief. To be shown what we ought to be, without having any method set before us by which we could attain to it, were to mock our misery. But Jesus first draws us up out of the horrible pit into which we were fallen, takes us out of the miry clay, by the efficacy of his atoning sacrifice, and then, having set our feet upon a rock by virtue of his merits, he himself leads the way onward to perfection, and so is a Saviour both in life and in death.

> "That JESUS saves from sin and hell,
> Is truth divinely sure;
> And on this rock our faith may rest
> Immovably secure."

Still bearing the name of Jesus, *our Lord rose from the dead.* The evangelists delight in calling him Jesus; in his appearance to Magdalen in the garden, in his manifestation of himself to the disciples, when they were met together, the doors being shut. He is always Jesus with them as the risen One. Beloved, since we are justified by his resurrection, we may well regard him as Saviour under that aspect. Salvation is still more linked with a risen Christ, because we see him by his resurrection destroying death, breaking down the prison of the sepulchre, bearing away like another Samson the gates of the grave. He is a Saviour for us since he has vanquished the last enemy that shall be destroyed, that we having been saved from sin by his death should be saved from death through his resurrection. Jesus is the title under which he is called *in glory,* for "him hath God exalted with his right hand to be a Prince and a Saviour, for to give repentance to Israel, and forgiveness of sins." He is to-day "the Saviour of the body." We adore him as the only-wise God, and our Saviour. "He is able also to save them to the uttermost that come unto God by him, seeing he ever liveth to make intercession for them." As Jesus *he shall shortly come,* and we are "Looking for that blessed hope, and the glorious appearing of the great God and our Saviour Jesus Christ." Our daily cry is, "Even so, come, Lord Jesus." Ay, and this is the name, the name "Jesus," by which he is known *in heaven at this hour.* Thus the angel spake of him before he was conceived by the virgin; thus the angels serve him and do his bidding, for he saith to John in Patmos, "I, Jesus, have sent mine angel to testify these things." The angels prophesied his coming under that sacred name. They came to those who stood looking up into heaven, and they said, " Ye men of Galilee, why stand ye gazing up into heaven? this same Jesus, which is taken up from you into heaven, shall so come in like manner as ye have seen him go into heaven." Under this name the devils fear him, for said they not, " Jesus we know, and Paul we know, but who are ye?" This is the spell that binds the hearts of cherubim in chains of love, and this is the word that makes the hosts of hell to tremble and to quail. This name is the joy of the church on earth; it is the joy of the church above. It is a common word, a household name for our dear Redeemer amongst the family of God below, and up there they still sing it.

> " Jesus, the Lord, their harps employs:—
> Jesus, my Love, they sing!
> Jesus, the life of both our joys,
> Sounds sweet from every string."

That man of God, Mr. Henry Craik, of Bristol, who, so much to our regret, was lately called away to his rest, tells us in his little work upon the study of the Hebrew tongue, as an instance of how much may be gathered from a single Hebrew word, that the name Jesus is particularly rich and suggestive to the mind of the Hebrew scholar. It comes from a root signifying amplitude, spaciousness, and then it comes to mean setting at large, setting free, delivering, and so comes to its common use among us, namely, that of Saviour. There are two words in the name Jesus. The one is a contraction of the word " Jehovah," the other is the word which I have just now explained to you as ultimately coming to mean " salvation." Taken to pieces, the word Jesus means JEHOVAH-SALVATION. You have the glorious essence and nature of Christ revealed to you as Jehovah, " I am that I am," and then you have in the second part of his name his great work for you in setting you at large and delivering you from all distress. Think, beloved fellow Christian, of the amplitude, the spaciousness, the breadth, the abundance, the boundless all-sufficiency laid up in the person of the Lord Jesus. "It pleased the Father that in him should all fulness dwell." You have no contracted Christ, you have no narrow Saviour. Oh, the infinity of his love, the abundance of his grace, the exceeding greatness of the riches of his love towards us! There are no words in any language that can bring out sufficiently the unlimited, the infinite extent of the riches of the glory of Christ Jesus our Lord. The word which lies at the root of this name " Jesus," or " Joshua," has sometimes the meaning of riches; and who can tell what a wealth of grace and glory are laid up in our Immanuel? Mr. Craik tells us that another form of the same word signifies " a cry." " Hearken unto the voice of my *cry*, my King and my God." Thus salvation, riches, and a cry, are all derived from the same root, and all find their answer in our Joshua or Christ. When his people cry out of their prison houses, then he comes and sets them at large, comes with all the amplitude and wealth of his eternal grace, all the plenitude of his overflowing power, and delivering them from every form of bondage, gives them to enjoy the riches of the glory treasured up in himself. If this interpretation should make the name of Jesus one particle more dear to you, I am sure I shall be exceedingly rejoiced. What think you, if there is so much stored up in the one single name, what must be laid up in himself! And if we can honestly say that it would be difficult to give the full bearing of this one Hebrew name which belongs to Christ, how much more difficult will it ever be to give the full bearing of all his character? If his bare name be such a mine of excellence, what must his person be? If this, which is but a part of his garment, doth so smell of myrrh, and aloes, and cassia, O what must his blessed person be but a bundle of myrrh, which shall lie for ever betwixt our breasts, to be the perfume of our life, and the delight of our soul?

> " Precious is the name of Jesus,
>   Who can half its worth unfold?
> Far beyond angelic praises,
>   Sweetly sung to harps of gold.
>
> Precious when to Calvary groaning,
>   He sustain'd the cursèd tree;
> Precious when his death atoning,
>   Made an end of sin for me.
>
> Precious when the bloody scourges
>   Caused the sacred drops to roll;
> Precious when of wrath the surges
>   Overwhelm'd his holy soul.
>
> Precious in his death victorious,
>   He the host of hell o'erthrows;
> In his resurrection glorious,
>   Victor crown'd o'er all his foes.
>
> Precious, Lord! beyond expressing,
>   Are thy beauties all divine;
> Glory, honour, power, and blessing,
>   Be henceforth for ever Thine.

Thus much have we spoken upon the Hebrew name. Now reverently consider the second title—*Christ*. That is a Greek name, a Gentile name—Anointed. So that you see you have the Hebrew Joshua, Jesus, then the Greek Christos, Christ; so that we may see that no longer is there either Jew or Gentile, but all are one in Jesus Christ. The word Christ, as you all know, signifies anointed, and as such our Lord is sometimes called "the Christ," "the very Christ;" at other times "the Lord's Christ, and sometimes "the Christ of God." He is the Lord's Anointed, our King, and our Shield.

This word "Christ" teaches us three great truths; first, *it indicates his offices*. He exercises offices in which anointing is necessary, and these are three:—the office of the King, of the Priest, and of the Prophet. He is King in Zion, anointed with the oil of gladness above his fellows, even as it was said of old, " I have found David my servant; with my holy oil have I anointed him : with whom my hand shall be established : mine arm also shall strengthen him. . . . I will set his hand also in the sea, and his right hand in the rivers. . . . Also I will make him my firstborn, higher than the kings of the earth." Saul, the first king of Israel, was anointed with but a vial of oil, David, with a horn of oil, as if to signify the greater plenitude of his power and excellence of his kingdom; but as for our Lord Jesus Christ, he has received the spirit of anointing without any measure, he is the Lord's Anointed, for whom an unquenchable lamp is ordained. " There will I make the horn of David to bud: I have ordained a lamp for mine anointed.[1] Beloved, as we think of that name, Christ, let us reverently yield our souls up to him whom God has anointed to be King. Let us stand up for his rights over his church, for he is King of Zion, and none have a right to rule there but under and in subjection to the great Head over all, who in all things shall have the pre-eminence. Let us stand up for his rights within our own hearts, seeking to thrust out all rival objects, desirous to keep our souls chaste for Christ, and to make every member of our body, though it may have surrendered itself aforetime unto sin, to become subservient to the anointed King who hath a right to rule over it.

Next, the Lord Christ is Priest. Priests were anointed. They were not to undertake this office of themselves, nor without passing through the ceremony which set them apart. Jesus Christ our Lord hath grace given to him that no priest ever had. Their outward anointing was but symbolical, his was the true and the real. He hath received that which their oil did but set forth in type and shadow, he hath the real anointing from the Most High. Beloved, let us always look at Christ as the anointed Priest. My soul, thou canst never come to God except through the only everliving and truly anointed High Priest of our profession. O never for a moment seek to come without him, nor through any pretender who may call himself a priest. High Priest of the house of God, we see thee thus ordained, and we give our cause into thy hands. Offer our sacrifices for us, present our prayers, take thou our praises and put them into the golden censer, and thyself offer them before thy Father's throne. Rejoice, my brethren, every time you hear the name Christ, that he who wears it is anointed to be Priest.

So with regard to the prophetic office. We find Elisha anointed to prophesy, and so is Jesus Christ the prophet anointed amongst his people. Peter spake to Cornelius of "how God anointed Jesus of Nazareth with the Holy Ghost and with power: who went about doing good and healing all that were oppressed of the devil; for God was with him." He was anointed to preach the glad tidings, and to sit as Master in Israel. We hold no man's teaching to be authoritative among us, but the testimony of the Christ. The teaching of the Lord's Christ is our creed, and nothing else. I thank God that in this church we have not to divide our allegiance between some venerable set of articles and the teaching of our Lord. One is our Master, and we own no right of any man to bind another's conscience; even though they be great in piety and deep in learning, like Augustine and Calvin, whose names we honour, for God honoured them, still they have no dominance over private judgment in regard to the people of God. Jesus Christ is the Prophet of Christendom. His words must always be the first and the last appeal. This, then, is the meaning of the word "Christos." He is anointed as King, Priest, and Prophet.

But it means more than that. The name Christ *declares his right to those offices.* He is not King because he sets himself up as such. God has set him as King upon his holy hill of Zion, and anointed him to rule. He is also Priest, but he has not taken the priesthood upon himself, for he is the propitiation whom God has set forth for human sin. He is the mediator whom the Lord God hath appointed, and set to be the only mediator between God and man. And as for his prophesying he speaketh not of himself; those things which he hath learnt of the Father, he hath revealed unto us. He comes not as a prophet who assumes office, but God hath anointed him to preach glad tidings to the poor, and to come among his people with the welcome news of eternal love.

Moreover, this anointing signifies a third thing, that as he has the office, and as it is his by right, so *he has the qualifications for the work.* He is anointed to be king. God has given him royal power, and wisdom, and government; he has made him fit to rule in the church, and to reign over the world. No better king than Christ, none so majestic as he who wore the thorn-crown, but who shall put upon his head the crown of universal monarchy. He has the qualifications for a priest too, such qualifications as even Melchisedec had not; such as cannot be found in all the house of Aaron, in all its length of pedigree. Blessed Son of God, perfect in thyself, and needing not a sacrifice for thine own sake, thou hast presented unto God an offering which hath perfected for ever those whom thou hast set apart, and now needing not to make a further offering, thou hast for ever put away sin. So is it with our Lord's prophesying, he hath the power to teach. " Grace is poured into thy lips: therefore God hath blessed thee for ever." All the words of Christ are wisdom and truth. The substance of true philosophy and certain knowledge are to be found in him who is the wisdom and the power of God. Oh, that word " Christ !" it seems to grow upon us as we think it over; it shows us the offices of Christ, his right to those offices, and his qualifications for them:

> " Christ, to thee our spirits bow !
> Prophet, Priest, and King art thou !
> Christ, anointed of the Lord,
> Evermore be thou adored."

Now, put the two titles together and ring out the harmony of the two melodious notes: Jesus Christ, Saviour-anointed. Oh, how blessed ! See ye not that our Beloved is a Saviour duly appointed, a Saviour abundantly qualified ! My soul, if God appoints Christ a Saviour of sinners, why dost thou raise a question ? God set him forth as a sinner's Saviour. Come, then, ye sinners, take him, accept him, and rest in him. Oh, how foolish we are when we begin raising questions, quibbles, and difficulties ! God declares that Christ is a Saviour to all who trust in him. My poor heart trusts him : she hath peace. But wherefore do some of you imagine that he cannot save you, or ask, " How can it be that this man shall save me ? " God has appointed him, take him, rest in him. Moreover, God has qualified him, given him the anointing of a Saviour. What, dost thou think God has not girded him with power enough, or furnished him with enough of merit with which to save such as thou art ? Wilt thou limit what God hath done ? Wilt thou think that his anointing is imperfect and cannot qualify Jesus to meet thy case ? O do not so slander the grace of heaven ! Do not such despite to the wisdom of the Lord ; but honour the Saviour of God's anointing by coming now, just as thou art, and putting thy trust in him.

II. We shall now examine the second point, HIS MEMORABLE ATTRIBUTES.

He is said to be the same. Now, Jesus Christ has not been the same in condition at all times, for he was once adored of angels but afterwards spit upon by menials. He exchanged the supernal splendours of his Father's court for the poverty of the earth, the degradation of death, and the humiliation of the grave. Jesus Christ is not, and will not be always the same as to occupation. Once he came to seek and to save that which was lost, but we very truly sing, "The Lord shall come, but not the same as once in lowliness he came." He shall come with a very different object; he shall come to scatter his enemies and break them as with a rod of iron. We are not to take the expression then, "the same," in the most unlimited sense conceivable. Looking at the Greek, one notices that it might be read thus, "Jesus Christ *himself* yesterday, and to-day, and for ever." The anointed Saviour is always himself. He is always Jesus Christ; and the word "same" seems to me to bear the most intimate relation to the two titles of the text, and does as good as say that Jesus Christ is always Jesus Christ, yesterday, and to-day, and for ever. Jesus Christ is always himself; at any rate, if that be not the correct translation, it is a very correct and blessed sentence: it is sweetly true that Jesus Christ is always himself. Immutability is ascribed to Christ, and we remark that *he was evermore to his people what he now is*, for he was the same yesterday. Distinctions have been drawn by certain exceedingly wise men (measured by their own estimate of themselves), between the people of God who lived before the coming of Christ, and those who lived afterwards. We have even heard it asserted that those who lived before the coming of Christ do not belong to the church of God! We never know what we shall hear next, and perhaps it is a mercy that these absurdities are revealed one at a time, in order that we may be able to endure their stupidity without dying of amazement. Why, every child of God in every place stands on the same footing; the Lord has not some children best beloved, some second-rate offspring, and others whom he hardly cares about. These who saw Christ's day before it came, had a great difference as to what they knew, and perhaps in the same measure a difference as to what they enjoyed while on earth in meditating upon Christ; but they were all washed in the same blood, all redeemed with the same ransom price, and made members of the same body. Israel in the covenant of grace is not natural Israel, but all believers in all ages. Before the first advent, all the types and shadows all pointed one way— they pointed to Christ, and to him all the saints looked with hope. Those who lived before Christ were not saved with a different salvation to that which shall come to us. They exercised faith as we must; that faith struggled as ours struggles, and that faith obtained its reward as ours shall. As like as a man's face to that which he seeth in a glass is the spiritual life of David to the spiritual life of the believer now. Take the book of Psalms in your hand, and forgetting for an instant that you have the representation of the life of one of the olden time, you might suppose that David wrote but yesterday. Even in what he writes of Christ, he seems as though he lived after Christ instead of before, and both in what he sees of himself and in what he sees of his Saviour, he appears to be rather a Christian writer than a Jew; I mean that living before Christ he has the same hopes and the same fears, the same joys and the same sorrows, there is the same estimate of his blessed Redeemer which you and I have in these times. Jesus was the same yesterday as an anointed Saviour to his people as he is to-day, and they under him received like precious gifts. If the goodly fellowship of the prophets could be here to-day, they would all testify to you that he was the same in every office in their times as he is in these our days.

Jesus Christ is the same now as he was in times gone by, for the text saith, "The same yesterday, and to-day." He is the same to-day as he was from old eternity. Before all worlds he planned our salvation; he entered into covenant with his Father to undertake it. His delights were with the sons of men in prospect, and now to-day he is as steadfast to that covenant as ever. He will not lose those who were then given to him, nor will he fail nor be discouraged till every stipulation of that covenant shall be fulfilled. Whatever was in the heart of Christ before the stars began to shine, that same infinite love is there to-day. Jesus is the same to-day as he was when he was here on earth. There is much comfort in this thought. When he tabernacled among men, he was most willing to save. "Come unto me, all ye that labour and are heavy laden," was the burden of his cry; he is still calling to the weary and the heavy laden to come to him. In the days of his flesh he would not curse the woman taken in adultery, neither would he reject the publicans and sinners who gathered to hear him; he is pitiful to sinners still, and saith to them yet, "Neither do I condemn thee: go, and sin no more." That delightful sentence which so graciously came from his lips, "Thy sins, which are many, are forgiven thee," is still his favourite utterance in human hearts. O think not that Christ in heaven has become distant and reserved, so that you may not approach him. Such as he was here, a Lamb, gentle and meek, a man to whom men drew near without a moment's hesitation, such is he now. Come boldly to him, ye lowliest and guiltiest ones, come near to him with broken hearts and weeping eyes. Though he be King and Priest, surrounded with unknown splendour, yet still he retains the same loving heart, and the same generous sympathies towards the sons of men. He is still the same in his ability as well as in his willingness to save. He is Jesus Christ the anointed Saviour still. In his earthly days, he touched the leper and said, "I will; be thou clean;" he called Lazarus from the tomb, and Lazarus came; sinner, Jesus is still as able to heal or quicken thee now as then. "He is able also to save them to the uttermost that come unto God by him, seeing he ever liveth to make intercession for them." Now that the blood is spilt indeed, and the sacrifice is fully offered, there is no limit to the ability of Christ to save. O come and rely upon him, and find salvation in him now. Believer, it will cheer you also to remember that when our Lord was here upon earth, he showed great perseverance in his art of saving. He could say, "Of them which thou gavest me have I lost none." Rejoice that he is the same to-day. He will not cast one of you away, nor suffer his little ones to perish. He brought all safe in the days of his flesh; he takes care to keep all safely in these the days of his glory. He is the same to-day, then, as he was on earth.

Blessed be his name, Jesus Christ is the same to-day as in apostolic days. Then, he gave the fulness of the Spirit; then, when he ascended up on high, he gave gifts to men, apostles, preachers, teachers of the word. Do not let us think we shall not see as good days now as they saw at Pentecost. He is the same Christ. He could as readily convert three thousand under one sermon to-day, as in Peter's time; his Holy Spirit is not exhausted, for God giveth it not by measure unto him. We ought to pray that he would raise up among us eminent men to proclaim the gospel. We do not pray enough for the ministry. The ministry is peculiarly the gift of the ascension. When he ascended on high he received gifts for men, and he gave—what? Why, men, apostles, teachers, preachers. If we ask for salvation, we plead the blood: why do we not ask for ministers, and plead the ascension? If we would do this more, we should see raised up amongst us more Whitfields and Wesleys, more Luthers and Calvins, more men of the apostolic stock, and the church would be revived. Jesus is the same to enrich his people with all spiritual gifts in this year 1869, as in the year when he ascended to his throne. " He is the same yesterday, and to-day."

He is the same to-day as he was to our fathers. These have gone to their rest, but they told us before they went what Christ was to them; how he succoured them in their time of peril; how he delivered them in their hour of sorrow. He will do for us just what he did for them. Some who lived before us went to heaven in a chariot of fire, but Christ was very precious to them at the stake. We have our martyrologies which we read with wonder. How sustaining the company of Christ was to those that did lie in prison, to those that were cast to the lions, to those that wandered about in sheep skins and goat skins! England, Scotland—all the countries where Christ was preached—have been dyed with blood and ennobled with the testimonies of the faithful. Whatever Jesus was to these departed worthies, he is to his people still. We have only to ask of God, and we shall receive the selfsame benefit.

" Jesus Christ the same to day," says the text. Then he is the same to-day as he has been to us in the past. We have had great enjoyments of God's presence; we do remember the love of our espousals, and if we have not the same joys to-day, it is no fault of his. There is the same water in the well still, and if we have not drawn it, it is our fault. We have come away from the fire, and therefore we are cold; we have walked contrary to him, and therefore he walks contrary to us. Let us return to him and he will be as glad to receive us now as in our first moment of repentance. Let us return to him. His heart is as full of love, and as ready to weep upon our neck as when we first came and sought pardon from his hands. There is much sweetness in the text, but I cannot linger longer upon that part of the subject; enough for us is it to remember that Jesus Christ is the same to-day as he always was.

Now, further, *Christ shall be to-morrow what he has been yesterday and is to-day.* Our Lord Jesus Christ will be changed in no respect throughout the whole of our life. It may be long before we shall descend to our graves, but let these hairs all be grey, and these limbs begin to totter, and these eyes grow dim, Jesus Christ shall have the dew of his youth upon him, and the fulness of his love shall still flow to us. And after death, or if we die not, at the coming Christ and in his glorious reign, Jesus will be the same to his people then as now. There seems to be a notion abroad amongst some that after his coming

Christ will deal differently with his people than now. I have been informed by a modern school of inventors (and, as I tell you, we live to learn) that some of us will be shut out from the kingdom when Christ comes. Saved by precious blood and brought near, and adopted into the family, and our names written upon the breastplate of Christ, and yet some of us will be shut out from the kingdom! Nonsense. I see nothing in the word of God, though there may be a great deal in the fancies of men, to support these novelties. The people of God, equally bought with blood, and equally dear to Jesus' heart, shall be treated on the same scale and footing. they will never be put under the law, never come to Christ, and find him rule them as a legal Judge, and beat them with many stripes in a future state, or shut them out of his estate of millennial Majesty. He will give to none, as a mere matter of reward, such rule and government so as to exclude others of his redeemed family; but they shall find him always treating them all as unchanging love and immutable grace shall dictate; and the rewards of the millennial state shall be always those of grace, shall be such as not to exclude the very least of all the family, but all shall have tokens of reward from the dear Saviour's hand. I know he will not love me to-day, and give me the glimpses of his face, give me to delight in his name, and yet after all when he comes, tell me I must stand out in the cold, and not enter into his kingdom. I have not a shade of faith in the purgatory of banishment, which certain despisers of the ministry have chosen to set up. I marvel that in a Protestant sect there should rise up a dogma as villanous as the dogma of purgatory, and that, too, from those who say they are no sectarians. We all are wrong but these, brethren; these are deeply taught and can discover what the ablest divines have never seen. That Jesus will love his people in time to come as strongly as he does now, seems to be a doctrine which if destroyed or denied, would cast sorrow into the whole family of God. Throughout eternity, in heaven, there shall still be the same Jesus Christ, with the same love to his people, and they shall have the same familiar intercourse with him, nay, shall see him face to face, and rejoice for ever in him as their unchangeably, anointed Saviour.

III. Our time has failed us, and therefore just two or three words only upon our Lord's EVIDENT CLAIMS.

If our Lord be " the same yesterday, and to-day, and for ever," then, according to the connection of our text, *he is to be followed to the end.* Observe the seventh verse, " Remember them which have the rule over you, who hath spoken unto you the word of God; whose faith follow, considering the end of their conversation;" the meaning being—these holy men ended their lives with Christ; their exit was to go to Jesus, and to reign with him. Beloved, if the Lord is still the same, follow him till you reach him. Your exit out of this life shall bring you where he is, and you will find him then what he always was. You shall see him as he is. If he were a will-o'-the-wisp, for ever changing, it were dangerous to follow him, but since he is ever and equally worthy of your admiration and example, follow him evermore. That was an eloquent speech of Henry the Sixth of France, when on the eve of battle, he said to his soldiers, "'Gentlemen, you are Frenchmen, I am your King. There is the enemy!'" Jesus Christ saith, "You are my people;

I am your leader. There is the foe !" How shall we dare to do any-thing unworthy of such a Lord as he is, or of such a citizenship as that which he has bestowed upon us? If we be indeed his, and he be indeed immutable, let us by his Holy Spirit's power persevere to the end, that we may obtain the crown.

The next evident claim of Christ upon us is that *we should be stead-fast in the faith.* Notice the ninth verse : " Jesus Christ the same yesterday, and to-day, and for ever. Be not carried about with divers and strange doctrines." There is nothing new in theology but that which is false. All that is true is old, though I say not that all that is old is true. Some speak of developments as though we had not the whole Christian religion discovered yet ; but the religion of Paul is the religion of every man who is taught by the Holy Spirit. We ought not, therefore, to indulge for a moment the idea that something has been discovered which may correct the teaching of Christ ; that some new philosophy or discovery of science has uprisen to correct the declared testimony of our Redeemer. Let us hold fast that which we have received, and never depart from " the truth once delivered unto the saints " by Christ himself.

If Jesus Christ be thus immutable, *he has an evident claim to our most solemn worship.* Immutability can be the attribute of none but God. Whoever is " the same yesterday, and to-day, and for ever," must be divine. Ever, then, believer, bring your adoration to Jesus ; at the feet of him that was crucified cast down your crown. Give royal and divine honours unto him who stooped to the ignominy of crucifixion. Let no one stop you of this you glory in—you boast the Son of God made man for you. Worship him as God over all, blessed for ever.

He claims also of us next, that *we should trust him.* If he be always the same, here is a rock that cannot be moved ; build on it. Here is an anchorage, cast your anchor of hope into it and hold fast in time of storm. If Christ were variable, he were not worthy of your confidence. Since he is evermore unchanged, rest on him without fear.

And, lastly, if he be always the same, rejoice in him, and rejoice always. If you ever had cause to rejoice in Christ, you always have cause, for he never alters. If yesterday you could sing of him, to-day you may sing of him. If he changed, your joy might change; but if the stream of your gladness springs solely and only out of this great deep of the immutability of Jesus, then it need never stay its flow. Beloved, let us "rejoice in the Lord alway: and again I say, rejoice ; " and, until the day break and the shadows flee away, till the blest hour arrive when we shall see him face to face, and be made like him, be this our joy, that " he is the same yesterday, and to-day, and for ever." Amen.

This Year Also

" This year also."—Luke xiii. 8.

AT the opening of another year, and at the commencement of another volume of sermons, we earnestly desire to utter the word of exhortation : but alas, at this present, the preacher is a prisoner, and must speak from his pillow instead of his pulpit. Let not the few words which we can put together come with diminished power from a sick man, for the musket fired by a wounded soldier sends forth the bullet with none the less force. Our desire is to speak with living words, or not at all. He who enables us to sit up and compose these trembling sentences is entreated to clothe them with his Spirit, that they may be according to his own mind.

The interceding vine-dresser pleaded for the fruitless fig-tree, "let it alone *this year also*," dating as it were a year from the time wherein he spoke. Trees and fruitbearing plants have a natural measurement for their lives : evidently a year came to its close when it was time to seek fruit on the fig-tree, and another year commenced when the vine-dresser began again his digging and pruning work. Men are such barren things that their fruitage marks no certain periods, and it becomes needful to make artificial divisions of time for them ; there seems to be no set period for man's spiritual harvest or vintage, or if there be, the sheaves and the clusters come not in their season, and hence we have to say one to another,—" This shall be the beginning of a new year." Be it so, then. Let us congratulate each other upon seeing the dawn of " this year also," and let us unitedly pray that we may enter upon it, continue in it, and come to its close under the unfailing blessing of the Lord to whom all years belong.

I. The beginning of a new year SUGGESTS A RETROSPECT. Let us take it, deliberately and honestly. "*This year also :*"—then there had been former years of grace. The dresser of the vineyard was not for the first time aware of the fig-tree's failure, neither had the owner come for the first time seeking figs in vain. God, who gives us " this year also," has given us others before it ; his sparing mercy is no novelty, his patience has already been taxed by our provocations. First came our *youthful years*, when even a little fruit unto God is peculiarly sweet to him. How did we spend them? Did our strength run all into wild wood and wanton branch? If so, we may well bewail that wasted vigour, that life misspent, that sin exceedingly multiplied. He who saw us misuse those golden months of youth nevertheless affords us " this year also," and we should enter upon it with a holy jealousy, lest what of strength and ardour may be left to us should be allowed to run away into the same wasteful courses as aforetime. Upon the heels of our youthful years came those of *early manhood*, when we began to muster a household, and to become as a tree fixed in its place; then also fruit would have been precious. Did we bear any? Did we present unto the Lord a basket of summer fruit? Did we offer him the firstling of our strength? If we did so, we may well adore the grace which so early saved us; but if not, the past chides us, and, lifting an admonitory finger, it warns us not to let " this year also " follow the way of the rest of our lives. He who has wasted youth and the morning of manhood has surely had enough of fooling : the time past may well suffice him to have wrought the will of the flesh : it will be a superfluity of naughtiness to suffer " this year also " to be trodden down in the service of sin. Many of us are now in the *prime of life*, and our years already spent are not few. Have we still need to confess that our years are eaten up by the grasshopper and the canker-worm? Have we reached the half-way house, and still know not whither we are going? Are we fools at forty? Are we half a century old by the calendar and yet far off from years of discretion? Alas, great God, that there should be men past this age who are still without knowledge! Unsaved at sixty, unregenerate at seventy, unawakened at eighty, unrenewed at ninety! These are each and all startling. Yet, peradventure, they will each one fall upon ears which they should make to tingle, but they will hear them as though they heard them not. Continuance in evil breeds callousness of heart, and when the soul has long been sleeping in indifference it is hard to arouse it from the deadly slumber.

The sound of the words " this year also " makes some of us remember *years of great mercy*, sparkling and flashing with delight. Were those years laid at the Lord's feet? They were comparable to the silver bells upon the horses—were they " holiness unto the Lord "? If not, how shall we answer for it if " this year also " should be musical with merry mercy and yet be spent in the ways of carelessness? The same words recall to some of us our *years of sharp affliction* when we were, indeed, digged about and dunged. How went those years? God was doing great things for us, exercising careful and expensive husbandry, caring for us with exceeding great and wise care,—did we render according to the benefit received? Did we rise from the bed more patient and gentle, weaned from the world, and welded to Christ? Did we bring forth clusters to reward the dresser of the vineyard? Let us not refuse these questions of self-examination, for it may be this is to be another of these years of captivity, another season of the furnace and the fining-pot. The Lord grant that the coming tribulation may take more chaff out of us than any of its predecessors, and leave the wheat cleaner and better.

The new year also reminds us of *opportunities for usefulness*, which have come and gone, and of *unfulfilled resolutions* which have blossomed only to fade; shall "this year also" be as those which have gone before? May we not hope for grace to advance upon grace already gained, and should we not seek for power to turn our poor sickly promises into robust action?

Looking back on the past we lament the follies by which we would not willingly be held captive "this year also," and we adore the forgiving mercy, the preserving providence, the boundless liberality, the divine love, of which we hope to be partakers "this year also."

II. If the preacher could think freely he could wherry the text at his pleasure in many directions, but he is feeble, and so must let it drive with the current which bears it on to a second consideration : the text MENTIONS A MERCY. It was in great goodness that the tree which cumbered the soil was allowed to stand for another year, and prolonged life should always be regarded as a boon of mercy. We must view "this year also" as a grant from infinite grace. It is wrong to speak as if we cared nothing for life, and looked upon our being here as an evil or a punishment; we are here "this year also" as the result of love's pleadings, and in pursuance of love's designs.

The wicked man should count that the Lord's longsuffering points to his salvation, and he should permit the cords of love to draw him to it. O that the Holy Spirit would make the blasphemer, the Sabbath-breaker, and the openly vicious to feel what a wonder it is that their lives are prolonged "this year also"! Are they spared to curse, and riot, and defy their Maker? Shall this be the only fruit of patient mercy? The procrastinator who has put off the messenger of heaven with his delays and half promises, ought he not to wonder that he is allowed to see "this year also"? How is it that the Lord has borne with him and put up with his vacillations and hesitations? Is this year of grace to be spent in the same manner? Transient impressions, hasty resolves, and speedy apostasies— are these to be the weary story over and over again? The startled conscience, the tyrant passion, the smothered emotion! Are these to be the tokens of yet another year? May God forbid that any one of us should hesitate and delay through "this year also." Infinite pity holds back the axe of justice, shall it be insulted by the repetition of the sins which caused the uplifting of the instrument of wrath? What can be more tantalizing to the heart of goodness than indecision? Well might the Lord's prophet become impatient and cry, "How long halt ye between two opinions?" Well may God himself push for a decision and demand an immediate reply. O undecided soul, wilt thou swing much longer between heaven and hell, and act as if it were hard to choose between the slavery of Satan and the liberty of the Great Father's home of love? "This year also" wilt thou sport in defiance of justice, and pervert the generosity of mercy into a licence for still further rebellion? "This year also" must divine love be made an occasion for continued sin? O do not act so basely, so contrary to every noble instinct, so injuriously to thine own best interests.

The believer is kept out of heaven "this year also" in love, and not in anger. There are some for whose sake it is needful he should abide in the flesh, some to be helped by him on their heavenward way, and others to be led to the Redeemer's feet by his instruction. The heaven of many saints is not yet prepared for them, because their nearest companions have not yet arrived, and their spiritual children have not yet gathered in glory in sufficient number to give them a thoroughly heavenly welcome : they must wait " this year also " that their rest may be the more glorious, and that the sheaves which they will bring with them may afford them greater joy. Surely, for the sake of souls, for the delight of glorifying our Lord, and for the increase of the jewels of our crown, we may be glad to wait below " this year also." This is a wide field, but we may not linger in it, for our space is little, and our strength is even less.

III. Our last feeble utterance shall remind you that the expression, " This year also," IMPLIES A LIMIT. The vine-dresser asked no longer a reprieve than one year. If his digging and manuring should not then prove successful he would plead no more, but the tree should fall. Even when Jesus is the pleader, the request of mercy has its bounds and times. It is not for ever that we shall be let alone, and allowed to cumber the ground ; if we will not repent we must perish, if we will not be benefited by the spade we must fall by the axe.

There will come a last year to each one of us : therefore let each one say to himself—Is this my last? If it should be the last with the preacher, he would gird up his loins to deliver the Lord's message with all his soul, and bid his fellow-men be reconciled to God. Dear friend, is " this year also " to be *your* last? Are you ready to see the curtain rise upon eternity ? Are you now prepared to hear the midnight cry, and to enter into the marriage supper ? The judgment and all that will follow upon it are most surely the heritage of every living man, blessed are they who by faith in Jesus are able to face the bar of God without a thought of terror.

If we live to be counted among the oldest inhabitants we must depart at last : there must be an end, and the voice must be heard—" Thus saith the Lord, this year thou shalt die." So many have gone before us, and are going every hour, that no man should need any other *memento mori*, and yet man is so eager to forget his own mortality, and thereby to forfeit his hopes of bliss, that we cannot too often bring it before the mind's eye. O mortal man, bethink thee! Prepare to meet thy God ; for thou must meet him. Seek the Saviour, yea, seek him ere another sun sinks to his rest.

Once more, "this year also," and it may be for this year only, the cross is uplifted as the pharos of the world, the one light to which no eye can look in vain. Oh that millions would look that way and live. Soon the Lord Jesus will come a second time, and then the blaze of his throne will supplant the mild radiance of his cross : the Judge will be seen rather than the Redeemer. Now he saves, but then he will destroy. Let us hear his voice at this moment. He hath limited a day, let us be eager to avail ourselves of the gracious season. Let us believe in Jesus this day, seeing it may be our last. These are the pleadings of one who now falls back on his pillow in very weakness. Hear them for your souls' sakes and live.

The Covenant Pleaded

"Have respect unto the covenant."—Psalm lxxiv. 20.

HE will succeed in prayer who understands the science of pleading with God. "Put me in remembrance: let us plead together," is a divine command. "Come now, let us reason together" is a sacred invitation. "Bring forth your strong reasons, saith the Lord," is a condescending direction as to the way of becoming victorious in supplication. Pleading is wrestling: arguments are the grips, the feints, the throes, the struggles with which we hold and vanquish the covenant angel. The humble statement of our wants is not without its value, but to be able to give reasons and arguments why God should hear us is to offer potent, prevalent prayer. Among all the arguments that can be used in pleading with God, perhaps there is none stronger than this—"Have respect unto the covenant." Like Goliath's sword, we may say of it, "There is none like it." If we have God's word for a thing we may well pray, "Do as thou hast said, for as a good man only needs to be reminded of his own word in order to be brought to keep it, even so is it with our faithful God; he only needs that for these things we put him in remembrance to do them for us." If he has given us more than his word, namely, his covenant, his solemn compact, we may then with the greatest composure of spirit cry to him, "Have respect unto the covenant," and then we may both hope and quietly wait for his salvation.

I need not tell you, for you are, I trust, well-grounded in that matter, that the covenant here spoken of is the covenant of grace. There is a covenant which we could not plead in prayer, the covenant of works, a covenant which destroys us, for we have broken it. Our first father sinned, and the covenant was broken; we have continued in his perverseness, and that covenant condemns us. By the covenant of works can none of us be justified, for we continue still to break our portion of it, and to bring upon ourselves wrath to the uttermost. The Lord hath made a new covenant with the second Adam, our federal head, Jesus Christ our Lord,—a covenant without conditions, except such conditions as Christ has already fulfilled, a covenant, ordered in all things and sure, which now consists of promises only, which run after this fashion—"I will be to them a God, and they shall be to me a people": "A new heart also will I give them, and a right spirit will I put within them": "From all their transgressions will I cleanse them ":—a covenant, I say, which had once conditions in it, all of which our Lord Jesus fulfilled when he finished transgression, made an end of sin, and brought in everlasting righteousness; and now the covenant is all of promise, and consists of infallible and eternal shalls and wills, which shall abide the same for ever.

We shall talk of the text thus, *What is meant by the plea before us*— " Have respect unto the covenant "? Then we will think a little *of whence it derives its force*: thirdly, we will consider *how and when we may plead it*: and we will close by noticing *what are the practical inferences from it*.

I. Let us begin by this—WHAT IS MEANT BY THE PLEA " Have respect unto the covenant "? It means this, does it not? "*Fulfil thy covenant*, O God: let it not be a dead letter. Thou hast said this and that; now do as thou hast said. Thou hast been pleased by solemn sanction of oath and blood to make this covenant with thy people. Now be pleased to keep it. Hast thou said, and wilt thou not do it? We are persuaded of thy faithfulness, let our eyes behold thy covenant engagements fulfilled.

It means again, "*Fulfil all the promises of thy covenant*," for indeed all the promises are now in the covenant. They are all yea and amen in Christ Jesus, to the glory of God by us; and I may say without being unscriptural that the covenant contains within its sacred charter every gracious word that has come from the Most High, either by the mouth of prophets or apostles, or by the lips of Jesus Christ himself. The meaning in this case would be—" Lord, keep thy promises concerning thy people. We are in want: now, O Lord, fulfil thy promise that we shall not want any good thing. Here is another of thy promises: ' When thou passest through the waters, I will be with thee.' We are in rivers of trouble. Be with us now. Redeem thy promises to thy servants. Let them not stand on the book as letters that mock us, but prove that thou didst mean what thou didst write and say, and let us see that thou hast power and will to make every jot and tittle good of all thou hast spoken. For hast thou not said, ' Heaven and earth shall pass away, but my word shall not pass away'? Oh then have respect unto the promises of thy covenant."

In the connection of our text there is no doubt that the suppliant meant, " O Lord, prevent anything from turning aside thy promises." The church was then in a very terrible state. The temple was burnt, and the assemblage broken up, the worship of God had ceased, and idolatrous emblems stood even in the holy place where once the glory of God shone forth. The plea is, " Do not suffer the power of the enemy to be so great as to frustrate thy purposes, or to make thy promises void." So may we pray—" O Lord, do not suffer me to endure such temptation that I shall fall. Do not suffer such affliction to come upon me that I shall be destroyed; for hast thou not promised that no temptation shall happen to us but such as we are able to bear, and that with the temptation there shall be a way of escape? Now have respect unto thy covenant, and so order thy providence that nothing shall happen to us contrary to that divine agreement."

And it means also, " So order everything around us that the covenant may be fulfilled. Is thy church low? Raise up again in her midst men who preach the gospel with power, who shall be the means of her uplifting. Creator of men, Master of human hearts, thou who canst circumcise human lips to speak thy word with power, do this, and let thy covenant with thy church that thou wilt never leave her be fulfilled. The kings of the earth are in thy hand. All events are controlled by thee. Thou orderest all things, from the minute to the immense. Nothing, however small, is too small for thy purpose : nothing, however great, is too great for thy rule. Manage everything so that in the end each promise of thy covenant shall be fulfilled to all thy chosen people."

That, I think, is the meaning of the plea, " Have respect unto the covenant." Keep it and see it kept. Fulfil the promise, and prevent thy foes from doing evil to thy children. Precious plea, assuredly.

II. And now let us see WHENCE IT DERIVES ITS FORCE. " Have respect unto the covenant."

It derives its force, first, from *the veracity of God*. If it be a covenant of man's making we expect a man to keep it ; and a man who does not keep his covenant is not esteemed amongst his fellows. If a man has given his word, that word is his bond. If a thing be solemnly signed and sealed it becomes even more binding, and he that would run back from a covenant would be thought to have forfeited his character among men. God forbid that we should ever think the Most High could be false to his word. It is not possible. He can do all things except this—he cannot lie ; it is not possible that he should ever be untrue. He cannot even change : the gifts and calling of God are without repentance. He will not alter the thing that hath gone out of his lips. When then we come before God in prayer for a covenant mercy we have his truthfulness to support us. " O God, thou must do this. Thou art a sovereign : thou canst do as thou wilt, but thou hast bound thyself by bonds that hold thy majesty ; thou hast said it, and it is not possible that thou shouldst go back from thine own word." How strong our faith ought to be when we have God's truth to lean upon. What dishonour we do to our God by our weak faith ; for it is virtually a suspicion of the fidelity of our covenant God.

Next, to support us in using this plea we have God's sacred *jealousy for his honour*. He has told us himself that he is a jealous God ; his name is jealousy ; he has great respect unto his honour among the sons of men. Hence this was Moses's plea—" What will the enemy say ? And what wilt thou do unto thy great name ?" Now, if God's covenant could be trifled with, and if it could be proved that he had not kept the promise that he made to his creatures, it would not only be a dreadful thing for us, but it would bring grievous dishonour upon his name ; and that shall never be. God is too pure and holy, and he is withal too honourable ever to run back from the word that he has given to his servants. If I feel that my feet have almost gone I may still be assured that he will not suffer me wholly to perish, else were his honour stained, for he hath said, " They shall never perish, neither shall any pluck them out of my hand." He might give me up to mine enemies so far as my deserts are concerned, for I deserve to be destroyed by them—but then his honour is engaged to save the meanest of his people, and he has said, " I give unto them eternal life." He will not, therefore, for his honour's sake, suffer me to be the prey of the adversary ; but will preserve me, even me, unto the day of his appearing. Here is good foothold for faith.

The next reflection that should greatly strengthen us is *the venerable character of the covenant.* This covenant was no transaction of yesterday: or ever the earth was this covenant was made. We may not speak of first or last with God, but speaking after the manner of men the covenant of grace is God's first thought. Though we usually put the covenant of works first in order of time as revealed, yet in very deed the covenant of grace is the older of the two. God's people were not chosen yesterday, but before the foundations of the world ; and the Lamb slain to ratify that covenant, though slain eighteen hundred years ago, was in the divine purpose slain from before the foundations of the world. It is an ancient covenant : there is nothing so ancient. It is to God a covenant which he holds in high esteem. It is not one of his light thoughts, not one of those thoughts which lead him to create the morning dew that melts ere the day has run its course, or to make the clouds that light up the setting sun with glory but which soon have lost their radiance ; but it is one of his great thoughts, yea, it is his eternal thought, the thought out of his own inmost soul—this covenant of grace. And because it is so ancient, and to God a matter so important, when we come to him with this plea in our mouths we must not think of being staggered by unbelief, but may open our mouths wide, for he will assuredly fill them. Here is thy covenant, O God, which of thy own spontaneous sovereign will thou didst ordain of old, a covenant in which thy very heart is laid bare, and thy love which is thyself is manifested. O God, have respect unto it, and do as thou hast said, and fulfil thy promise to thy people.

Nor is this all. It is but the beginning. In one sermon I should not have time to show you all the reasons that give force to the plea ; but here is one. The covenant has upon it *a solemn endorsement.* There was the stamp of God's own word—that is enough. The very word that created the universe is the word that spake the covenant. But, as if that were not sufficient, seeing we are unbelieving, God has added to it his oath, and because he could swear by no greater, he has sworn by himself. It were blasphemy to dream that the Eternal could be perjured, and he has set his oath to his covenant, in order that, by two immutable things wherein it is impossible for God to lie, he might give to the heirs of grace strong consolation.

But more, that venerable covenant thus confirmed by oath was *sealed with blood.* Jesus died to ratify it. His heart's blood bedewed that Magna Charta of the grace of God to his people. It is a covenant now which God the just *must* keep. Jesus has fulfilled our side of it—has executed to the letter all the demands of God upon man. Our Surety and our Substitute has at once kept the law and suffered all that was due by his people on account of their breach of it ; and now shall not the Lord be true and the everlasting Father be faithful to his own Son ? How can he refuse to his Son the joy which he set before him and the reward which he promised him ? "He shall see his seed : he shall see of the travail of his soul and shall be satisfied." My soul, the faithfulness of God to his covenant is not so much a matter between thee and God as between Christ and God, for now it so stands—Christ as their representative puts in his claim before the throne of infinite justice for the salvation of every soul for whom he shed his blood, and he must have what he has purchased. Oh what confidence is here ! The rights of the Son, blended with the love and the veracity of the Father, makes the covenant to be ordered in all things and sure.

Moreover, remember, and I will not detain you much longer with this, that up till now nothing in the covenant has ever failed. The Lord has been tried by ten thousand times ten thousand of his people, and they have been in trying emergencies and serious difficulties ; but it has never been reported in the gates of Zion that the promise has become naught, neither have any said that the covenant is null and void. Ask ye those before you who passed through deeper waters than yourselves. Ask the martyrs who gave their lives up for their Master, " Was he with them to the end ? " The placid smiles upon their countenances while enduring the most painful death were evident testimonies that God is true. Their joyous songs, the clapping of their hands amidst the fire, and their exultation even on the rack, or when rotting in some loathsome dungeon—all these have proved how faithful the Lord has been.

And have you not heard with your own ears the testimony of God's dying people ? They were in conditions in which they could not have been sustained by mere imagination, nor buoyed up by frenzy, and yet they have been as joyful as if their dying day had been their wedding day. Death is too solemn a matter for a man to play a masquerade there. But what did your wife say in death? or your mother now with God? or what your child, who had learnt the Saviour's love ? Can you not recall their testimonies even now ? I think I hear some of them, and amongst the things of earth that are like to the joys of heaven, I think this is one of the foremost,—the joy of departed saints when they already hear the voices of angels hovering near, and turn round and tell us in broken language of the joys that are bursting in upon them— their sight blinded by the excess of brightness, and their hearts ravished with the bliss that floods them. Oh it has been sweet to see the saints depart !

I mention these things now, not merely to refresh your memories, but to establish your faith in God. He has been true so many times and false never, and shall we now experience any difficulty in resting on his covenant ? No, by all these many years in which the faithfulness of God has been put to the test, and has never failed, let us be confident that he will still regard us, and let us pray boldly,—"Have respect unto the covenant." For, mark you, as it has been in the beginning, it is now, and ever shall be, world without end. It shall be to the last saint as it was with the first. The testimony of the last soldier of the host shall be, "Not one good thing hath failed of all that the Lord God hath promised."

Only one more reflection here. Our God has taught many of us to trust in his name. We were long in learning the lesson, and nothing but Omnipotence could have made us willing to walk by faith, and not by sight ; but with much patience the Lord has brought us at last to have no reliance but on himself, and now we are depending on his faithfulness and his truth. Is that thy case, brother ? What then ?

Thinkest thou that God has given thee this faith to mock thee? Believest thou that he has taught thee to trust in his name, and thus far has brought thee to put thee to shame? Has his Holy Spirit given thee confidence in a lie? and has he wrought in thee faith in a fiction? God forbid! Our God is no demon who would delight in the misery which a groundless confidence would be sure to bring to us. If thou hast faith, he gave it to thee, and he that gave it to thee knows his own gift, and will honour it. He was never false yet, even to the feeblest faith, and if thy faith is great, thou shalt find him greater than thy faith, even when thy faith is at its greatest; therefore be of good cheer. The fact that thou believest should encourage thee to say, " Now, O Lord, I have come to rest upon thee, canst thou fail me? I, a poor worm, know no confidence but thy dear name, wilt thou forsake me? I have no refuge but thy wounds, O Jesus, no hope but in thy atoning sacrifice, no light but in thy light: canst thou cast me off?" It is not possible that the Lord should cast off one who thus trusts him. Can a woman forget her sucking child, that she should not have compassion on the son of her womb? Can any of us forget our children when they fondly trust us in the days of their weakness? No, the Lord is no monster: he is tender and full of compassion, faithful and true; and Jesus is a friend which sticketh closer than a brother. The very fact that he has given us faith in his covenant should help us to plead,—
" Have respect unto the covenant."

III. Having thus shown you, dear friends, the meaning of the plea, and whence it derives its force, we will now pause a minute and observe HOW AND WHEN THAT COVENANT MAY BE PLEADED.

First, it may be pleaded *under a sense of sin*—when the soul feels its guiltiness. Let me read to you the words of our apostle, in the eighth chapter of the Hebrews, where he is speaking of this covenant at the tenth verse. " For this is the covenant that I will make with the house of Israel after those days, saith the Lord; I will put my laws into their mind, and write them in their hearts: and I will be to them a God, and they shall be to me a people. And they shall not teach every man his neighbour, and every man his brother, saying, Know the Lord: for all shall know me, from the least to the greatest. For I will be merciful to their unrighteousness, and their sins and their iniquities will I remember no more." Now, dear hearer, suppose that thou art under a sense of sin; something has revived in thee a recollection of past guilt, or it may be that thou hast sadly stumbled this very day, and Satan whispers, "Thou wilt surely be destroyed, for thou hast sinned." Now go to the great Father, and open this page, putting thy finger on that twelfth verse, and say, " Lord, thou hast in infinite, boundless, inconceivable mercy entered into covenant with me, a poor sinner, seeing I believe in the name of Jesus, and now I beseech thee have respect unto thy covenant. Thou hast said, *I will be merciful to their unrighteousness:*—O God be merciful to mine. *Their sins and their iniquities will I remember no more:* Lord, remember no more my sins: forget for ever my iniquity." That is the way to use the covenant: when under a sense of sin, run to that clause which meets your case.

But suppose, beloved brother or sister, you are *labouring to overcome inward corruption*, with intense desire that holiness should be wrought in you. Then read the covenant again as you find it in the thirty-first chapter of Jeremiah at the thirty-third verse. It is the same covenant, only we are reading another version of it. "This shall be the covenant that I will make with the house of Israel; after those days, saith the Lord, I will put my law in their inward parts, and write it in their hearts." Now, can you not plead that and say, "Lord, thy commandments upon stone are holy, but I forget them, and break them; but, O my God, write them on the fleshy tablets of my heart. Come now and make me holy; transform me; write thy will upon my very soul, that I may live it out, and from the warm impulses of my heart serve thee as thou wouldst be served. Have respect unto thy covenant and sanctify thy servant."

Or suppose you desire to be *upheld under strong temptation,* lest you should go back and return to your old ways. Take the covenant as you find it in Jeremiah at the thirty-second chapter at the fortieth verse. Note these verses and learn them by heart, for they may be a great help to you some of these days. Read the fortieth verse of the thirty-second chapter of Jeremiah. "And I will make an everlasting covenant with them, that I will not turn away from them, to do them good; but I will put my fear in their hearts, that they shall not depart from me." Now go and say, "O Lord, I am almost gone, and they tell me I shall finally fall, but O, my Lord and Master, there stands thy word. Put thy fear in my heart and fulfil thy promise, that I shall not depart from thee." This is the sure road to final perseverance.

Thus I might take you through all the various needs of God's people, and show that in seeking to have them supplied they may fitly cry, "Have respect unto the covenant." For instance, suppose you were in great distress of mind and needed comfort, you could go to him with that covenant promise, "As a mother comforteth her children, even so will I comfort thee,—out of Zion will I comfort thee." Go to him with that and say, "Lord, comfort thy servant." Or if there should happen to be a trouble upon us, not for yourselves, but for the church; how sweet it is to go to the Lord and say, "Thy covenant runs thus—'the gates of hell shall not prevail against her.' O Lord, it seems as though they would prevail. Interpose thy strength and save thy church." If it ever should happen that you are looking for the conversion of the ungodly, and desiring to see sinners saved, and the world seems so dark, look at our text again—the whole verse—"Have respect unto the covenant, for the dark places of the earth are full of the habitations of cruelty," to which you may add, "but thou hast said that thy glory shall cover the earth, and that all flesh shall see the salvation of God. Lord, have respect unto thy covenant. Help our missionaries, speed thy gospel, bid the the mighty angel fly through the midst of heaven to preach the everlasting gospel to every creature. Why, it is a grand missionary prayer. "Have respect unto the covenant." Beloved, it is a two-edged sword, to be used in all conditions of strife, and it is a holy balm of Gilead, that will heal in all conditions of suffering.

IV. And so I close with this last question, WHAT ARE THE PRACTICAL INFERENCES FROM ALL THIS? "Have respect unto the covenant." Why, that if we ask God to have respect unto it *we* ought to have respect unto it ourselves, and in this way.

Have a grateful respect for it. Bless the Lord that he ever condescended to enter into covenant with you. What could he see in you even to give you a promise, much more to make a covenant with you? Blessed be his dear name, this is the sweet theme of our hymns on earth, and shall be the subject of our songs in heaven.

Next, *have a believing respect for it.* If it is God's covenant, do not dishonour it. It stands sure. Why do you stagger at it through unbelief?

> " His every work of grace is strong
> As that which built the skies ;
> The voice that rolls the stars along
> Speaks all the promises."

Next, *have a joyful respect for it.* Wake your harps, and join in praise with David : " Although my house be not so with God, yet hath he made with me an everlasting covenant." Here is enough to make a heaven in our hearts while yet we are below—the Lord hath entered into a covenant of grace and peace with us, and he will bless us for ever.

Then have a jealous respect for it. Never suffer the covenant of works to be mixed with it. Hate that preaching—I say not less than that—hate that preaching which does not discriminate between the covenant of works and the covenant of grace, for it is deadly preaching and damning preaching. You must always have a straight, clear line here between what is of man and what is of God, for cursed is he that trusteth in man and maketh flesh his arm ; and if you have begun with the Spirit under this covenant do not think of being made perfect in the flesh under another covenant. Be ye holy under the precepts of the heavenly Father ; but be ye not legal under the taskmaster's lash. Return not to the bondage of the law, for ye are not under law, but under grace.

Lastly, *have a practical respect for it.* Let all see that the covenant of grace, while it is your reliance, is also your delight. Be ready to speak of it to others. Be ready to show that the effect of its grace upon you is one that is worthy of God, since it has a purifying effect upon your life. He that hath this hope in him purifieth himself even as he is pure. Have respect unto the covenant by walking as such people should who can say that God is to them a God, and they are to him a people. The covenant says, " From all their idols will I cleanse them." Don't love idols then. The covenant says, " I will sprinkle pure water upon them, and they shall be clean." Be ye clean then, ye covenanted ones, and may the Lord preserve you and make his covenant to be your boast on earth and your song for ever in heaven. Oh that the Lord may bring us into the bonds of his covenant, and give us a simple faith in his dear Son, for that is the mark of the covenanted ones. Amen and Amen.

The Beginning of Months

"And the Lord spake unto Moses and Aaron in the land of Egypt, saying, this month shall be unto you the beginning of months : it shall be the first month of the year to you."—Exodus xii. 1, 2.

In all probability up to that time the year had been supposed to begin in the autumn. The question has been raised at what season of the year did God create man, and it has been decided by many that it must have been in autumn, so that when Adam was placed in the garden he might at once find fruits ripe and ready for his use. It has not seemed probable that he would have begun his career while as yet all fruits were raw and green ; therefore many have concluded that the first year of human history began in the time of harvest, when fruits were mellowed for man's food. For this reason, perhaps, in the old time the new year began when the feast of harvest had been celebrated. Here at the point of the Exodus, by a decree of God, the commencement of the year was altered, and so far as Israel was concerned the opening of the year was fixed for the time of our spring—in the month called Abib, or Nisan. We know that a little before the barley was in the ear (see Exodus ix. 31), and on the Sabbath after the passover, the produce of the earth was so far advanced that the firstfruits were offered, and a sheaf of new barley was waved before the Lord. Of course, when I speak of spring, and then of ears of barley, you must remember the difference of climate, for in that warm region the seasons are far in advance of ours. You must pardon me if my ideas should become a little mixed ; you can correct them easily at your leisure. From the time when the Lord saved his people from destruction by passing them over the ecclesiastical year began in the month Abib, in which the passover was celebrated. The jubilee year was not altered, but began in the autumnal equinox. The Jews seem to have had two or three beginnings of the year in relation to different purposes ; but the ecclesiastical year, the great year by which Israel reckoned its existence, commenced henceforth in the month Abib, when the Lord brought his people out with a high hand and an out-stretched arm.

It is with God to change times and seasons as he pleases, and he has done so for great commemorative purposes. The change of the Sabbath is on the same manner, for whereas the day of rest was formerly the seventh, it is now merged in the Lord's-day, which is the first day of the week. As Herbert says, " He did unhinge the day," and he set the Sabbath on golden hinges by consecrating the day of his resurrection. To every man God makes such a change of times and seasons when he deals with him in a way of grace ; for all things are become new within him, and therefore he begins a new chronology. Some of us used to think our birthday fell at a certain time of the year ; but now we regard with much more delight another day as our true birthday, since on that second natal day we began truly to live. Our calendar has been altered and amended by a deed of divine grace.

This morning I want to bring to your mind this fact, that, just as the people of Israel when God gave them the passover had a complete shifting and changing of all their dates, and began their year on quite a different day, so when God gives to his people to eat the spiritual passover there takes place in their chronology a very wonderful change. Saved men and women date from the dawn of their true life ; not from their first birthday, but from the day wherein they were born again of the Spirit of God, and entered into the knowledge and enjoyment of spiritual things. The passover is, as we all know, a type of the great work of our redemption by the blood of Jesus, and it represents the personal application of it to each believer. When we perceive the Lord's act of passing us over because of Christ's atoning sacrifice, then it is that we begin to live, and from that day we date all future events.

So this morning we shall first *describe the event;* secondly, *mention varieties of its recurrence;* and thirdly, *consider in what light the date of this grand event is to be regarded* according to the law of the Lord.

I. First, then, let us DESCRIBE THIS REMARKABLE EVENT, which was henceforth to stand at the head of the Jewish year, and, indeed, at the commencement of all Israelitish chronology.

First, this event was *an act of salvation by blood.* You know how the elders and heads of families each one took the lamb and shut it up, that they might examine it carefully. Having chosen a lamb without blemish, in the prime of its life, they kept it by itself as a separated and consecrated creature, and after four days they slew it, and caught its blood in a basin. When this was done they took hyssop and dipped it in the blood, and therewith sprinkled the lintel and the two side posts of their houses. By this means the houses of Israel were preserved on that dark and dreadful night, when with unsheathed sword the angel of vengeance sped through every street of Pharaoh's domain and slew the firstborn of all the land, both of men and of cattle. You will remember, dear friends, the time when you yourselves perceived that God's vengeance was out against sin ; you can even now recollect your terror and your trembling. Many of us can never forget the memorable time when we first discovered that there was a way of deliverance from the wrath of God. Memory may drop all else from her enfeebled grasp, but this is graven on the palms of her hands. The mode of our deliverance is before us in the type as Moses describes it. The angel could not be restrained, his wing could not be bound, and his sword could not be sheathed: he must go forth, and he must smite. He must smite us among the rest, for sin was upon us, and there must be no partiality: "the soul that sinneth it shall die." But do you remember when you discovered God's new way, his blessed ordinance by which, without abrogating the destroying law, he brought in a glorious saving clause by which we were delivered?

The clause was this,—that if another could be found who could and would suffer instead of us, and if there could be clear evidence that this surety did so suffer, then the sight of that evidence should be enough for our deliverance. Do you remember your joy at that discovery? for, if so, you can enter into the feelings of the Israelites when they understood that God would accept an unblemished lamb in the place of their firstborn; and if the blood was displayed upon the doorpost as the clear evidence that a sacrifice had died, and a substitute had suffered, then the angel should know that in that house his work was done, and he might therefore pass over that habitation. The avenger was to demand a life; but the life was already paid, for there was the blood-mark which proved it, and the exactor might go on his way. It was the night of God's passover, not because the execution of vengeance was left undone in the houses passed over, but for a reason of the opposite kind,—because in those houses the death-blow had been struck, and the victim had died, and, as the penalty could not be exacted twice, that family was clear.

I do not know whether there is any truth in the statement of a correspondent that whatever part of the earth the lightning once strikes it never strikes it again : but whether it be so or not, it is certain that wherever the lightning of God's vengeance has once struck the sinner's substitute it will not strike the sinner. The best preservative for the Israelite's house was this,—vengeance had struck there and could not strike again. There was the insurance mark, the blood-streak; death had been there, no matter though it had fallen on a harmless lamb, it had fallen on a victim of God's own appointment, and in his esteem it had fallen upon his Christ, the Lamb slain from before the foundation of the world. Because the claims of retribution had been fully met there was no further demand, and Israel was secure. This is my eternal confidence, and here is my soul's sweet hymn:—

> " If thou hast my discharge procured,
>   And freely in my room endured
>   The whole of wrath divine :
>   Payment God cannot twice demand,
>   First at my bleeding Surety's hand,
>   And then again at mine.
>
> " Turn then, my soul, unto thy rest ;
>   The merits of thy great High Priest
>   Have bought thy liberty :
>   Trust in his efficacious blood,
>   Nor fear thy banishment from God,
>   Since Jesus died for thee."

It was to me the beginning of my life, that day in which I discovered that judgment was passed upon me in the person of my Lord, and that there is therefore now no condemnation to me. The law demands death, —" The soul that sinneth it shall die." Lo, there is the death it asks, and more. Christ, my Lord, has died, died in my stead: as it is written, "Who his own self bare our sins in his own body on the tree." Such a sacrifice is more than even the most rigorous law could demand. "Christ our passover is sacrificed for us." "Christ hath redeemed us from the curse of the law, being made a curse for us." Therefore do we sit securely within doors, desiring no guard without to drive away the destroyer; for, when God sees the blood of Jesus he will pass over us. "In his days Judah shall be saved, and Israel shall dwell safely: and this is his name whereby he shall be called, THE LORD OUR RIGHTEOUSNESS" (Jer. xxiii. 6). I say again, it was the beginning of life to me when I saw Jesus as dying in my stead. I beheld the first sight that was worth beholding, let all the rest be darkness and as the shadow of death. Then did my soul rejoice when I understood and accepted the substitutionary sacrifice of the appointed Redeemer. That is the first view of this event,—the blood of sprinkling made Israel secure.

Secondly, that night *they received refreshment from the lamb.* Being saved by its blood, the believing households sat down and fed upon the lamb. They never ate as they ate that night. Those who spiritually understood the symbol must have partaken of every morsel with a mysterious awe mingled with an unfathomable delight. I am sure there must have been a singular seriousness about the table as they stood there eating in haste; and especially if ever and anon they were startled with the shrieks that rose from every house in the land of Egypt, because of the slain of the Lord. It was a solemn feast, a meal of mingled hope and mystery. Do you remember, brothers and sisters, when first you fed upon Christ, when your hungry spirit enjoyed the first morsel of that food of the soul? It was dainty fare, was it not? It was better than angels' bread, for

> "Never did angels taste above
> Redeeming grace and dying love."

I hope you have never risen from that table, but are daily feeding upon Jesus. It is a very instructive fact that we do not go to our Lord's table, like Israel, to eat in haste, with a staff in our hand, but we come there to recline at ease with our heads in his bosom, reposing in his love. Christ Jesus is the daily bread of our spirits.

Observe that the refreshment which Israel ate that night was the Lamb "roast with fire." The best refreshment to a troubled heart is the suffering Saviour; the Lamb roast with fire. A poor sinner under a sense of sin goes to a place of worship, and he hears Christ preached as an example. This may be useful to the saint, but it is scant help to the poor sinner. He cries, "That is true; but it rather condemns than comforts me." It is not food for him: he wants the lamb roast with fire, Christ his substitute, Christ suffering in his place and stead. We hear a great deal about the beauty of Christ's moral character, and assuredly our blessed Lord deserves to be highly exalted on that score; but that is not the aspect under which he is food to a soul conscious of sin. The chief relish about our Lord Jesus to a penitent sinner is his sin-bearing, and his agonies in that capacity. We need the suffering Saviour, the Christ of Gethsemane, the Christ of Golgotha and Calvary, Christ shedding his blood in the sinner's stead, and bearing for us the fire of God's wrath. Nothing short of this will suffice to be meat for a hungry heart. Keep this back and you starve the child of God.

We are told in the chapter that they were not to eat of the lamb raw. Alas ! there are some who try to do this with Christ, for they preach a half-atoning sacrifice. They would make him in his Person and in his character to be meat for their souls, but they have small liking for his Passion, and they cast his Atonement into the background, or represent it to be an ineffectual expiation which does not secure any soul from vengeance. What is this but to devour a raw Christ ? I will not touch their half-roasted lamb; I will have nothing to do with their half substitution, their half-complete redemption. No, no ; give me a Saviour who has borne all my sins in his own body, and so has been roast with fire to the full. " It is finished," is the most charming note in all Calvary's music. " It is finished," the fire has passed upon the Lamb, he has borne the whole of the wrath that was due to his people : this is the royal dish of the feast of love.

What a multitude of teachers there are who must needs have the Lamb sodden with water, though the Scripture saith, " Eat not of it raw, nor sodden at all with water." I have heard it said that a great number of sermons are about Christ and about the gospel, but yet neither Christ nor his gospel are preached in them. If so, the preachers present the lamb sodden in the water of their own thoughts and speculations and notions. Now, the mischief of this boiling process is that the water takes away a good deal from the meat. Philosophical discoursings upon the Lord Jesus take away much of the essence and virtue of his person, offices, work, and glory. The real juice and vital nutriment of his glorious Word is carried off by interpretations which do not explain, but explain away. How many boil out the soul of the gospel by their carnal wisdom ! What is worse still, when meat is sodden, it is not only that the meat gets into the water, but the water gets into the meat ; and so, what truth these gospel-boilers do hand out to us is sodden with error, and you receive from them dishes made up partly of God's truth and partly of men's imaginings. We hear in some measure solid gospel and in larger measure mere watery reasoning. When certain divines preach atonement, it is not substitution pure and simple ; one hardly knows what it is. Their atonement is not the vicarious sacrifice, but a performance of something they are long in defining. They have a theory which is like the relics of meat after months of boiling, all strings and fibres. All manner of schemes are tried to extract the marrow and fatness from the grand soul-satisfying doctrine of substitution, which to my mind is the choicest truth that can ever be brought forth for the food of souls. I cannot make out why so many divines are afraid of the shedding of blood for the remission of sin, and must needs stew down the most important of all the truths of revelation. No, no ; as the type could only be correct when the lamb was roast with fire, so the gospel is not truly set forth unless we describe our Lord Jesus in his sufferings for his people, and those sufferings in the room, place, and stead of sinners, presenting absolutely and literally a substitution for them. I will have no dilution : it is substitution :—" he bore our sins." He was made sin for us. " The chastisement of our peace was upon him, and by his stripes we are healed." We must have no mystifying of this plain truth, it must not be " sodden at all with water," but we must have Christ in his sufferings fresh from the fire.

Now, this lamb they were to eat, and the whole of it. Not a morsel must be left. Oh that you and I would never cut and divide Christ so as to choose one part of him and leave another. Let not a bone of him be broken, but let us take in a whole Christ up to the full measure of our capacity. Prophet, Priest, and King, Christ divine and Christ human, Christ loving and living, Christ dying, Christ risen, Christ ascended, Christ coming again, Christ triumphant over all his foes—the whole Lord Jesus Christ is ours. We must not reject a single particle of what is revealed concerning him, but must feed upon it all as we are able.

That night Israel had to feed upon the lamb there and then. They might not put by a portion for to-morrow: they must consume the whole in some way or other. Oh, my brother, we need a whole Christ at this very moment. Let us receive him in his entirety. Oh for a splendid appetite and fine powers of digestion, so as to receive into my inmost soul the Lord's Christ just as I find him. May you and I never think lightly of our Lord under any light or in any one of his offices. All that you now know and all that you can find out concerning Christ you should now believe, appreciate, feed upon, and rejoice in. Make the most of all that is in the word concerning your Lord. Let him enter into your being to become part and parcel of yourself. If you do this the day in which you feed on Jesus will be the first day of your life, its day of days, the day from which you date all that follows. If once you have fed upon Christ Jesus you will never forget it in time or in eternity. That was the second event which was celebrated in each succeeding Passover.

The third event was *the purification of their houses from leaven*, for that was to go in a most important way side by side with the sprinkling of the blood and the eating of the lamb. They were told that they must not eat leaven for seven days, for whosoever did partake of leaven should be cut off from Israel. It shows the deep importance of this purification that it is put in equal position with the sprinkling of the blood; at any rate it might not be separated from it upon pain and penalty that he who divided the two should himself be divided from the congregation of Israel. Now, it is always a pity when we are preaching justification by faith so to bring in sanctification as to make it a part of justification; but it is also a horrible error when you are preaching justification so to preach it as to deny the absolute necessity of sanctification, for the two are joined together of the Lord. There must be the eating of the lamb as well as the sprinkling of the blood; and there must be the purging out of the old leaven, as well as the sprinkling of the blood and the eating of the lamb. Very carefully the Jewish householder looked into every closet, corner, drawer, and cupboard to sweep out every crumb of stale bread; and if they had any bread in store, even if it was new and they intended to eat it, they must put it all away, for there must not be a particle of leaven in the same house with the lamb. When you and I first came to Christ what a sweep there was of the leaven. I know I was clean delivered from the leaven of the Pharisees, for all trust in my own good works went, even the last crumb of it. All confidence in rites and ceremonies must go too. I have not a crust left of either of these two sour and corrupt confidences at the present moment, and I wish never to taste that old leaven any more. Some are always chewing at that leaven, glorying in their own prayers, and alms, and ceremonies; but when Christ comes in, this leaven all goes out. Moreover, the leaven of the Pharisees, which is hypocrisy, must be cleared out. " Blessed is he whose transgression is forgiven, whose sin is covered. Blessed is the man unto whom the Lord imputeth not iniquity, and in whose spirit there is no guile." Guile must go, or guilt will not go. The Lord sweeps the cunning out of his people, the craftiness, the deceit: he makes them true before his face. They wish that they were as clear of every sin as they are clear from insincerity. They once tried to dwell before the Lord with double dealing, pretending to be what they were not; but as soon as ever they ate of Christ, and the blood was sprinkled, then they humbled themselves in truth, and laid bare their sinnership, and stood before God as they were, with their hypocrisy rent away. Christ has not saved the man who still trusts in falsehood. You cannot feed on Christ and at the same time hold a lie in your right hand by vain confidence in yourself, or by love of sin. Self and sin must go. But oh what a day it is when the old leaven is put out,—we shall never forget it! This month is the beginning of months, the first month of the year to us, when the Spirit of truth purges out the spirit of falsehood.

A fourth point in the passover is not to be forgotten. On the passover night there came, as the result of the former things, *a wonderful, glorious, and mighty deliverance.* That night every Israelite received promise of immediate emancipation, and as soon as the morning dawned he quitted the house in which he had sheltered during the night, and quitting his home he quitted Egypt too. He left for ever the brick-kilns, washed the brick-earth for the last time from his hands, looked down on the yoke he used to carry when he worked amid the clay, and said, " I have done with you." He looked at every Egyptian taskmaster, remembered how often he had struck him with the stick, and he rejoiced that he would never strike him again, for there he was at his feet begging him to be gone lest all Egypt should die. Oh what joy! They marched out with their unleavened bread still on their backs, for they had some days in which they were still to eat it, and I think before the seventh day of unleavened bread was over they had reached the Red Sea. Still eating unleavened bread they went down into the depths of the Red Sea, and still with no flavour of leaven in their mouths they stood on its shore to sing unto the Lord the great Hallelujah, because he had triumphed gloriously, and the horse and his rider had been cast into the sea. Do you recollect when the Lord purged you from the love of sin, and from trust in self, and when he brought you clean out and set you free, and said, "Go on to the promised rest, go on to Canaan " ? Do you remember when you saw your sins drowned for ever, never to rise in judgment against you,—not merely your destruction prevented, not merely your soul fed with the finest food, not merely your heart and your house cleansed of hypocrisy, but yourself delivered and emancipated, the Lord's free man ? Oh, if so, I am sure you will grant the wisdom of the ordinance by which the Lord decreed,

—"this month shall be unto you the beginning of months, it shall be the first month of the year to you." Thus much, then, on describing the event.

II. Now, secondly, I want to MENTION THE VARIETIES OF ITS RECURRENCE among us at this day.

The first recurrence is of course on *the personal salvation of each one of us.* The whole of this chapter was transacted in your heart and mine when first we knew the Lord. Our venerable Brother and Elder White, when I saw him the other night, said to me, "Oh, sir, it is very precious to read the Bible, but it is infinitely more delightful to have it here in your own heart." Now I find it very profitable to read about the passover ; but oh, how sweet to have a passover transacted in your own soul by the work of the Holy Spirit! Moses wrote of something that happened thousands of years ago, but the substance of it all has happened to me in all its details, and to thousands who are trusting in the Lord. Can we not read this story in Exodus, and say, " Yes, it is even so " ? Every word of it is true, for it has all occurred to me, every atom of it, even to the eating of the bitter herbs ; for I recollect right well that, at the very moment when I had the sweet flavour of my Lord's atonement in my mouth, I felt the bitterness of repentance on account of sin, and the bitterness of struggling against the temptation to sin again. Even the minute touches of that typical festival are all correct, as thousands know who have participated in its antitype. This passover record is not a story of olden times alone, it is the record of your life and mine,—I hope it is. Thus by each separate saved man the paschal feast is kept.

But then it happens again in a certain sense *when the man's house is saved.* Remember, this was a family business. The father and mother were present when the lamb was slain. I dare say the eldest son helped to bring the lamb to the slaughter, another held the knife, a third held the basin, and the little boy fetched the bunch of hyssop, and they all united in the sacrifice. They all saw father strike the lintel and the side-posts, and they all ate of the lamb that night. Everyone that was in the house, all that were really part of the family, partook of the meal : they were all protected by the blood, they were all refreshed by the feast, and they all started the next morning to go to Canaan. Did you ever hold a family supper of that kind ? " Oh," some fathers might say, "it would be the beginning of family life to me if ever I might eat bread in the kingdom of God with all my sons and daughters. Oh that every chick and child around my table truly belonged to Christ." A family begins to live in the highest sense when as a family, without exception, it has all been redeemed, all sprinkled with the blood, all made to feed on Jesus, all purged from sin, and all set at liberty to go out of the domains of sin, bound for the Kingdom. Joy! joy! joy! " I have no greater joy than to hear that my children walk in truth." If any of you enjoy the privilege of family salvation, you may well set up a monument of praise, and make a generous offering to God, by whom you are thus favoured. Engrave it upon marble, and set it up for ever—This household is saved, and the day of its salvation is the beginning of its history in connection with the Lord's Israel.

117

Extend the thought—it was not only a family ordinance but *it was for all the tribes of Israel.* There were many families, but in every house the passover was sacrificed. Would it not be a grand thing if you that employ large numbers of men should ever be able to gather all together and hopefully say, "I trust that all these understand the sprinkling of the blood, and all feed upon Christ." Dear men and women that are placed in such responsible positions, you might indeed say, "This shall be the beginning of months to us." Labour for it, therefore, and make it your heart's desire. If you live to see a district in which you labour permeated with the gospel, what a joy! If we shall live to see London with every house sprinkled with the redeeming blood! If we should live to see all England feeding, not as many do at Christmas to excess on the delicacies of earth, but feasting spiritually, where there can be no excess, upon Christ. Oh, what a beginning of years it would be to our happy island! What a paradise it would be! If it should be so with France, if it should be so in any country, what a day to be remembered. Commence a nation's annals from its evangelization. Begin the chronicle of a people from the day when they bow at the feet of Jesus. There will come a day to this poor earth when all over it Jesus shall reign. It may be long yet, but the day shall come when Christ shall have dominion from sea to sea. The nations which are called Christians, although they so little deserve the title, do already date their chronology from the birth of Christ, and this is a sort of faint foreshadowing of the way in which men shall one day date all things from the reign of Jesus; for his unsuffering kingdom yet shall come. God hath decreed his triumph, and on all the wings of time it hastens. When he cometh that month shall be the beginning of months unto us. I say no more.

III. And now, in the last place, I come to SHOW IN WHAT LIGHT THIS DATE IS TO BE REGARDED, if it has occurred to us in the senses I have mentioned.

Primarily, if it has occurred in the first sense to us personally: what about it then? Why, first, the day in which we first knew the Saviour as the Paschal Lamb should always be *the most honourable day* that has ever dawned upon us. The Israelites placed the month Abib in the first rank because it was the month of the passover: put down the date at which you knew the Lord as the premier day, the noblest hour you have ever known. It eclipses your natural birthday, for then you were born in sin, then you were "born to trouble as the sparks fly upward;" but now you are born into spiritual life, born unto eternal bliss. It eclipses your marriage day, for union to Christ shall bring you greater felicity than the happpiest of conjugal bonds. If you have ever known a day in which you received the honours of the State, or gained distinction in learning, or attained to a position in society, or arrived at a larger wealth, all these were but dim, cloudy, foggy days compared with this "morning without clouds." On that day your sun rose never to go down again: the die was cast, your destiny for glory was openly declared. I pray you never in your thoughts degrade that blessed day by thinking more of any pleasure, honour, or advancement than you do of the blessing of salvation by the blood of Jesus. I am afraid that some are striving and struggling after other distinctions, and if they could once reach a certain event then they would be satisfied : is not your salvation worth vastly more than this? They would feel that they were made for life if a certain matter turned out right. Brother, you were made for life when you were made anew in Christ Jesus. You came to your estate when you came to Christ : you were promoted when he received you to his friendship. You gained all that you need desire when you found Christ, for a saint of old said, "He is all my salvation, and all my desire." Do not, therefore, if the Queen should knight you or the people should send you to Parliament, think that the event would overshadow your conversion and salvation. Think of that act of grace as the Lord thinks of it, for he says, "Since thou wast precious in my sight thou hast been honourable, and I have loved thee." Unto you that believe Jesus is honour ; in him you boast and glory, and well you may. The blood-mark is a believer's chief adornment and decoration, and his being cleansed and set free by grace is his noblest distinction. Glory in grace and in nothing else. Prize the work of grace beyond all the treasures of Egypt.

This date is to be regarded as *the beginning of life*. The Israelites reckoned that all their former existence as a nation had been death. The brick-kilns of Egypt, the lying among the pots, the mixing up with idolaters, the hearing of a language which they understood not— they looked on all Egyptian experience as death, and the month which ended it was to them the beginning of months. On the other hand, they looked upon all that followed after as being life. The passover was the beginning, and only the beginning : a beginning implies something to follow it. Now then, Christian men, whenever you speak about your existence before conversion always do it with shamefacedness, as one risen from the dead might speak of the charnel-house and the worm of corruption. I feel grieved when I hear or read of people who can stand up and talk about what they used to do before they were converted very much in the way in which an old seafaring man talks of his voyages and storms. No, no, be ashamed of your former lusts in your ignorance ; and if you must speak of them to the praise and glory of Christ, speak with bated breath and tears and sighs. Death, rottenness, corruption are all most fitly left in silence, or, if they demand a voice, let it be as solemn and mournful as a knell. Let your sin-story be told in a way which shall show that you wish it had never been true. Let your conversion be the burial of the old existence, and as for that which follows after, take care that you make it real life, worthy of the grace which has quickened you.

Suppose these Israelites had loitered about in Egypt : suppose one of them had said, " Well, I did not finish that batch of bricks. I cannot go out just yet. I should like to see them thoroughly well baked and prepared for the pyramid "—what a foolish fellow he would have been ! No, but they left the bricks, and the clay, and the stuff behind, and went straight away, and let Egypt take care of itself. Now, child of God, quit the ways of sin with determination, leave the world, leave its pleasures, leave its cares, and get right away to Jesus and his leadership. You are now the Lord's free man ; shall the blood be sprinkled for nothing ! Shall the lamb be eaten and mean nothing ! Shall the leavened bread be purged out in vain ! Shall the Red Sea be crossed, and the Egyptians drowned, and you remain a slave? The thought is abhorrent. That was the mischief about the Israelites, that they had still a hankering after the leeks and garlick of Egypt: these strong-smelling things had scented their garments, and it is hard to get such vile odours out of one's clothes. Alas, that Egyptian garlick clings to us, and the smell of it is not always so abominable to us as it ought to be. Besides, they pined for fish which they did eat in Egypt in plenty, muddy fish though it was. There were better fisheries for them in Jordan, and Gennesaret, and the Great Sea, if they had gone ahead; and sweeter herbs were on Canaan's hills than ever grew in Egypt's mire. Because of this evil lusting they were kept dodging about for forty years in the wilderness. They might have marched into Canaan in forty days if it had not been for that stinking garlick of theirs, and their Egyptian habits and memories. Oh, that God would cut us quite free, and enable us to forget those things whereof we are now ashamed.

I have nearly concluded when I have added this, that inasmuch as the passover was now the beginning of the year to them *it was the putting of all things right*. I told you that the year had formerly begun in autumn, according to most traditions: was this really the best season to pitch upon? Upon second thoughts, was autumn the best season in which to begin life, with winter all before you and everything declining? By the institution of the passover the year was made to begin in what is our spring. If I judge from the condition of our land I should ask,— When could the year begin more fitly than in the springtide of early May? It seems to me that it actually does begin in spring. I do not see that the year naturally begins to-day, though it does so arbitrarily. We are in about the middle of winter, and the year as yet lies dead. When the birds sing and the flowers rise from their beds of earth, then the year begins. It seems to me a strange supposition that our first parents commenced life in autumn, amid lengthening nights and declining forces. No, we say, by all means let the date be fixed in spring, so that the salutations of the new year shall be sweet with fragrant flowers and rich with joyous songs. Nor would the time of our spring in the East be a season without supplies, for in April and May the first ears of corn are ready, and many other fruits are fit for food. It was good for the Israelites to have the feast of the firstfruits in the month Abib, to bring the first ears to the Lord, and not to wait till they were ripe before they blessed the Giver of all good. We ought to be grateful for green mercies, and not tarry till everything come to ripeness. In some parts of the East there is fruit all the year round, and why not in Eden? In the delightful country where I have sojourned, which bears a very close resemblance to the East, there are fruits still ripening upon the trees, and one tree or another will be found to bear fruit every month all the year round, so that if Adam had been created in the month of April there would have been food for him, followed by a succession of fruits which would have supplied all his wants. Then he would have had summer before him with all its ripening beauties, and this is a more paradisaical outlook than winter. It is right that the year should begin with the firstfruits, and I am sure it is quite right that the year should begin with you and with me when we come to

Christ and receive the firstfruits of the Spirit. Everything is out of joint till a man knows Christ: everything is disorderly and bottom upwards till the gospel comes and turns him upside down, and then the right side is up again. Man is all wrong till the gospel puts him all right. Though grace is above nature it is not contrary to nature, but restores true nature. Our nature is never so truly the nature of a man as when it is no longer man's sinful nature. We become truly men, such as God meant men to be, when we cease to be men such as sin has made men to be.

Our life, beginning as it does at our spiritual passover, and at our feeding upon Christ, we ought always to regard our conversion as a festival and remember it with praise. Whenever we look back upon it the memory of it should excite delight in our hearts. I wonder how long a man ought to thank God for forgiving his sins? Is life long enough? Is time long enough? Is eternity too long? How long ought a man to thank God for saving him from going down to hell? Would fifty years suffice? Oh no, that would never do, the blessing is too great to be all sung of in a millennium. Suppose you and I never had a single mercy except this one, that we were made the children of God and co-heirs with Christ Jesus,—suppose we had nothing else to enjoy! We ought to sing about that alone for ever and ever. Ay, if we were sick, cast on the bed of pain with a hundred diseases, with the bone wearing through the skin, yet since God's everlasting mercy will sanctify every pain and every affliction, should we not still continue to lift up happy psalms to God and praise him for ever and ever? Therefore, be that your watchword all through the year—" Hallelujah, praise ye the Lord ! " The Israelite always closed the passover with a hymn of praise, and therefore let us close our sermon this morning with holy joy, and continue our happy music till this year ends, ay, till time shall be no more. Amen.

Sermon for New Year's Day

"And he that sat upon the throne said, Behold, I make all things new."—Revelation **xxi.** 5.

How pleased we are with that which is new! Our children's eyes sparkle when we talk of giving them a toy or a book which is called new; for our short-lived human nature loves that which has lately come, and is therefore like our own fleeting selves. In this respect, we are all children, for we eagerly demand the news of the day, and are all too apt to rush after the "many inventions" of the hour. The Athenians, who spent their time in telling and hearing some new thing, were by no means singular persons: novelty still fascinates the crowd. As the world's poet says—

"All with one consent praise new-born gawds."

I should not wonder, therefore, if the mere words of my text should sound like a pleasant song in your ears; but I am thankful that their deeper meaning is even more joyful. The newness which Jesus brings is bright, clear, heavenly, enduring. We are at this moment specially ready for *a new year*. The most of men have grown weary with the old cry of depression of trade and hard times; we are glad to escape from what has been to many a twelve-months of great trial. The last year had become wheezy, croaking, and decrepit, in its old age; and we lay it asleep with a psalm of judgment and mercy. We hope that this new-born year will not be worse than its predecessor, and we pray that it may be a great deal better. At any rate, it is new, and we are encouraged to couple with it the idea of happiness, as we say one to another, "I wish you a happy New Year."

"Ring out the old, ring in the new:
Ring, happy bells, across the snow;
The year is going, let him go;
Ring out the false, ring in the true."

We ought not, as men in Christ Jesus, to be carried away by a childish love of novelty, for we worship a God who is ever the same, and of whose years there is no end. In some matters "the old is better." There are certain things which are already so truly new, that to change them for anything else would be to lose old gold for new dross. The old, old gospel is the newest thing in the world ; in its very essence it is for ever good news. In the things of God the old is ever new, and if any man brings forward that which seems to be new doctrine and new truth, it is soon perceived that the new dogma is only worn-out heresy dexterously repaired, and the discovery in theology is the digging up of a carcase of error which had better have been left to rot in oblivion. In the great matter of truth and godliness, we may safely say, "There is nothing new under the sun."

Yet, as I have already said, there has been so much evil about ourselves and our old nature, so much sin about our life and the old past, so much mischief about our surroundings and the old temptations, that we are not distressed by the belief that old things are passing away. Hope springs up at the first sound of such words as these from the lips of our risen and reigning Lord: " Behold, I make all things new." It is fit that things so outworn and defiled should be laid aside, and better things fill their places.

This is the first day of a new year, and therefore a solemnly joyous day. Though there is no real difference between it and any other day, yet in our mind and thought it is a marked period, which we regard as one of the milestones set up on the highway of our life. It is only in imagination that there is any close of one year and beginning of another ; and yet it has most fitly all the force of a great fact. When men "cross the line," they find no visible mark : the sea bears no trace of an equatorial belt ; and yet mariners know whereabouts they are, and they take notice thereof, so that a man can hardly cross the line for the first time without remembering it to the day of his death. We are crossing the line now. We have sailed into the year of grace 1885 ; therefore, let us keep a feast unto the Lord. If Jesus has not made us new already, let the new year cause us to think about the great and needful change of conversion ; and if our Lord has begun to make us new, and we have somewhat entered into the new world wherein dwelleth righteousness, let us be persuaded by the season to press forward into the centre of his new creation, that we may feel to the full all the power of his grace.

The words he speaks to us to-night are truly divine. Listen,—"Behold, *I* make." Who is the great I ? Who but the eternal Son of God ? "Behold, *I make*." Who can make but God, the Maker of heaven and earth ? It is his high prerogative to make and to destroy. "Behold, I *make all things*." What a range of creating power is here ! Nothing stands outside of that all-surrounding circle. "Behold, I make all things *new*." What a splendour of almighty goodness shines out upon our souls ! Lord, let us enter into this new universe of thine. Let us be new-created with the "all things." In us also may men behold the marvels of thy renewing love.

Let us now, at the portal of the new year, sing a hymn to Jesus, as we hear these encouraging words which he speaks from his throne. O Lord, we would rejoice and be glad for ever in that which thou dost create. The former troubles are forgotten, and are hid from our eyes because of thine ancient promise,—" Behold, I create new heavens and a new earth: and the former shall not be remembered, nor come into mind." (Isaiah lxv. 17).

I am going to talk to-night for a little upon *the great transformation* spoken of in the text, "I make all things new;" and then upon *the earnest call* in the text to consider that transformation: "He that sat upon the throne said, '*Behold*': attend, consider, look to it!" "Behold, I make all things new." Oh for a bedewing of the Holy Spirit while entering upon this theme! I would that our fleece might now be so wet as never to become dry throughout the whole year. Oh for a horn of oil to be poured on the head of the young year, anointing it for the constant service of the Lord!

I. Briefly, then, here is one of the grandest truths that ever fell even from the lips of Jesus:—" Behold, I make all things new." Let us gaze upon THE GREAT TRANSFORMATION.

This renewing work has been in our Lord's hands from of old. We were under the old covenant, and our first father and federal head, Adam, had broken that covenant, and we were ruined by his fatal breach. The substance of the old covenant was on this wise,—" If thou wilt keep my command thou shalt live, and thy posterity shall live; but if thou shalt eat of the tree which I have forbidden thee, dying, thou shalt die, and all thy posterity in thee." This is where we were found, broken in pieces, sore wounded, and even slain by the tremendous fall which destroyed both our Paradise and ourselves. We died in Adam as to spiritual life, and our death revealed itself in an inward tendency to evil which reigned in our members. We were like Ezekiel's deserted infant unswaddled and unwashed, left in our pollution to die; but the Son of God passed by and saw us in the greatness of our ruin. In his wondrous love our Lord Jesus put us under *a new covenant*, a covenant of which he became the second Adam, a covenant which ran on this wise,—" If thou shalt render perfect obedience and vindicate my justice, then those who are in thee shall not perish, but they shall live because thou livest." Now, our Lord Jesus, our Surety and Covenant Head, has fulfilled his portion of the covenant engagement, and the compact stands as a bond of pure promise without condition or risk. Those who are participants in that covenant cannot invalidate it, for it never did depend upon them, but only upon him who was and is their federal head and representative before God. Of Jesus the demand was made and he met it. By him man's side of the covenant was undertaken and fulfilled, and now no condition remains; it is solely made up of promises which are unconditional and sure to all the seed. To-day believers are not under the covenant of "If thou doest this thou shalt live," but under that new covenant which says, "Their sins and their iniquities will I remember no more." It is not now "Do and live," but "Live and do;" we think not of merit and reward, but of free grace producing holy practice as the result of gratitude. What law could not do, grace has accomplished.

We ought never to forget this bottom of everything, this making of all things new by the fashioning of a new covenant, so that we have come out from under the bondage of the law and the ruin of the fall, and we have entered upon the liberty of Christ, into acceptance with God, and into the boundless joy of being saved in the Lord with an everlasting salvation, so that we "shall not be ashamed nor confounded world without end." You young people, as soon as ever you know the Lord, I exhort you to study well that word "covenant." It is a key-word opening the treasures of revelation. He that rightly understands the difference between the two covenants has the foundation of sound theology laid in his mind. This is the clue of many a maze, the open sesame of many a mystery. "I make all things new," begins with the bringing in of a better hope by virtue of a better covenant.

The foundation being made new, the Lord Jesus Christ has set before us *a new way of life*, which grows out of that covenant. The old way of life was, "If thou wilt enter into life, keep the commandments." There they are, perfect, and holy, and just, and good; but, alas, dear friends, you and I have broken the commandments. We dare not say that we have kept the ten commands from our youth up; on the contrary, we are compelled by our consciences to confess that in spirit and in heart, if not in act, we have continually broken the law of God; and we are therefore under sin and condemnation, and there is no hope for us by the works of the law. For this reason the gospel sets before us another way, and says, "It is of faith, that it might be by grace." "Believe on the Lord Jesus Christ, and thou shalt be saved." Hence we read of being "justified by faith," and being made acceptable to God by faith. To be "justified" means being made really just : though we were guilty in ourselves we are regarded as just by virtue of what the Lord Jesus Christ has done for us. Thus we fell into condemnation through another, and we rise into justification through another. It is written, "By his knowledge shall my righteous servant justify many; for he shall bear their iniquities"; and this scripture is fulfilled in all those who believe in the Lord Jesus unto eternal life. Our path to eternal glory is the road of faith,—"The just shall live by faith." We are "accepted in the Beloved" when we believe in him whom God has set forth to be our righteousness. "By the deeds of the law there shall no flesh be justified in his sight"; but we are "justified freely by his grace through the redemption that is in Christ Jesus."

What a blessing it is for you and for me that Jesus has made all things new in that respect! I am glad that I have not to stand here and say, "My dear hearers, do this and do that, and you will be saved" : because you would not do as you were commanded ; for your nature is weak and wicked. But I have to bid you—

> "Lay your deadly doing down, down at Jesus' feet;
> Stand in him, in him alone, gloriously complete."

I trust you will accept this most gracious and suitable way of salvation. It is most glorious to God and safe to you : do not neglect so great salvation. After you have believed unto life you will go and do all manner of holy deeds as the result of your new life ; but do not attempt them with the view of earning life. Prompted no longer by the servile and selfish motive of saving yourself, but by gratitude for the fact that you are saved, you will rise to virtue and true holiness. Faith has brought us into the possession of an indefeasible salvation ; and now for the love we bear our Saviour, we must obey him and become "zealous for good works."

By grace every believer is brought into *a new relationship* with God. Let us rejoice in this : " Thou art no more a servant but a son, and if a son, then an heir of God through Christ." Oh you who are now children, you were servants a little while ago ! Some of you, my hearers, are servants now, and as servants I would bid you expect your wages. Alas, your service has been no service, but a rebellion ; and if you get no more wages than you deserve you will be cast away for ever. You ought to be thankful to God that he has not yet recompensed you—that he has not dealt with you after your sins, nor rewarded you according to your iniquities. Do you not also know, you servants, what is likely to happen to you as servants ? What do you yourself do with a bad servant ? You say to him, " There are your wages : go." " A servant abideth not in the house for ever." You, too, will be driven out of your religious profession and your period of probation, and where will you go ? The wilderness of destruction lies before you. Oh that you may not be left to wander with Ishmael, the son of the bondwoman !

" Behold, I make all things new," says Jesus, and then he makes his people into sons. When we are made sons do we work for wages ? We have no desire for any present payment, for our Father says to us, " Son, thou art ever with me, and all that I have is thine "; and, moreover, we have the inheritance in reversion, entailed by the covenant. We cannot demand the servile wage because we have already all that our Father possesses. He has given us himself and his all-sufficiency for our everlasting portion ; what more can we desire ? He will never drive us from his house. Never has our great Father disowned one of his sons. It cannot be ; his loving heart is too much bound up in his own adopted ones. That near and dear relationship which is manifested in adoption and regeneration, binds the child of God to the great Father's heart in such a way that he will never cast him off, nor suffer him to perish. I rejoice in the fact that we are no longer bond-slaves but sons. " Behold," says Christ, " I make all things new."

There has also been wrought in us by the work of the Holy Spirit *a new life*, with all the new feelings, and new desires, and new works which go therewith. The tree is made new, and the fruits are new in consequence. That same Spirit of God who taught us that we were ruined in our old estate, led us gently by the hand till we came to the New Covenant promise and looked to Jesus, and saw in him the full atonement for sin. Happy discovery for us ; it was the kindling of new life in us. From the moment that we trusted in Jesus, a new life darted into our spirit. I am not going to say which is first, the new birth, or faith, or repentance. Nobody can tell which spoke of a wheel moves first ; it moves as a whole. The moment the divine life comes into the heart we believe : the moment we believe the eternal life is there. We repent because we believe, and believe while we repent. The life that we live in the flesh is no longer according to the lusts of the world, but we live by faith in the Son of God, who loved us and gave himself for us. Our spiritual life is a new-born thing, the creation of the Spirit of life. We have, of course, that natural life which is sustained by food, and evidenced by our breath ; but there is another life within which is not seen of men, nor fed by the provisions of earth.

We are conscious of having been quickened, for we were dead once, and we know it; but now we have passed from death into life, and we know it quite as certainly. A new and higher motive sways us now; for we seek not self but God. Another hand grasps the tiller and steers our ship in a new course. New desires are felt to which we were strangers in our former state. New fears are mighty within us,—holy fears which once we should have ridiculed. New hopes are in us, bright and sure, such as we did not even desire to know when we lived a mere carnal life. We are not what we were: we are new, and have begun a new career. We are not what we shall be, but assuredly we are not what we used to be. As for myself, my consciousness of being a new man in Christ Jesus is often as sharp and crisp as my consciousness of being in existence. I know I am not only and solely what I was by my first birth; I feel within myself another life—a second and a higher vitality which has often to contend with my lower self, and by that very contention makes me conscious of its existence. This new principle is, from day to day, gathering strength, and winning the victory. It has its hand upon the throat of the old sinful nature, and it shall eventually trample it like dust beneath its feet. I feel this within me: do not you? [*A loud voice, "Ay! ay!"*] Since you feel this, I know you can say to-night that Jesus Christ, who sits on the throne, makes all things new. Blessed be his name. [*Several voices, "Amen."*] It needed the Lord himself to make such as we are new. None but a Saviour on the throne could accomplish it; and therefore let him have the glory of it.

I believe that Jesus Christ has in some of you not only made you new, but *made everything new to you.* "Ah," said one, when she was converted, "either the world is greatly altered, or else I am." Why, either you and I are turned upside down in nature, or the world is. We used to think it a wise world once, but how foolish we think it now! We used to think it a brave gay world that showed us real happiness, but we are no longer deceived, we have seen Madame Bubble's painted face in its true deformity. "The world is crucified unto me," said Paul; and many of you can say the same. It is like a gibbeted criminal hung up to die. Meanwhile, there is no love lost, for the world thinks much the same of us, and therein we can sympathize with Paul when he said, "I am crucified unto the world." What a transformation grace makes in all things within our little world! In our heart there is a new heaven and a new earth. What a change in our joys! Ah, we blush to think what our joys used to be; but they are heavenly now. We are equally ashamed of our hates and our prejudices: but these have vanished once for all. Why, now we love the very things we once despised, and our heart flies as with wings after that which once it detested. What a different Bible we have now! Blessed book; it is just the same, but oh, how differently do we read it. The mercy-seat, what a different place it is now! Our wretched, formal prayers, if we did offer them—what a mockery they were! But now we draw near to God and speak with our Father with delight. We have access to him by the new and living way. The house of God, how different it is from what it used to be! We love to be found within its walls, and we feel delighted to join in the praises of the Lord. I do not know that I admire brethren for calling out in the service as our friends did just now; but I certainly do not blame them.

A person shook hands with me one day this week who does not often hear me preach, and he expressed to me his unbounded delight in listening to the doctrine of the grace of God, and he added, "Surely your people must be made of stone." "Why?" said I. "Why!" he replied, "if they were not they would all get up and shout 'Hallelujah' when you are preaching such a glorious gospel. I wanted to shout badly on Sunday morning; but as everybody else was quiet, I held my tongue." For which I thought he was a wise man: but yet I do not wonder if men who have tasted of the grace of God, and feel that the Lord has done great things for them, whereof they are glad, do feel like crying out for joy. Let us have a little indulgence to-night. Now, you that feel that you must cry aloud for joy, join with me and cry "Hallelujah." [*A great number of voices cried, "Hallelujah!"*] Hallelujah, glory be to our Redeemer's name. Why should we not lift up our voices in his praise? We will. He has put a new song into our mouths, and we must sing it. The mountains and the hills break forth before us into singing, and we cannot be dumb. Praise is our ever new delight; let us baptize the new year into a sea of it. In praise we will vie with angels and archangels, for they are not so indebted to grace as we are.

> " Never did angels taste above
> Redeeming grace and dying love."

But we have tasted these precious things, and unto God we will lift up our loudest song for ever and for ever.

The process which we have roughly described as taking place in ourselves is in other forms going on in the world. The whole creation is travailing, all time is groaning, providence is working, grace is striving, and all for one end,—the bringing forth of the new and better age. It is coming. It is coming. Not in vain did John write, "And I saw a new heaven and a new earth: for the first heaven and the first earth were passed away; and there was no more sea. And I John saw the holy city, new Jerusalem, coming down from God out of heaven, prepared as a bride adorned for her husband. And I heard a great voice out of heaven saying, Behold, the tabernacle of God is with men, and he will dwell with them, and they shall be his people, and God himself shall be with them, and be their God. And God shall wipe away all tears from their eyes; and there shall be no more death, neither sorrow, nor crying, neither shall there be any more pain: for the former things are passed away. And he that sat upon the throne said, Behold, I make all things new. And he said unto me, Write: for these words are true and faithful." What a prospect does all this open up to the believer! Our future is glorious; let not our present be gloomy.

II. But now, in the text there is AN EARNEST CALL for us to consider this work of our Lord. He that sitteth on the throne saith, "*Behold*, I make all things new." Why should he call upon us to behold it? All his works deserve study: "The works of the Lord are great, sought out of all them that have pleasure therein." Whatsoever the Lord doeth is full of wisdom, and the wise will search into it. But when the Lord himself sets up a light, and calls us to pause, and look, we cannot help beholding.

I think that the Lord Jesus Christ especially calls us to consider this, that we may, according to our condition, derive profit from it.

First, if the Lord Jesus makes all things new, then *a new birth is possible* to you, dear friend, though you have come here to-night in a wrong state of heart, with your sins upon you, binding you fast. There is enough of light in your soul for you to know that you are in darkness; and you are saying to yourself, " Oh, that I could reach to better things ! I hear how these people of God cry ' Hallelujah ! ' at what Christ has done for them. Can he do the same for me ? " Listen ! He that sitteth on the throne says in infinite condescension to you upon the dunghill, " Behold, I make all things new." There is nothing so old that he cannot make it new—nothing so fixed and habitual that he cannot change it. Dost thou not know, dear heart, that the Spirit of God has regenerated men and women quite as far gone as thou art ? They have been as deeply sunken in sin, and as hardened by habit as ever thou canst be, and they thought themselves given up to despair, as thou thinkest thyself to be; yet the Spirit of God carried out the will of the Lord Christ, and made them new. Why should he not make *thee* new ? Let every thief know that the dying thief entered heaven by faith in Jesus. Let every one that has been a great transgressor remember how Manasseh received a new heart, and repented of his evil deeds. Let every one who has left the paths of purity remember how the woman that was a sinner loved much, because much had been forgiven her. I cannot doubt of the possibility of your salvation, my dear friend, whenever I think of my own. A more determined, obstinate rebel than I could scarce have been. Child as I was, and under holy restraint as I was, so as to be kept from gross outward sin, I had a powerful inner nature which would not brook control. I strove hard and kicked against the pricks. I laboured to win heaven by self-righteousness, and this is as real a rebellion as open sin. But, oh, the grace of God, how it can tame us ! How it can turn us ! With no bit or bridle, but with a blessed suavity of tenderness, it turns us according to its pleasure. O anxious one, it can turn you ! I want, then, to drop into your ear—and may the Spirit of God drop into your heart—this word, you may be born again. The Lord can work a radical change in you. He that sitteth on the throne can do for you what you cannot do for yourself; and, as he made you once, and you became marred by sin, he can new make you; for he saith, " Behold, I make all things new."

Furthermore, you will say to me, " I desire to lead *a new life*." To do this you must be new yourself ; for as the man is, so his life will be. If you leave the fountain foul the streams cannot be pure. Renewal must begin with the heart. Dear friend, the Lord Jesus Christ is able to make your life entirely new. We have seen many transformed into new parents and new children. Friends have said in wonder, " What a change in John ! What an alteration in Ellen ! " We have seen men become new husbands, and women become new wives. They are the same persons, and yet not the same. Grace works a very deep, striking, and lasting change. Ask those that have had to live with converted people whether the transformation has not been marvellous. Christ makes new servants, new masters, new friends, new brothers, new sisters. The Lord can so change us that we shall scarcely know ourselves : I mean he can thus change you who now despair of yourselves. O dear hearts, there is no absolute necessity that you should always go downward in evil till you descend to hell. There is a hand that can give you a gravitation in the opposite direction. It would be a wonderful thing if Niagara when it is in its full descent should be made to leap upwards, and the St. Lawrence and the sea should begin to climb backward to the lakes. Yet God could do even that; and so he can reverse the course of your fallen nature, and make you act as a new man. He can stay the tide of your raging passion; he can make you, who were like a devil, become as an angel of God; for thus he speaks from the throne of his eternal majesty, "Behold, I make all things new." Come and lay yourself down at his feet, and ask him to make you new. I beseech you, do this at once!

"Well, I am going to mend myself," says one : "I have taken the pledge, and I am going to be honest, and chaste, and religious." This is commendable resolving, but what will come of it? You will break your resolutions, and be nothing bettered by your attempts at reform. I expect that if you go into the business of mending yourself, you will be like the man who had an old gun, and took it to the gunsmith, and the gunsmith said, "Well, this would make a very good gun if it had a new stock, and a new lock, and a new barrel." So you would make a very good man by mending, if you had a new heart, and new life, and were made new all over, so that there was not a bit of the old stuff left. It will be easier, a great deal, depend upon it, even for God to make you new, than to mend you; for the fact is that "the carnal mind is enmity against God," and is not reconciled to God, neither, indeed, can be ; so that mending will not answer; you must be made anew. "Ye must be born again." What is wanted is that you should be made a new creature in Christ Jesus. You must be dead and buried with Christ, and risen again in him; and then all will be well, for he will have made all things new. I pray God to bless these feeble words of mine for the helping of some of his chosen out of the darkness of their fears.

But now, beloved, farther than this. There are children of God who need this text, "Behold, I make all things new," whose sigh is that they so soon grow dull and weary in the ways of God, and therefore they need *daily renewing.* A brother said to me some time ago, "Dear sir, I frequently grow very sleepy in my walk with God. I seem to lose the freshness of it ; and especially by about Saturday I get I hardly know where; but," he added, "as for you, whenever I hear you, you seem to be all alive and full of fresh energy." "Ah, my dear brother," I said, "that is because you do not know much about me." That was all I was able to say just then. I thank God for keeping me near himself; but I am as weak, and stale, and unprofitable as any of you. I say this with very great shame—shame for myself, and shame for the brother who led me to make the confession. We are both wrong. With all our fresh springs in God, we ought to be always full of new life. Our love to Christ ought to be every minute as if it were new-born. Our zeal for God ought to be as fresh as if we had just begun to delight in him. "Ay, but it is not," says one ; and I am sorry I cannot contradict him. After a few months a vigorous young Christian will begin to cool down ; and those who have been long in the ways of God find that final perseverance must be a miracle if ever it is to be accomplished, for naturally they tire and faint.

Well, now, dear friends, why do you and I ever get stale and flat ? Why do we sing,

> " Dear Lord, and shall we ever live
> At this poor dying rate ? "

Why do we have to cry—

> "In vain we tune our formal songs,
> In vain we strive to rise;
> Hosannas languish on our tongues,
> And our devotion dies " ?

Why, it is because we get away from him who says, " Behold, I make all things new." The straight way to a perpetual newness and freshness of holy youth is to go to Christ again, just as we did at the first.

A better thing still is never to leave him, but to stand for ever at the cross-foot delighting yourself in his all-sufficient sacrifice. They that are full of the joy of the Lord never find life grow weary. They that walk in the light of his countenance can say of the Lord Jesus, " Thou hast the dew of thy youth " ; and that dew falls upon those who dwell with him. Oh, I am sure that if we kept up perpetual communion with him, we should keep up a perpetual stream of delights.

> " Immortal joys come streaming down,
> Joys, like his griefs, immense, unknown ; "

but these joys only come from him. We shall be young if we keep with the ever young and fresh Beloved, whose locks are bushy and black as a raven. He saith, and he performs the saying, " Behold, I make all things new."

He can make that next sermon of yours, my dear brother minister, quite new and interesting. He can make that prayer-meeting no longer a dreary affair, but quite a new thing to you and all the people. My dear sister, next time you go to your class, you may feel as if you had only just begun teaching. You will not be at all tired of your godly work, but love it better than ever. And you, my dear brother, at the corner of the street where you are often interrupted, perhaps, with foul language, you will feel that you are pleased with your position of self-denial. Getting near to Christ, you will partake in his joy, and that joy shall be your strength, your freshness, the newness of your life. God grant us to drink of the eternal founts, that we may for ever overflow.

And, further, dear friends, there may be some dear child of God here who is conscious that he lives on a very low platform of spiritual life, and he knows that the Lord can raise him to *a new condition*. Numbers of Christians seem to live in the marshes always. If you go through the valleys of Switzerland, you will find yourself get feverish and heavy in spirit, and you will see many idiots, persons with the goitre, and people greatly afflicted. Climb the sides of the hills, ascend into the Alps, and you will not meet with that kind of thing in the pure fresh air. Many Christians are of the sickly-valley breed. Oh that they could get up to the high mountains, and be strong !

I want to say to such, if you have been all your lifetime in bondage, you need not remain there any longer; for there is in Jesus the power to make all things new, and to lift you into new delights. It will seem to be a dead lift to you; but it is within the power of that pierced hand to lift you right out of doubt, and fear, and despondency, and spiritual lethargy, and weakness, and just to make you now, from this day forward, "strong in the Lord, and in the power of his might."

Now breathe a silent prayer, dear brother, dear sister, to him who makes all things new. "Lord, make thy poor, spiritually sick child to be strong in spiritual health." Oh, what a blessing it would be for some workers if God would make them strong! All the church would be the better because of the way in which the Lord would help them to do their work. Why should some of you be living at a penny a day and starving yourselves, when your Father would give you to live like princes of the blood royal if you would but trust him? I am persuaded that the most of us are beggars when we might be millionaires in spiritual things. And here is our strength for rising to a nobler state of mind, "Behold I make all things new."

Another application of this truth will be this:—"Oh," says one, "I do not know what to make of myself. I have had a weary time of late. Everything seems to have gone wrong with me. My family cause me great anxiety. My business is a thorny maze. My own health is precarious. I dread this year. In fact, I dread everything." We will not go on with that lamentation, but we will hear the cheering word,— "Behold, I make all things new." The Lord, in answer to believing prayer, and especially in answer to a full resignation to his will, is able to make *all providential surroundings new for you.* I have known the Lord on a sudden to turn darkness into light, and take away the sackcloth and the ashes from his dear children, for "he doth not afflict willingly, nor grieve the children of men." Sometimes all this worry is mere discontent; and when the child of God gets right himself, these imaginary troubles vanish like the mist of the morning; but when they are real troubles, God can as easily change your condition, dear child of God, as he can turn his hand. He can make your harsh and ungodly husband to become gentle and gracious. He can bring your children to bow at the family altar, and to rejoice with you in Christ. He can cause your business to prosper; or, if he does not do that, he can strengthen your back to bear the burden of your daily cross. Oh, it is wonderful how different a thing becomes when it is taken to God. But you want to make it all new yourself; and you fret and you worry, and you tease, and you trouble, and you make a burden of yourself. Why not leave that off, and in humble prayer take the matter to the Lord, and say, "Lord, appear for me, for thou hast said, 'I make all things new.' Make my circumstances new"? He is certainly able to turn your captivity as he turns the sun when it has reached the southern tropic.

Come, there is one more application, and that is that *the Lord can convert those dear friends about whose souls you have been so anxious.* The Lord who makes all things new can hear your prayers. One of the first prayers that I heard to-night in the prayer-meeting was by a dear brother that God would save his relatives. Then another with great tenderness prayed for his children. I knew it came from an aching heart.

Some of you have heart-breakers at home: the Lord break *their* hearts. You have grievous trouble because you hear the dearest that you have blaspheming the God you love. You know that they are Sabbath-breakers, and utterly godless, and you tremble for their eternal fate. Certain persons attend this Tabernacle—I do not see them to-night—but I can say of them that I never enter this pulpit without looking to their pews to see whether they are there, and breathing my heart to God for them. I forget a great many of you who are saved; but I always pray for *them*. And they will be brought in, I feel assured; but, oh, that it may be this year! I liked what a brother said at the church-meeting on Monday night, when his brother was introduced to the church. (Ah, there he sits.) I asked about his brother's conversion, and I said, " I suppose you were surprised to see him converted." He said, " I should have been very much surprised if he had not been." " But why, my dear brother?" I said. " Because I asked the Lord to convert him, and I kept on praying that he might be converted; and I should have been very much surprised if he had not been." That is the right sort of faith. I should be very much surprised if some of you that come here, time after time, are not converted. You shall be : blessed be God. We will give him no rest until he hears us. But come! Are we to be praying for you, and you not praying for yourselves? Do you not agree with our prayers? Oh, I trust you may. But, even if you do not, we shall pray for you ; and if we were sure that you opposed our intercessions, and were even angry with them, we should pray all the more, for we mean to have you won for Jesus, by the grace of God, and you may as well come soon as late. We are bound to have you in the church confessing your faith in Jesus. We will never let you go, neither will we cease from our importunate prayers until we get an answer from the throne, and see you saved. Oh that you would yield on this first night of the year to him who can make new creatures of you. God grant you may !

The Lord answer our prayer now, for Jesus' sake, for we seek the salvation of every hearer and every reader of this sermon. Amen.

Our Own Dear Shepherd

"I am the good Shepherd, and know my *sheep*, and am known of mine. As the Father knoweth me, even so know I the Father: and I lay down my life for the sheep."—John x. 14, 15.

As the passage stands in the Authorized Version, it reads like a number of short sentences with scarcely any apparent connection. Even in that form it is precious; for our Lord's pearls are priceless even when they are not threaded together. But when I tell you that in the Greek the word "and" is several times repeated, and that the translators have had to leave out one of these "ands" to make sense of the passage on their line of translation, you will judge that they are none too accurate in this case. To use many "ands" is after the manner of John; but there is usually a true and natural connection between his sentences. The "and" with him is usually a real golden link, and not a mere sound; we need a translation which makes it so. Observe also that in our Version the word "sheep" is put in italics, to show that it is not in the original. There is no need for this alteration if the passage is more closely rendered. Hear, then, the text in its natural form—

"*I am the good Shepherd; and I know mine own, and mine own know me, even as the Father knoweth me, and I know the Father; and I lay down my life for the sheep.*"

This reading I have given you is that of the Revised Version. For that Revised Version I have but little care as a general rule, holding it to be by no means an improvement upon our common Authorized Version. It is a useful thing to have it for private reference, but I trust it will never be regarded as the standard English translation of the New Testament. The Revised Version of the Old Testament is so excellent, that I am half afraid it may carry the Revised New Testament upon its shoulders into general use. I sincerely hope that this may not be the case, for the result would be a decided loss. However, that is not my point. Returning to our subject, I believe that, on this occasion, the Revised Version is true to the original. We will therefore follow it in this instance, and we shall find that it makes most delightful and instructive sense. " I am the good Shepherd; and I know mine own, and mine own know me, even as the Father knoweth me, and I know the Father; and I lay down my life for the sheep."

He who speaks to us in these words is the Lord Jesus Christ. To our mind every word of Holy Scripture is precious. When God speaks to us by priest or prophet, or in any way, we are glad to hear. Though when, in the Old Testament, we meet with a passage which begins with " Thus saith the Lord " we feel specially charmed to have the message directly from God's own mouth, yet we make no distinction between this Scripture and that. We accept it all as inspired; and we are not given to dispute about different degrees and varying modes of inspiration, and all that. The matter is plain enough if learned unbelievers did not mystify it; "all Scripture is given by inspiration of God, and is profitable for doctrine, for reproof, for correction, for instruction in righteousness " (2 Tim. iii. 16). Still, there is to our mind a peculiar sweetness about words which were actually spoken by the Lord Jesus Christ himself: these are as honey in the comb. You have before you, in this text, not that which comes to you by prophet, priest, or king, but that which is spoken to you by one who is Prophet, Priest, and King in one, even your Lord Jesus Christ. He opens his mouth, and speaks to you. You will open your ear, and listen to him, if you be indeed his own.

Observe here, also, that we have not only Christ for the speaker, but we have Christ for the subject. He speaks, and speaks about himself. It were not seemly for you, or for me, to extol ourselves; but there is nothing more comely in the world than for Christ to commend himself. He is other than we are, something infinitely above us, and is not under rules which apply to us fallible mortals. When he speaketh forth his own glory, we feel that his speech is not vain-glory ; nay, rather, when he praises himself, we thank him for so doing, and admire the lowly condescension which permits him to desire and accept honour from such poor hearts as ours. It were pride for us to seek honour of men ; it is humility in him to do so, seeing he is so great an One that the esteem of beings so inferior as we are cannot be desired by him for his own sake. Of all our Lord's words, those are the sweetest in which he speaks about himself. Even he cannot find another theme which can excel that of himself.

My brethren, who can speak of Jesus but himself ? He masters all our eloquence. His perfection exceeds our understanding ; the light of his excellence is too bright for us, it blinds our eyes. Our Beloved must be his own mirror. None but Jesus can reveal Jesus. Only he can see himself, and know himself, and understand himself ; and therefore none but he can reveal himself. We are most glad that in his tenderness to us he sets himself forth by many choice metaphors, and instructive emblems, by which he would make us know some little of that love which passeth knowledge. With his own hand he fills a golden cup out of the river of his own infinity, and hands it to us that we may drink and be refreshed. Take, then, these words as being doubly refreshing, because they come directly from the Well-beloved's own mouth, and contain rich revelations of his own all-glorious self. I feel that I must read them again;—" I am the good Shepherd; and I know mine own, and mine own know me, even as the Father knoweth me, and I know the Father; and I lay down my life for the sheep."

In this text there are three matters about which I shall speak. First, I see here *complete character.* " I am the good Shepherd." He is not a half shepherd, but a shepherd in the fullest possible sense. Secondly, I see *complete knowledge,* " and I know mine own, and mine own know me, even as the Father knoweth me, and I know the Father." Thirdly, here is *complete sacrifice.* How preciously that sentence winds up the whole, " and I lay down my life for the sheep" ! He goes the full length to which sacrifice can go. He lays down his soul in the stead of his sheep ; so the words might be not incorrectly translated. He goes the full length of self-sacrifice for his own.

I. First, then, here is COMPLETE CHARACTER. Whenever the Saviour describes himself by any emblem, that emblem is exalted, and expanded; and yet it is not able to bear all his meaning. The Lord Jesus fills out every type, figure, and character ; and when the vessel is filled there is an overflow. There is more in Jesus, the good Shepherd, than you can pack away in a shepherd. He is the good, the great, the chief Shepherd ; but he is much more. Emblems to set him forth may be multiplied as the drops of the morning, but the whole multitude will fail to reflect all his brightness. Creation is too small a frame in which to hang his likeness. Human thought is too contracted, human speech too feeble, to set him forth to the full. When all the emblems in earth and heaven shall have described him to their utmost, there will remain a somewhat not yet described. You may square the circle ere you can set forth Christ in the language of mortal men. He is inconceivably above our conceptions, unutterably above our utterances.

But notice that he here sets himself forth as a shepherd. Dwell on this for a moment. A shepherd is hardly such a man as we employ in England to look after sheep for a few months, till they are large enough to be slaughtered ; a shepherd after the Oriental sort, such as Abraham, Jacob, or David, is quite another person.

The Eastern shepherd is generally *the owner* of the flock, or at least the son of their owner, and so their proprietor in prospect. The sheep are his own. English shepherds seldom, or never, own the sheep : they are employed to take care of them, and they have no other interest in them. Our native shepherds are a very excellent set of men as a rule —those I have known have been admirable specimens of intelligent working-men—yet they are not at all like the Oriental shepherd, and cannot be ; for he is usually the owner of the flock which he tends. He remembers how he came into possession of the flock, and when and where each of the present sheep was born, and where he has led them, and what trials he had in connection with them ; and he remembers this with the emphasis that they are his own inheritance.

His wealth consists in them. He very seldom has much of a house, and he does not usually own much land. He takes his sheep over a good stretch of country, which is open common for all his tribe ; but his possessions lie in his flocks. Ask him, " How much are you worth ?"

He answers, " I own so many sheep." In the Latin tongue the word for money is akin to the word " sheep," because, to many of the first Romans, wool was their wealth, and their fortunes lay in their flocks. The Lord Jesus is our Shepherd: we are his wealth. If you ask what is his heritage, he tells you 'of " the riches of the glory of his inheritance in the saints." Ask him what are his jewels, and he replies, " *They* shall be mine in that day." If you ask him where his treasures are, he will tell you, " The Lord's portion is his people. Jacob is the lot of his inheritance." The Lord Jesus Christ has nothing that he values as he does his own people. For their sakes he gave up all that he had, and died naked on the cross. Not only can he say, " I gave Ethiopia and Seba for thee," but he " loved his church, and gave himself for it." He regards his church as being his own body, " the fulness of him that filleth all in all."

The shepherd, as he owns the flock, is also *the caretaker*. He takes care of them always. One of our brethren now present is a fireman ; and, as he lives at the fire-station, he is always on duty. I asked him whether he was not off duty during certain hours of every day ; but he said, " No ; I am never off duty." He is on duty when he goes to bed, he is on duty while he is eating his breakfast, he is on duty if he walks down the street. Any time the bell may ring the alarm, and he must be in his place, and hasten to the fire. Our Lord Jesus Christ is never off duty. He has constant care of his people day and night. He has declared it,—" For Zion's sake will I not hold my peace, and for Jerusalem's sake I will not rest." He can truly say what Jacob did. " In the day the drought consumed me, and the frost by night." He says of his flock what he says of his garden, " I the Lord do keep it ; I will water it every moment: lest any hurt it, I will keep it night and day." I cannot tell you all the care a shepherd has over his flock, because his anxieties are of such a various kind. Sheep have about as many complaints as men. You do not know much about them, and I am not going to enter into details, for the all-sufficient reason that I do not know much about them myself ; but the shepherd knows, and the shepherd will tell you that he leads an anxious life. He seldom has all the flock well at one time. Some one or other is sure to be ailing, and he spies it out, and has eye and hand and heart ready for its succour and relief. There are many varieties of complaints and needs, and all these are laid upon the shepherd's heart. He is both possessor and care-taker of the flock.

Then he has to be *the provider* too, for there is not a woolly head among them that knows anything about the finding and selecting of pasturage. The season may be very dry, and where there once was grass there may be nothing but a brown powder. It may be that herbage is only to be found by the side of the rippling brooks, here and there a bit ; but the sheep do not know anything about *that ;* the shepherd must know everything for them. The shepherd is the sheep's providence. Both for time and for eternity, for body and for soul, our Lord Jesus supplies all our need out of his riches in glory. He is the great storehouse from which we derive everything. He has provided, he does provide, and he will provide ; and each one of us may therefore sing, " The Lord is my Shepherd ; I shall not want."

But, dear friends, we often dream that we are the shepherds, or that we, at any rate, have to find some of the pasture. I could not help saying just now to our friends at our little prayer-meeting, " There is a passage in the Psalms which makes the Lord do for us what one would have thought we could have done for ourselves—' He maketh me to lie down in green pastures.' " Surely, if a sheep can do nothing else it can lie down. Yet to lie down is the very hardest thing for God's sheep to do. It is here that the full power of the rest-giving Christ has to come in to make our fretful, worrying, doubtful natures lie down and rest. Our Lord is able to give us perfect peace, and he will do so if we will simply trust to his abounding care. It is the shepherd's business to be the provider; let us remember this, and be very happy.

Moreover, he has to be *the leader*. He leads the sheep wherever they have to go. I have often been astonished at the shepherds in the South of France, which is so much like Palestine, to see where they will take their sheep. Once every week I saw the shepherd come down to Mentone, and conduct all his flock to the sea-beach. I could see nothing for them but big stones. Folk say that perhaps this is what makes the mutton so hard; but I have no doubt the poor creatures get a little taste of salt, or something which does them good. At any rate, they follow the shepherd, and away he goes up the steep hillsides, taking long steps, till he reaches points where the grass is growing on the sides of the hills. He knows the way, and the sheep have nothing to do but to follow him wherever he goes. Theirs not to make the way; theirs not to choose the path; but theirs to keep close to his heel.

Do you not see our blessed Shepherd leading your own pilgrimage? Cannot you see him guiding your way? Do you not say, " Yes, he leadeth me, and it is my joy to follow"? Lead on, O blessed Lord; lead on, and we will follow the traces of thy feet!

The shepherd in the East has also to be *the defender* of the flock, for wolves yet prowl in those regions. All sorts of wild beasts attack the flock, and he must be to the front. Thus is it with our Shepherd. No wolf can attack us without finding our Lord in arms against him. No lion can roar upon the flock without arousing a greater than David. " He that keepeth Israel shall neither slumber nor sleep."

He is a shepherd, then, and he completely fills the character—much more completely than I can show you just now.

Notice that the text puts an adjective upon the shepherd, decorating him with a chain of gold. The Lord Jesus Christ himself says, " I am the *good* Shepherd." " The *good* Shepherd "—that is, he is not a thief that steals, and only deals with the sheep as he bears them from the fold to the slaughter. He is not a hireling: he does not do merely what he is paid to do, or commanded to do, but he does everything *con amore*, with a willing heart. He throws his soul into it. There is a goodness, a tenderness, a willingness, a powerfulness, a force, an energy in all that Jesus does that makes him to be the best possible Shepherd that can be. He is no hireling; neither is he an idler. Even shepherds that have had their own flocks have neglected them, as there are farmers who do not well cultivate their own farms; but it is never so with Christ. He is the good Shepherd: good up to the highest point of goodness, good in all that is tender, good in all that is kind, good in all the directions in which a shepherd can be needed; good at fight, and good at rule; good in watchful oversight, and good in prudent leadership; good every way most eminently.

And then notice he puts it, "I am *the* good Shepherd." That is the point I want to bring out. Of other shepherds we can say, he is *a* shepherd; but this is *the* Shepherd. All others in the world are shadows of the true Shepherd; and Jesus is the substance of them all. That which we see in the world with these eyes is after all not the substance, but the type, the shadow. That which we do not see with our eyes, that which only our faith perceives, is after all the real thing. I have seen shepherds; but they were only pictures to me. *The* Shepherd, the real, the truest, the best, the most sure example of shepherdry is the Christ himself; and you and I are the sheep. Those sheep we see on yonder mountain-side are just types of ourselves: but we are the true sheep, and Jesus is the true Shepherd. If an angel were to fly over the earth to find out the real sheep, and the real Shepherd, he would say, "The sheep of God's pasture are men; and Jehovah is their Shepherd. He is the true, the real Shepherd of the true and real sheep." All the possibilities that lie in a shepherd are found in Christ. Every good thing that you can imagine to be, or that should be, in a shepherd, you find in the Lord Jesus Christ.

Now, I want you to notice that, according to the text, the Lord Jesus Christ greatly rejoices in this. He says, "I am the good Shepherd." He does not confess that fact as if he were ashamed of it, but he repeats it in this chapter so many times that it almost reads like the refrain of a song. "I am the good Shepherd": he evidently rejoices in it. He rolls it under his tongue as a sweet morsel. Evidently it is to his heart's content. He does not say, "I am the Son of God, I am the Son of man, I am the Redeemer"; but this he does say, and he congratulates himself upon it: "I am the good Shepherd."

This should encourage you and me to get a full hold of the word. If Jesus is so pleased to be my Shepherd, let me be equally pleased to be his sheep; and let me avail myself of all the privileges that are wrapped up in his being my Shepherd, and in my being his sheep. I see that it will not worry him for me to be his sheep. I see that my needs will cause him no perplexity. I see that he will not be going out of his way to attend to my weakness and trouble. He delights to dwell on the fact, "I am the good Shepherd." He invites me, as it were, to come and bring my wants and woes to him, and then look up to him, and be fed by him. Therefore I will do it.

Does it not make you feel truly happy to hear your own Lord say himself, and say it to you out of this precious Book, "I am the good Shepherd"? Do you not reply, "Indeed thou art a good Shepherd. Thou art a good Shepherd to me. My heart lays emphasis upon the word 'good,' and says of thee, 'there is none good but One, but thou art that good One.' Thou art the good Shepherd of the sheep"?

So much, then, concerning the complete character.

II. May the Holy Spirit bless the word still more, while I speak in my broken way upon the next point: THE COMPLETE KNOWLEDGE.

The knowledge of Christ towards his sheep, and of the sheep towards him, is wonderfully complete. I must read the text again—"I know mine own, and mine own know me, even as the Father knoweth me, and I know the Father."

First, then, consider *Christ's knowledge of his own, and the comparison by which he sets it forth:* " As the Father knows me." I cannot conceive a stronger comparison. Dost thou know how much the Father knows the Son, who is his glory, his darling, his *alter ego,* his other self—yea, one God with him? Dost thou know how intimate the knowledge of the Father must be of his Son, who is his own wisdom, ay, who is his own self? The Father and the Son are one spirit. We cannot tell how intimate is that knowledge ; and yet so intimately, so perfectly, does the great Shepherd know his sheep.

He knows their *number.* He will never lose one. He will count them all again in that day when the sheep shall pass again under the hand of him that telleth them, and then he will make full tale of them. " Of all that thou hast given me," says he, " I have lost none." He knows the number of those for whom he paid the ransom-price.

He knows their *persons.* He knows the age and character of every one of his own. He assures us that the very hairs of our head are all numbered. Christ has not an unknown sheep. It is not possible that he should have overlooked or forgotten one of them. He has such an intimate knowledge of all who are redeemed with his most precious blood that he never mistakes one of them for another, nor misjudges one of them. He knows their constitutions,—those that are weak and feeble, those that are nervous and frightened, those that are strong, those that have a tendency to presumption, those that are sleepy, those that are brave, those that are sick, sorry, worried, or wounded. He knows those that are hunted by the devil, those that are caught up between the jaws of the lion, and shaken till the very life is almost driven out of them. He knows their feelings, fears, and frights. He knows the secret ins and outs of every one of us better than any one of us knows himself.

He knows our *trials,*—the particular trial under which you are now bowed down, my sister ; our difficulties,—that special difficulty which seems to block up your way, my brother, at this very time. All the ingredients of our life-cup are known to him. " I know mine own, as the Father knoweth me." It is impossible to conceive a completer knowledge than that which the Father has of his only-begotten Son ; and it is equally impossible to conceive a completer knowledge than that which Jesus Christ has of every one of his chosen.

He knows our *sins.* I often feel glad to think that he always did know our evil natures, and what would come of them. When he chose us, he knew what we were, and what we should be. He did not buy his sheep in the dark. He did not choose us without knowing all the devious ways of our past and future lives.

> " He saw us ruined in the fall,
> Yet loved us notwithstanding all."

Herein lieth the splendour of his grace. " Whom he did foreknow, he also did predestinate." His election implies foreknowledge of all our ill manners. They say of human love that it is blind ; but Christ's love has many eyes, and all its eyes are open, and yet he loves us still.

I need not enlarge upon this. It ought, however, to be very full of comfort to you that you are so known of your Lord, especially as he knows you not merely with the cold, clear knowledge of the intellect, but with the knowledge of love and of affection. He knows you in his heart. You are peculiarly dear to him. You are approved of him. You are accepted of him. He knows you by acquaintance with you ; not by hearsay. He knows you by communion with you ; he has been with you in sweet fellowship. He has read you as a man reads his book, and remembers what he reads. He knows you by sympathy with you : he is a man like yourself.

> " He knows what sore temptations mean,
> For he has felt the same."

He knows your weaknesses. He knows the points wherein you suffer most, for

> " In every pang that rends the heart
> The Man of sorrows had a part."

He gained this knowledge in the school of sympathetic suffering. " Though he were a Son, yet learned he obedience by the things which he suffered." " He was in all points made like unto his brethren ; " and by being made like to us he has come to know us, and he does know us in a very practical and tender way. You have a watch, and it will not go, or it goes very irregularly, and you give it into the hands of one who knows nothing about watches ; and he says, " I will clean it for you." He will do it more harm than good. But here is the very person who made the watch. He says, " I put every wheel into its place ; I made the whole of it, from beginning to end." You think to yourself, " I feel the utmost confidence in trusting that man with my watch ; he can surely put it right, for he made it." It often cheers my heart to think that since the Lord made me he can put me right, and keep me so to the end. My Maker is my Redeemer. He that first made me has made me again, and will make me perfect, to his own praise and glory. That is the first part of this complete knowledge.

The second part of the subject is *our knowledge of the Lord, and the fact by which it is illustrated.* "And mine own know me, even as I know the Father." I think I hear some of you say, " I do not see so much in that. I can see a great deal more in Christ's knowing us." Beloved, I see a great deal in our knowing Christ. That he should know me is great condescension, but it must be easy to him to know me. Being so divine, with such a piercing eye as his, it is amazingly condescending, as I say, but it is not difficult for him to know me. The marvel is that I should ever know him. That such a stupid, blind, deaf, dead soul as mine should ever know him, and should know him as he knows the Father, is ten thousand miracles in one. Oh, sirs, this is a wonder so great that I do not think you and I have come at it yet to the full, or else we should sit down in glad surprise, and say,—This proves him to be the good Shepherd indeed, not only that he knows his flock, but that he has taught them so well that they know him ! With such a flock as Christ has, that he should be able to train his sheep so that they should be able to know him, and to know him as he knows the Father, is miraculous.

O beloved, if this be true of us, that we know our Shepherd, we may clap our hands for very joy! And yet I think it is true even now. At any rate, I know so much of my Lord that nothing gives me so much joy as to hear of him. Brethren, there is no boasting in this personal assertion of mine. It is only the bare truth. You can say the same; can you not? If anybody were to preach to you the finest sermon that was ever delivered, would it charm you if there was no Christ in it? No. But you will come and hear me talk about Jesus Christ in words as simple as ever I can find, and you cry one to another, "It was good to be there."

> "Thou dear Redeemer, dying Lamb,
>   We love to hear of thee :
> No music's like thy charming name,
>   Nor half so sweet can be."

Now mark that this is the way in which Jesus knows the Father. Jesus delights in his Father, and you delight in Jesus. I know you do; and herein the comparison holds good.

Moreover, does not the dear name of Jesus stir your very soul? What is it that makes you feel as if you wish to hasten away, that you might be doing holy service for the Lord? What makes your very heart awake, and feel ready to leap out of your body? What but hearing of the glories of Jesus? Play on what string you please, and my ear is deaf to it; but when you once begin to tell of Calvary, and sing the song of free grace, and dying love, oh, then my soul opens all her ears, and drinks in the music, and then her blood begins to stir, and she is ready to shout for joy! Do you not even now sing—

> "Oh, for this love let rocks and hills
>   Their lasting silence break,
> And all harmonious human tongues
>   The Saviour's praises speak.

> "Yes, we will praise thee, dearest Lord,
>   Our souls are all on flame,
> Hosanna round the spacious earth
>   To thine adorèd name?"

Yes, we know Jesus. We feel the power of our union with him. We know him, brethren, so that we are not to be deceived by false shepherds. There is a way nowadays of preaching Christ against Christ. It is a new device of the devil to set up Jesus against Jesus, his kingdom against his atonement, his precepts against his doctrines. The half Christ in his example is put up, to frighten souls away from the whole Christ, who saves the souls of men from guilt as well as from sin, from hell as well as from folly. But they cannot deceive us in that way. No, beloved, we know our Shepherd from all others. We know him from a statue covered with his clothes. We know the living Christ, for we have come into living contact with him, and we cannot be deceived any more than Jesus Christ himself can be deceived about the Father. "Mine own know me, even as I know the Father." We know him by union with him, and by communion with him. "We have seen the Lord." "Truly our fellowship is with the Father, and with his Son Jesus Christ."

We know him by love: our soul cleaves to him, even as the heart of Christ cleaves to the Father. We know him by trusting him—"He is all my salvation, and all my desire." I remember once feeling many questions as to whether I was a child of God or not. I went into a little chapel, and I heard a good man preach. He was a simple working-man. I heard him preach, and I made my handkerchief sodden with my tears as I heard him talk about Christ, and the precious blood. When I was preaching the same things to others I was wondering whether this truth was mine, but while I was hearing for myself I knew it was mine, for my very soul lived upon it. I went to that good man, and thanked him for the sermon. He asked me who I was. When I told him, he turned all manner of colours. "Why," he said, "Sir, that was your own sermon." I said, "Yes, I knew it was, and it was good of the Lord to feed me with food that I had prepared for others." I perceived that I had a true taste for what I myself knew to be the gospel of Jesus Christ. Oh, yes, we do love our good Shepherd! We cannot help it.

And we know him also by a deep sympathy with him ; for what Christ desires to do, we also long to do. He loves to save souls, and so do we. Would we not save all the people in a whole street if we could? Ay, in a whole city, and in the whole world! Nothing makes us so glad as that Jesus Christ is a Saviour. "There is news in the paper," says one. That news is often of small importance to our hearts. I happened to hear that a poor servant girl had heard me preach the truth, and found Christ; and I confess I felt more interest in that fact than in all the rise and fall of Whigs or Tories. What does it matter who is in Parliament, so long as souls are saved? That is the main thing. If the kingdom of Christ grows, all the other kingdoms are of small account. That is the one kingdom for which we live, and for which we would gladly die. As there is a boundless sympathy between the Father and the Son, so is there between Jesus and ourselves.

We know Christ as he knows the Father, because we are one with him. The union between Christ and his people is as real and as mysterious as the union between the Son and the Father.

We have a beautiful picture before us. Can you realize it for a minute ? The Lord Jesus here among us—picture him! He is the Shepherd. Then, around him are his own people, and wherever he goes they go. He leads them into green pastures, and beside the still waters. And there is this peculiarity about them: he knows them as he looks upon every one of them, and they every one of them know him. There is a deeply intimate and mutual knowledge between them. As surely as he knows them, they know him. The world knows neither the Shepherd nor the sheep, but they know each other. As surely as truly, and as deeply, as God the Father knows the Son, so does this Shepherd know his sheep ; and as God the Son knows his Father, so do these sheep know their Shepherd. Thus in one band, united by mutual intercourse, they travel through the world to heaven. "I know mine own, and mine own know me, even as the Father knoweth me, and I know the Father." Is not that a blessed picture ? God help us to figure in it !

III. The last subject is COMPLETE SACRIFICE. The complete sacrifice is thus described,—"*I lay down my life for the sheep.*"

These words are repeated in this chapter in different forms some four times. The Saviour keeps on saying, " I lay down my life for the sheep." Read the eleventh verse: " The good Shepherd giveth his life for the sheep." The fifteenth verse: "I lay down my life for the sheep." The seventeenth verse: " I lay down my life, that I may take it again." The eighteenth verse: " I have power to lay it down, and I have power to take it again." It looks as if this was another refrain of our Lord's personal hymn. I call this passage his pastoral song. The good Shepherd with his pipe sings to himself and to his flock, and this comes in at the end of each stanza, " I lay down my life for the sheep."

Did it not mean, first, that he was always doing so ? All his life long he was, as it were, laying it down for them ; he was divesting himself of the garments of life, till he came to be fully disrobed on the cross. All the life he had, all the power he had, he was always laying it out for his sheep. It means that, to begin with.

And then it means that the sacrifice was actively performed. It was ever in the doing as long as he lived ; but he did it actively. He did not die for the sheep merely, but he laid down his life, which is another thing. Many a man has died for Christ : it was all that he could do. But we cannot lay down our lives, because they are due already as a debt of nature to God, and we are not permitted to die at our own wills. That were suicidal and improper. With the Lord Christ it was totally different. He was, as it were, actively passive. " I lay down my life for the sheep. I have power to lay it down, and I have power to take it again. This commandment have I received of my Father."

I like to think of our good Shepherd, not merely as dying for us, but as willingly dying—laying down his life : while he had that life, using it for us ; and when the time came, putting off that life on our behalf. This has now been actually done. When he spoke these words, it had not been done. At this time it has been done. " I lay down my life for the sheep " may now be read, " I have laid down my life for the sheep." For you, beloved, he has given his hands to the nails, and his feet to the cruel iron. For you he has borne the fever and the bloody sweat ; for you he has cried " Eloi, Eloi, lama sabachthani ;" for you he has given up the ghost.

And the beauty of it is that he is not ashamed to avow the object of it. " I lay down my life *for the sheep.*" Whatever Christ did for the world—and I am not one of those who would limit the bearings of the death of Christ upon the world—yet his peculiar glory is, " I lay down my life *for the sheep.*

Great Shepherd, do you mean to say that you have died for such as these ? What ! for these sheep ? Died for them ? What ! die for sheep, Shepherd ? Surely you have other objects for which to live beside sheep. Have you not other loves, other joys ? We know that it would grieve you to see the sheep killed, torn by the wolf, or scattered ; but you really have not gone so far in love for them that for the sake of those poor creatures you would lay down your life ? " Ah, yes," he says, " I would, I have ! " Carry your wondering thoughts to Christ Jesus. What ! What ! What ! Son of God, infinitely great and inconceivably glorious Jehovah, wouldst thou lay thy life down for men and women ? They are no more in comparison with thee than so many ants and wasps, pitiful and obnoxious creatures. Thou couldst make ten thousand millions of them with a word, or crush them out of existence at one blow of thy hand. They are poor things, make the most you can of them. They have hard hearts, and wandering wills; and the best of them are no better than they should be. Saviour, didst thou die for such? He looks round, and says, "Yes, I did. I did. I laid down my life for the sheep. I am not ashamed of them, and I am not ashamed to say that I died for them." No, beloved, he is not ashamed of his dying love. He has told it to his brethren up yonder, and made it known to all the servants in his Father's house, and this has become the song of that house, "Worthy is the Lamb that was slain!" Shall not we take it up, and say, "For thou wast slain, and hast redeemed us to God by thy blood"? Whatever men may talk about particular redemption, Christ is not ashamed of it. He glories that he laid down his life for the sheep. *For the sheep,* mark you. He says not for the world. There is a bearing of the death of Christ towards the world; but here he boasts, and glories in the specialty of his sacrifice. "I lay down my life *for the sheep,*"—"instead of the sheep," it might be read. He glories in substitution for his people. He makes it his boast, when he speaks of his chosen, that he suffered in their stead—that he bore, that they might never bear, the wrath of God on account of sin. What he glories in, we also glory in. "God forbid that I should glory save in the cross of our Lord Jesus Christ, by whom the world is crucified unto me, and I unto the world!"

O beloved, what a blessed Christ we have who loves us so, who knows us so—whom we also know and love! May others be taught to know him, and to love him! Yea, at this hour may they come and put their trust in him, as the sheep trust to the shepherd! We ask it for Jesu's sake. Amen.